THE
FASTEST MEN
ON EARTH

THE FASTEST MEN ON EARTH

Neil Duncanson

WILLOW BOOKS
Collins
8 Grafton Street, London W1
1988

Neil Duncanson, an assistant producer with Thames Sport, devised and researched the television series 'The Fastest Men on Earth', and interviewed athletic veterans and contemporary track stars worldwide for the project.

He is an experienced journalist who has worked for some of the major newspapers on Fleet Street. As a news journalist at Thames Television he worked both on and off camera. He has also been a freelance writer for the press and television.

Willow Books
William Collins Sons & Co Ltd
London . Glasgow . Sydney . Auckland
Toronto . Johannesburg

Designed and produced by Sackville Design Group Ltd
Art director: Al Rockall
Art editor: Joyce Chester
Editor: Heather Thomas

First published 1988
© Thames Television PLC
and Neil Duncanson 1988

BRITISH LIBRARY CATALOGUING IN PUBLICATION DATA
Duncanson, Neil
Fastest men on earth
1. Olympic Games. Athletics. Running.
Sprinting. Biographies. Collections
I. Title
796.4′26′0922

ISBN 0-00-218313-7

Set in Century by Hourds Typographica, Stafford
Printed and bound in Spain by Cronion S.A., Barcelona

CONTENTS

INTRODUCTION

At 1.30pm on Saturday, 24 September, 1988, eight men will line up on the track in Seoul's Olympic Stadium for the start of the 100 metres final. All their past performances will be forgotten, all their hard-won titles ignored and all their records completely irrelevant. In less than 10 seconds, one man will flash past the finish line, claim a priceless gold medal and take the coveted title of 'The Fastest Man on Earth'.

World records will always be broken and other competitions long forgotten, but Olympic titles last for ever, so this is the sporting peak of any

WORLD RECORD HOLDERS		
100 metres		
10.6	D. Lippincott	USA	1912
10.4	C. Paddock	USA	1921
10.3	P. Williams	Canada	1930
10.2	J. Owens	USA	1936
10.1	W. Williams	USA	1956
10.0	A. Hary	West Germany	1960
9.99	J. Hines	USA	1968
9.95	J. Hines	USA	1968
9.93	C. Smith	USA	1983
9.83	B. Johnson	Canada	1987

sprinter's career. They are the world's fastest humans – men with reactions like lightning and wings on their heels. If they win on the day they will be feted as heroes, but if they make even one small mistake they will be demoted to history, for in the sprint there is no margin for error. When the winner of the Seoul 100 metres climbs up to the winner's rostrum he will become only the twenty first man to do so. There have been 20 champions in 20 Olympic Games, and so far no man has ever won the coveted gold medal twice.

So the new champion will be following in the footsteps of some of the most illustrious names in athletic history – ghosts of the past whose feats are now just fading memories in the record books. But who were these fast men, how did they win their titles and, perhaps more intriguingly, how did their speed and their gold medals affect the

rest of their lives? To most of us, 10 seconds is the blink of an eye, but to these men it was a very special short period of time after which life would never be the same again. For some, just getting to the Olympics was a triumph over tragedy and hardship, whereas to others, winning the gold would change their lives irrevocably, sometimes for the good and sometimes otherwise. This is the story of those fast men and it takes us from the earliest days of speed running to the dominance of the professionals in the nineteenth century, when thousands of pounds were wagered on races by wealthy Victorians and where bribery and corruption were the order of the day.

It takes us to the dawn of the modern Olympic movement where the creed of the amateur ruled and running was the sport of gentlemen. The early Olympic years were dominated by such men, but gradually, as the Games grew in size and stature, the personalities began to emerge – men like the tiny American Archie Hahn, probably the finest sprinter of the early Olympic era; teenager Reg Walker who had to pay his own way from South Africa to the London Games, because his country judged him too young to compete; and California's Charley Paddock, the first great showman of the track, who went on to become a movie star and whose life was so tragically cut short. There is also the real story of Britain's Harold Abrahams, who was glamourized in the film *Chariots of Fire*; the sad tale of the unknown Canadian kid Percy Williams, who had to hitch-hike his way to the country's Olympic trials; and tiny Eddie Tolan, who looked more like a bank clerk, with his spectacles, but whose speed earned him the title, 'The Midnight Express'.

As time moved on, the big names began to appear – like the legendary Jesse Owens and the real truth behind the so-called Hitler snub and how he was thrown out of the sport by his own country. Owens' athletic prowess spawned successive champions, including Harrison Dillard, who only concentrated on the sprint because he failed at the hurdles; the Cinderella story of 'no-hoper' Lindy Remigino; and the exploitation of America's 'Mr Clean', Bobby Morrow, after his Olympic triumph. It is true that all that glisters was not necessarily gold for some

Harold
Abrahams

Jesse
Owens

*Pictured from left to
right are: Jim Hines, Bob
Hayes, Lindy Remigino,
Hasely Crawford, Bobby
Morrow, Harrison Dillard
and Allan Wells*

Charley
Paddock

Eddie
Tolan

OLYMPIC CHAMPIONS
100 metres

1896	T. Burke	USA
1900	F. Jarvis	USA
1904	A. Hahn	USA
1908	R. Walker	South Africa
1912	R. Craig	USA
1920	C. Paddock	USA
1924	H. Abrahams	Great Britain
1928	P. Williams	Canada
1932	E. Tolan	USA
1936	J. Owens	USA
1948	H. Dillard	USA
1952	L. Remigino	USA
1956	B. Morrow	USA
1960	A. Hary	West Germany
1964	B. Hayes	USA
1968	J. Hines	USA
1972	V. Borzov	USSR
1976	H. Crawford	Trinidad
1980	A. Wells	Great Britain
1984	C. Lewis	USA
1988		

of these men, and the sad story of West Germany's Armin Hary, a 'bad boy' both on and off the track, was punctuated by controversy and, finally, prison. However, he was not alone – his successor on the Olympic rostrum was 'Bullet' Bob Hayes, possibly the greatest sprinter ever and certainly one of the top American football players, but only now back on the rails after a nightmare of alcoholism, drugs and prison. He was succeeded by Jimmy Hines, another man now on the way up after struggling for so long to find his way.

The Russians were accused of manufacturing sprinter Valeri Borzov to counter the American domination of the event, but just how true were those 'robot' jibes, and can the Soviet system teach the rest of the world how to treat its retired athletes? Haseley Crawford was a national hero in Trinidad when he won the 100 metres gold. His fellow countrymen even named a jet after him, and today he is still a revered figure, but can Britain's Allan Wells expect the same kind of treatment when he finally decides to hang up his spikes and retire from the track?

Today there is more interest in the sprints than at any other time in their history, due partly to the general increase in popularity of the sport, but even more to the personalities who currently dominate it. Enthusiasm grew during the 1984 Olympic Games in Los Angeles, where Carl Lewis captured the popular imagination in flying to seemingly effortless victories, winning four gold medals and laying claim to the title of the world's greatest athlete. However, even for him, the path to Seoul has not been an easy one, both off the track where he has been dogged by the media, which he claims does not understand him, and on the track where he now has to contend with the awesome presence of the Canadian powerhouse Ben Johnson, who not only beat Lewis so convincingly in the 1987 World Championships, but in so doing obliterated the world record with an astonishing run of 9.83, a mark that the experts say could remain intact until well into the next century. These two athletes have raised the levels of awareness and appreciation of the sprint, and their confrontation in Seoul will be one of the highlights of the Games, and one of the few occasions when the promoters will not have to pay out enormous amounts of money to lure them on to the track.

Today's top athletes, the best examples of whom are probably Lewis and Johnson, can demand huge appearance fees, and now the promoters have had to start their calculations for these two at a staggering £25,000 each per race, plus bonuses for winning and extra money if a record happens to be broken along the way. Last year they met on the lucrative European circuit and for one 100 metre race earned an incredible £37,000 each – that amounts to £3,700 per second! There is no doubt that the sport is changing rapidly and the 1988 Olympics, in South Korea, will be the first to totally embrace the new 'professional' athletes rather than just the off-track marketing of years gone by. Up-front cash, whether it is in the form of sponsorship, appearance or prize money, is now the driving force in a sport that has existed for so long on a gentleman's handshake, secret brown envelopes or a furtive nod and a wink, and while the stadiums stay full, the sponsors queue up to pump in more money, and television and press coverage remains at a premium, athletics will continue to ride the crest of a wave.

Of course, traditionalists worry that athletics is now threatened by rampant commercialism and drug abuse. They may be right about the drug scene, but in terms of finance these opponents of paid athletes are now a waning, as well as an ageing, force in a sport that has taken a long time to catch up with the 'real' world, especially in marketing, and is only now beginning to realise its true potential. Those who wag foreboding fingers about how track and field has changed out of all recognition are forgetting that amateur athletics, certainly at the highest level, has really only existed in the relatively recent past and that the new professionalism seen today is actually taking the sport full circle back to its roots.

FROM PROFESSIONAL TO AMATEUR

1896 Tom Burke

1900 Frank Jarvis

1904 Archie Hahn

1908 Reg Walker

1912 Ralph Craig

Below: this scene from an ancient Greek athletic tournament shows what appears to be the finish of a contemporary sprint race
Bottom: the scene at Olympia today. All that remains of the once great Olympic stadium of the ancient world is this flat stone surface, a few crumbling walls and some decaying steps

Baron Pierre de Coubertin, the founding father of the Olympic movement, would be amazed at how money and not the Corinthian spirit dominates the modern Games, but times have changed and even he would have to admit that the origins of the Olympics were always cash orientated. In fact, from the earliest days of organised racing, the key motivation was always a tangible reward rather than purely personal kudos and the joy of competing. Man has always wanted to know who is the fastest, whether it be faster than a pursuing animal or just faster than another man. The first record of organised sprints comes from 5,000BC in Syria, where pottery drawings show that they were part of religious festivals, and the culture subsequently spread throughout the Middle East and the Mediterranean, particularly Greece.

Homer often related tales of sprint races in his works and even identified the legendary Achilles as the first great Greek sprinter. The passion throughout the nation for athletics soon turned into the first Olympic Games, held on the sacred site of Olympia, and by about 800BC they had developed into a highly organised event, the technology of which was not improved upon until the middle of the twentieth century. Foot racing became so popular that in some areas of Ancient Greece the Queen even chose her King by means of a sprint, and the sport became embedded in Greek philosophy, striking a balance between mind and body. As time went on, some magnificent stadiums were built, but the Greeks had to iron out several early teething problems with the sprint races, most notably the starts, which were often marred by cheating. At first they combatted this by placing a judge on the start line armed with a menacing trident. Thus if an athlete (and remember that they were all naked) tried to get away before the rest of the field he was given an extremely painful reminder of his transgression! The very first Olympic race was a sprint, called the 'stade' because it was the length of the stadium, about 192 metres, and the first winner was a young man called Coroebus.

After a few years, more scientific means of starting these popular sprint races were introduced, much to the relief of the athletes, including starting sills, which were simple grooved slots; starting stones, a crude type of block; starting holes; and there is even evidence of an impressive starting gate system, or 'husplex', which was controlled by a single judge and is reminiscent of modern-day horse racing stalls. The winners of the Olympic sprints became lifelong heroes in the ancient world, and in addition to winning prize money for their achievements at the Games, they often received public property in their home towns, free meals

A powerful illustration of ancient sprinting is depicted on this Greek vase, showing the characteristic high knee lift and well defined muscles of the early sprinters

for life, and all kinds of gifts. These athletes seldom worked again and their kinsmen often worshipped them as Gods, so it was not unusual to discover coercion and bribery taking place in order to ensure victory.

The culture for sprinting lasted about a thousand years until the Roman Emperor Theodosius I decided to abolish the Olympics in AD393, and although small pockets of athletic activity remained their memory gradually faded. There is little evidence to suggest any widespread sprinting between that time and the early nineteenth century, although foot races were popular in some countries. Regular athletic meetings with money prizes have been recorded throughout Europe, in the Middle East and in North America, where the Indians were particularly renowned exponents of sprinting. By the end of the eighteenth century in Britain, professional running was beginning to increase in popularity. One of the early heroes was the Reverend Lord Frederick Beauclerk, who raced all over London and was reputed to be the great-grandson of King Charles II and Nell Gwynne. However, the hot bed of this new attraction was Kent, and the men of the county were reckoned to be the swiftest in England. Throughout the nineteenth century, the sport continued to grow in the new industrial centres, especially London and the northern cities. Among the early professional racing personalities was Jem Wantling, who was discovered in a Derby pottery factory, and by 1824 had virtually run out of opponents in England. A powerful man, he ran in constant fear of pulling muscles and always turned out with his legs strapped with leather thongs. He was reputed to have run regular 100-yard races in nine seconds flat – on gravel roads!

An almost comical start to a typical 100 yards race in the 1880s. It shows all four athletes still using the tried and trusted standing start

He was followed by George Seward, the 'American Wonder', who arrived in England in 1843, having run out of competition in the United States. The following year, in front of more than 3,000 people, he ran 100 yards in 9.25 seconds on a turnpike road in Hammersmith, although it later transpired that the course was downhill. Seward was a big crowd-puller, especially in London, and in 1847, on one of the new running grounds in Barnet, he achieved 19½ seconds for 200 yards, a record that remained intact until the end of the century. It took him less than five years to exhaust the competition in England, so he had to tour the country offering to run against six different men over 100 yards, racing them at five-minute intervals – he always won.

The old turnpike roads were a favourite location for professional sprinting in the early days but later grass cricket fields were used, and finally, when sprinting became really popular, purpose-built cinder tacks, or 'running paths' as they were known, were constructed around the country. However, despite its success, the professional racing circuit was always shrouded in disrepute because of its domination by a collection of greedy and selfish promoters, rather than one overall ruling body. Therefore spectators could never be certain whether the races they were watching were genuine or 'fixed', which they were more often than not. There were no rules to govern procedure and it was common for spectators to try to interfere with the runners, or even for rival sprinters to clash during a race. When contracts were drawn up for races, which were between two men only, the small print included details on how the race should be started. In the early days, this was known as 'starting by consent', whereby one runner would just take off when he felt so inclined, but if the other did not wish to start at the same time, the first competitor would have to return to the start. This sometimes continued for hours – in one case, four hours and 200 false starts – and eventually a rule was made stipulating that the athletes had to begin racing within 15 minutes or a pistol would be used to start the race. It was only a matter of time before common sense prevailed, and from 1857 onwards, starting sprint races by pistol became the standard practice.

At about the same time, the first 'spikes' came into use, and athletes who had been running either barefooted, or in moccasins or boots, began to wear custom-made cricket shoes with spiked soles, which enabled them to run quickly on cinders. However, it was not until the 1870s that athletic spikes were custom-made and widely used.

Harry Hutchens was probably the finest sprinter from the professional ranks, and was still capable of top-class running when well into his forties

Despite the proliferation of races and runners in the nineteenth century, one man stood out head and shoulders above the other 'pros', and that was Londoner Harry Hutchens. Born in Putney in 1856, Hutchens would become the greatest sprinter of his day, and his record suggests that he was one of the fastest men ever, although it is difficult to determine exactly how good he was as timing was always somewhat haphazard in those days. However, Olympic sprint champions, right up to World War I, held him in very high regard, and in a magazine article written by Harold Abrahams in the 1930s, he was still a sufficiently big name to warrant serious comparison with Jesse Owens.

Hutchens first realised his fleet of foot when working as a delivery boy for the newsagents W.H. Smith, and even as a teenager he found a sponsor and took up a career in sprinting. He won his first race in Wimbledon with a first prize of an electro-plated silver tea service, but after that the real money began to pour in. The purses on offer for the big sprint races were large enough to attract would-be fast men from all over the world, and the boom period for the sport began around 1870, when two prestigious purpose-built stadiums were erected – Powderhall in Edinburgh and Lillie Bridge in West London – and with only a few exceptions all the top races were held at these two venues.

From the mid-1870s onwards, Hutchens established himself as the fastest man in Britain, if not the world, with a series of handicap wins around the country. He was a big crowd-puller for the promoters, but with his long shorts and big, droopy moustache, he hardly looked like a typical athlete, standing about 5ft 10in, with a wiry frame that belied his natural speed. However what made him particularly viable as a business proposition for the promoters was that he did what he was told, and thus he ran to form whenever the book-

Left: a single policeman attempts to stop a rampaging mob of angry spectators from wrecking Lillie Bridge stadium after the so-called 'Race of the Century' was called off at the last minute
Above: the burning of the stadium in September 1887 marked the end of the once-great home of British athletics

ies backed him to win, and also lost a few races, which he should have won easily, when his backers wanted to make money. Of course, he received a share of the proceeds, but the management and the promoters made their money, too. However, when Hutchens ran seriously there was no-one who could stay with him at any distance from 100 to 300 yards.

In 1878, Hutchens won his first Sheffield Handicap, and the following year he threw down the gauntlet in the press for anyone to challenge him over 130 yards for £500. However, there were no takers and when he ran at Powderhall his fans from all over the country packed into special trains to make the journey. In fact, a crowd of more than 10,000 paid to see him run. On this occasion, however, he failed to get out of first gear and lost his one and only heat in the handicap competition. When he attempted a world record over 600 yards he pulled out just after the halfway mark.

But it was on the same track, in the winter of 1884, at the famous New Year Sprint, which became something of a tradition in Scotland and continued there until the 1960s, that he set the pro racing world alight. After running a 300-yard heat in the freezing cold in the morning, he sat down to a big, traditional English lunch of roast beef and potatoes, and then went out less than an hour later to run the distance in 30 seconds exactly – a record that stood until well after World War II. In 1887 he went to Australia for the winter where he made a great deal of money winning – and losing – a series of sprint races against some of the top Australian runners, but on returning home he discovered that a new man was calling himself 'Britain's No.1'.

Harry Gent, a 26-year-old Geordie, had won some important handicap races in Hutchens' absence and fancied his chances against the older man. Therefore, the promoters, who could see a big pay day on the horizon, arranged for the two men to race over 120 yards at Lillie Bridge for the official championship of the world with prize money of £200. Although the size of the purse was small in comparison to some other races, the promoters knew that they would more than recoup it on admissions to the ground and betting. The date for the big race, which attracted a tremendous amount of publicity, was set for September 1887, and the promoters must have been rubbing their hands in glee when they saw the thousands of people streaming into the ground to watch what the papers had dubbed 'The Race of the Century'. A massive crowd, reckoned to be around 15,000, had paid a shilling each to be admitted, and queues formed immediately around the stalls of the various bookmakers inside.

However, the promoters' masterplan had one fatal flaw and it would not only cost them their small fortune but would ultimately sound the death knell for the entire professional running culture in England. While Hutchens and Gent thrilled the crowds with a short warm-up routine on the track, back in the dressing-room a fearful row had broken out between the rival backers as to who should be the winner of the race. It was generally agreed that the result should be 'fixed' so that they could place some heavy bets. However, the pride of both runners, or the lack of suitable financial compensation, prevented either from giving way and agreeing to lose. The argument culminated in Hutchens' backers whisking their man out of the dressing-room into a waiting carriage and away from the ground, hastily followed by Gent and his entourage.

Meanwhile, outside in the stadium, the patience of the big crowd was rapidly fading, especially when it became apparent that the race was not going to be run and that both the runners whom they had paid to see had long gone. Their surprise quickly turned to anger and then to violence and, in scenes never witnessed before in Victorian England, the beautiful ground was smashed to pieces, with a huge mob of hooligans, hell-bent on revenge, tearing down the wooden stadium buildings, uprooting the perimeter railings and then setting fire to everything that stood. The majority of the crowd tried desperately to get away and the small police presence was powerless to stop the rampage, with one local newsman describing 'groups of men dancing like savages around the embers of the ruined stadium'. Such was the scale of the violence that terrified spectators climbed over the fence between the stadium and the local railway and ran along the tracks to get to the nearest station. The ageing stationmaster tried vainly to stop the first bunch but when he saw the huge mob behind them he dropped dead on the spot.

This black day destroyed Britain's premier athletics stadium and it was never re-built – today it is an overflow car park for the Earls Court exhibition centre. However, more importantly, the riot killed off the popularity of professional sprinting in England, although it continued on a much smaller scale in the North and was always popular in Scotland. As for Hutchens and Gent, they finally got together in a park in Gateshead, about a month later, where some 9,000 people turned out to see Gent beat the favourite, this time with an apparently suitable agreement on finances.

In the following year at Powderhall, after a decade as the top sprinter, Hutchens had to give way to Gent in the New Year competition, but he continued to run and the records show that he won his fourth Sheffield Handicap in 1891 at 35 years old and even finished fourth in the same race in 1898 at the amazing age of 42. Hutchens

maintained a keen interest in the sport, coaching promising youngsters on the professional circuit during the early 1900s. He died in relative obscurity in 1939, at the advanced aged of 81, at his home in Catford, South London. Incredibly, even his own local paper did not seem to realise his reputation and gave his death scant coverage, whereas the *New York Times*, the premier newspaper in the United States, gave him a substantial obituary, with tributes from some of the top American sprinters. Timekeeping being what it was and race fixing being the order of the day, it is difficult to conclude with any conviction just how good Hutchens really was, although if only some of his recorded times were genuine he has to be bracketed in the top class. At the turn of the century, he had no less than nine world records still to his name, between 50 and 350 yards, including a 9.75 for 100 yards and 21.8 for 220 yards.

After the Lillie Bridge scandal many fans turned to other sports, such as soccer, and their

Scotsman Alf Downer demonstrates his crouch start. He was one of the great 'amateur' sprinters of the 1890s, but was later thrown out of the sport when he admitted to taking money from the sports promoters of the day

growing disillusionment with professional sprinting, together with the lack of a proper governing body and the mercenary attitude of the promoters, meant that fans of the track also began to look elsewhere.

Inadvertently, the popularity of the professionals had encouraged the development of amateur athletics in Britain, which had been growing steadily from about the 1860s but had hitherto been confined mainly to the Armed Services, a few up-market clubs and the universities. However, as the new century approached, it was the amateurs who began to take over the athletics scene, and thus a new breed of sprinters began to arrive, including a Jamaican-born Scot called Alf Downer. He was rated as the fastest amateur in the world in the early 1890s but was thrown out of the sport in sensational fashion after he dared to disclose some of the shady, 'shamateur' dealings that went on even in those days. He revealed that he was regularly paid under-the-table money for running, usually about ten pounds a time, by clubs up and down the country who saw his value as a big crowd puller. Downer's revelations hit the sport like a bombshell and the AAAs reacted by embarking on a witch-hunt – throwing out selected athletes for receiving illegal payments. Downer always spoke disparagingly about their selective action as he claimed that 99 per cent of British athletes were not real amateurs, and the AAAs had not penalized the clubs that had made the payments. At the famous hearing in London in 1896, Downer and five other top athletes were suspended for life from amateur competition an ordeal that he later described as something akin to being tried for manslaughter. So Downer and the AAAs went their separate ways – he into professional running while the amateur body continued to grow into an even more powerful force.

Despite the Downer episode the amateur movement around the world was going from strength to strength, but it was a young French aristocrat, Baron Pierre de Coubertin, who really put the sport on the international map. He had visited Britain during the 1880s and toured the top public schools, including Eton, Harrow and Rugby, where he was particularly impressed by the strong sporting traditions that ran hand-in-hand with the academic schooling. He went away convinced that the entire edifice of the British Empire was founded on the sports orientation of these schools, building such qualities as leadership, loyalty, national pride, character and morale; a kind of muscular Christianity that he had read about in such books as *Tom Brown's*

Baron Pierre de Coubertin, the founding father of the modern Olympic movement. He based his revival of the Games more on the sporting philosophy of the British public school system than the ethos of the Olympics of the ancient world

Schooldays and had now seen for himself.

He had a vision of uniting the nations of the world in sporting competition, and that dream would soon become the modern Olympic movement, although it owed more to Tom Brown and the British Empire than the ancient games of the same name. Central to de Coubertin's thinking was the Victorian notion of the amateur – of gentlemen running together without the taint of money prizes – and that this was the future of sport. With this philosophy, he captured the mood of the times, and by 1894 he had won international approval to stage the very first modern Olympic Games.

So it was that in Athens, on Monday, 6 April 1896, King George I of Greece stood in the flower-covered royal box of the magnificent new stadium, paid for by a rich Greek merchant, and resurrected the Games after a lapse of more than fifteen centuries. Although the organization was good, it was an unusual competition, which included such diverse events as mountain climbing, bell-ringing and choral singing, as well as the more traditional athletic endeavours. The white marble stadium, erected on the ruins of an ancient sports complex, was an impressive sight, and every day during the Games it held a capacity 40,000 spectators. However, the construction was too narrow – in fact, the pillared corners of the track were so tight that the athletes kept slowing down, running into each other and even falling over whilst trying to negotiate them. For some unknown reason, the races were run in the opposite direction to that of today.

Thirteen nations entered the competition, although they could hardly be described as truly international teams – rather as groups of individuals who happened to be in Greece, or small parties of athletes sent by schools and clubs. The US team comprised such a party, mainly from the East Coast clubs and most notably from the famous Boston Athletics Association. However, it was this last group of athletes who almost missed the Games completely as they had not been notified that designated dates were set using the Greek calendar. Thus instead of arriving with a relaxed 17 days for training and preparation, the angry Boston contingent landed in Athens, after a two week boat journey, just 10 minutes before the opening ceremony was due to commence.

Among the latecomers was the only reigning American champion to make the trip. Tom Burke was rated as probably the best middle-distance runner in the world and a red-hot favourite to win the 400 metres. However, he knew that some of the world's top sprinters had not made the journey to Athens, notably the great Bernie Wefers, who had been breaking many sprint records but was more than 4,000 miles away running in the Boston College Indoor Games. So Burke decided to take advantage of this dearth of sprinting talent and have a go at the 100 metres himself. After all, he had not travelled such a long way to compete in just one event!

In the 100 metre heats, the three American sprinters, Burke, Tom Curtis and Frank Lane, adopted their usual crouch start, much to the amazement of the crowd and the European athletes, who had never seen such a stance before. Resolutely sticking to their standing start, they watched the three Americans win their heats easily, albeit against very mediocre opposition, and qualify for the final. Curtis then dropped out, deciding to conserve his energy for his favourite

event, the 110 metres hurdles, which was the next final on the programme.

So five men – two Americans, a German, a Hungarian and a Greek – eventually lined up on the rough cinder track for the start of the first 100 metres Olympic final, surrounded by spectators who had crowded on to the track itself for a better view. The sun was shining brightly, the stadium was packed, and contemporary newspapers reported that the hills above were bristling with another 60,000 spectators. As the pistol cracked, a great roar went up from the crowds both inside and outside the stadium as Tom Burke powered away from the rest of the field, his long legs easing him across the line in a sedate 12 seconds flat, a poor time and a fifth of a second slower than he had run already in the heats, but sufficiently fast to beat off the challenge of second placed Fritz Hoffman, better known for rope climbing, and Hungarian Alajos Szokolyi who came in third.

A few days later he went out for the final of the 400 metres and again won easily – a feat that he probably would have repeated had all the world's top athletes been on show, although his Olympic time of 54.2 seconds was six seconds slower than his best time for the distance. So Burke collected his two silver medals (there were no gold medals at the Athens Games) and returned home a hero. The Americans won nine of the 12 track and field events, and when the all-conquering Boston athletes finally returned home, the city went wild and turned out in force to show its appreciation, parading their new heroes through the streets and staging sumptuous banquets for them.

After retiring from the track, Burke practised law in his native Boston and coached briefly at Mercersburg Academy, but his real passion was for writing. During the Olympics he had sent back regular despatches about his experiences to the *Boston Post*, and he worked regularly as a columnist for both the *Post* and the *Boston Journal* in the years that followed. His interest in athletics continued right up to his death, following a heart attack in 1929, at the relatively early age of 54. In an obituary in his old paper, the *Boston Post*, his great running rival Bernie Wefers said that few could equal Burke's great running achievements, and the newspaper mourned the passing of 'one of the greatest athletes of all time'.

The author of the article was journalist Arthur Duffey, who had gone to the 1900 Olympic Games in Paris as the out-and-out favourite to succeed Burke as the 100 metres champion. Duffey had beaten everyone out of sight during the time leading up to the Games, and while in Europe before leaving for Paris, he beat his two closest rivals, the

Americans Frank Jarvis and J.W. Tewkesbury, in the British Championships in London. However, once in the French capital all kinds of things began to go wrong. Instead of one US team, there were 55 American competitors who had been sent from a variety of colleges. They had all been told that they were competing in an international exhibition meeting which was to run alongside the giant Paris Exposition. They subsequently insisted that they never knew that they were competing in the Olympic Games until they received their medals some months later. Indeed, the newspaper reports of the day did not mention the 'Olympics' at all.

The Games were organised badly from the start, mainly due to the fact that de Coubertin had lost his grip on them. Although he had successfully

Left: Boston AC's Tom Burke, the 1896 Olympic 100 and 400 metres champion
Below: the start of the first Olympic 100 metres final held in the magnificent newly built stadium in Athens in 1896

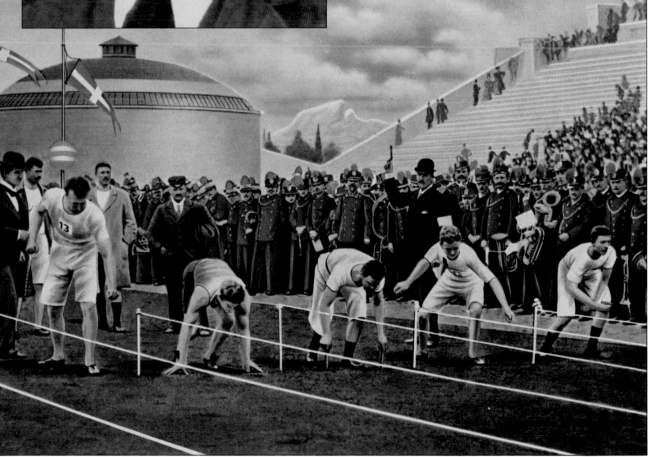

fought off an attempt by the Greeks to keep the Games permanently in Athens, he had little influence and plenty of enemies in France, and thus the Olympics were wrenched from his control and run by a group of French officials, merely as an unimportant sporting sideshow to the trade exposition. The athletics were held at the Racing Club, in the Bois de Boulogne, but there was not even a proper cinder track, so the officials marked out a course on a grass arena, with a 100 metre stretch which rose and fell like a roller coaster and was littered with bumps and holes. The French decided to open the Games on Sunday, July 15, but the USA protested at this 'ungodly' act and demanded that they should start on Saturday. The French countered that this was Bastille Day and opening the competition then would be impossible. After a long and bitter battle it was decided that the Games should open on the Saturday and that some athletes would then miss Sunday and start in earnest again on Monday.

The 100 metres competition, the heats and the final, were staged on the opening Saturday, so consequently only a handful of people turned out to watch. As one newspaper remarked, there were more people on the track than in the stands, and most of those were American tourists. Arthur Duffey, the pride of Georgetown University, was still the clear favourite to win, despite both Jarvis and Tewkesbury equalling the world record of 10.8 seconds in their heats. However, there was some evidence that the French timekeeping was a little on the generous side to say the least. In glorious sunshine, the final field of just four men shot out of their marks at the sound of the gun and, as expected, Duffey charged into an early lead and the race looked over. Then disaster struck. At 50 metres he suddenly leaped into the air and then crashed spectacularly to the ground, while Jarvis hurtled past him and crossed the line in first place with the watches stopping at 11 seconds dead, Tewkesbury being just a step behind him.

Duffey told waiting pressmen: 'I don't know why my leg gave way. I felt a peculiar twitching after going 20 yards. I then seemed to lose control of my leg and suddenly it gave out, throwing me on my face. But that is one of the fortunes of sport and I cannot complain. But I don't think I can compete here again.' He later confirmed that he had pulled a tendon and subsequently tripped over the rope that separated his lane from the next while trying to keep his balance. Nearly all

the press reports majored on Duffey's catastrophic fall and hardly a mention was made of the actual winner of the event, Frank Jarvis. But the Princeton star, who was a direct descendant of George Washington, took it all in good part. However, it would be unfair to dismiss him merely as someone who was lucky enough to pick up the crumbs of Duffey's bad fortune. He was regarded as a top-class performer in the United States, where he won many titles, including the coveted AAU 100 yards in 1898.

Although Jarvis did not compete any further in Paris, the Games went ahead, and from a crowd-pulling point of view proved to be the dismal failure everyone expected. While Duffey found fame as a top sports writer, Jarvis returned home to the quiet life and soon after the Games he graduated from Princeton and later practised as an attorney in Pittsburgh until his death in 1933 at the age of 55, and such was his prominence in the city, both within his own profession and the

Right: Princeton University's contribution to the United States' Olympic team for the 1900 Games. Frank Jarvis is on the right
Below: Arthur Duffey (far right) wins the British 100 yards championship from Jarvis (21)

community, that all the federal, state and county courts were adjourned as a mark of respect on the day of his funeral.

However, by the time of the 1904 Olympics, Frank Jarvis had gone and the big sporting news of the day was all about how heavyweight boxing champion James J. Jeffries had run out of opponents, so there was little excitement being

generated about what might happen on the track in St Louis, home of that year's Games. As an international competition the 1904 Olympics were laughable, with hardly anyone, bar the United States, sending a truly representative team. Britain and France did not send one at all, and those countries that did, and there were only eleven, sent merely a handful of athletes, such were the financial realities of taking a large squad of athletes halfway across the world. So, in effect, the Games, which were held as a sporting adjunct to the World's Fair, were just an over-blown American club meeting, but with the great rivals New York AC and Chicago AC battling it out to determine which was the best club in the country, the performances remained very much in the major league.

While newspapers around the world devoted their attention to the Russo-Japanese war, President Theodore Roosevelt opened both the Fair and the Games, in late August, but whereas tens of thousands flocked to the Fair, only a few thousand watched the Olympics. The United States won every track and field event except one, where a Montreal policeman, Etienne Desmonteau, triumphed in throwing the 56lb weight. But that victory aside, it was an apparently poor performance by the world's athletes until you realise that only 92 foreign athletes took part in the entire competition, and 41 of those were from Canada. In the sprints, Chicago AC considered that they had the fastest man in Bill Hogenson, but the events were dominated by the diminutive figure of fast-starting Archie Hahn, christened the 'Milwaukee Meteor' by the sports writers at the Games.

Hahn, the son of a tobacconist, was born and raised in Dodgeville, a small farming town in Wisconsin, and never set foot on a track until he was 19-years-old. His high school did not have a track team and, despite his height of just 5ft 5in and weight of around 130lb, he was a regular on the football team. He eventually ran his first race in 1899 at a county fair and finished third in a 100 yards dash, but he returned the following year and won the event at a canter, impressing the crowd with a time of 10.1 seconds, especially the observers from the University of Michigan, who invited him to study law and turn out for their track team. Archie wanted to play football but the coach, Fielding Yost, dismissed the idea saying that he was too small. So Hahn turned all his energies to running, particularly running very fast over short distances.

In the four years that he was at Michigan, Archie was the sprint champion of the 'Big Ten'

The diminutive figure of American sprinter Archie Hahn, the 1904 Olympic sprint champion, with gold medals in the 60, 100 and 200 metres events in St Louis. A great early Olympic star

colleges every season and served notice of his Olympic intent when he won both the US and Canadian sprint titles in 1903. But to qualify to run in the Olympics during this period meant membership of an athletics club, not a college as it became some years later, so Archie signed up with the Milwaukee AC and joined them for the trip to St Louis. There were three sprint events at the Games, at 60, 100 and 200 metres, and Hahn outpaced his rivals in the shortest dash in just seven seconds. With that edge, he entered the 200 metres, which was a straight course rather than the familiar curve of today, and of the four starters – all American – three of them false-started in successive attempts to get the race underway and were penalized with a two-yard deficit. Thus, all Hahn's rivals started behind him and they never caught him. He crossed the line a comfortable three metres ahead of them with the powerful Louisville sprinter Nat Cartmell in second place and Hogenson in third. Hahn's time of 21.6 remained the Olympic record until the Games returned to the United States in 1932. All he needed for a clean sweep of the sprint event

Above: Michigan University's Archie Hahn wins the first of his first three gold medals at the 1904 St Louis Games. His time in the 60 metres event was 7.0 seconds flat

Below: Athens 1906, the so-called 'Renegade' Games. Archie Hahn (right) returned to the Olympic arena to win a gold medal in the 100 metres race despite a somewhat dubious start

was a victory in the classic 100 metres, and again all six finalists were American. At the gun, the field got away together and powered into a strong head-wind, but by the 20-metre mark Hahn was already edging ahead of his two nearest rivals, Cartmell and Hogenson, and he hit the tape a good two yards clear to claim his third gold medal of the Games, one of four athletes to achieve the feat in St Louis.

Shortly after returning home, Hahn graduated from Michigan with a law degree, but he never practised his profession, deciding instead to devote his life to sport, particularly the track. At about this time it was decided that Athens would stage an 'interim' Games in 1906 to try and bring back the international flavour to the Olympics, something that had been lost by the lack of foreign participants in St Louis. So Hahn decided to go back into training to compete for the USA in the sprints and took a job as a teacher in a Michigan high school while he prepared for the competition.

For the first time in American track history, a genuine US team was selected from the clubs and colleges, ruled over by the newly formed American Olympic Committee, headed by Teddy Roosevelt, and Hahn was selected for the 100 metres. He won it easily, with his toughest rivals, Cartmell and Hogenson, not taking part. However, it was rumoured that Hahn took advantage of a lenient starter by tearing out of his marks when the Greek command *etami* or 'get set' was made. He apparently left his rivals on the start line and actually eased up as he won the race, but the starter did not recall the runners and so the result stood. Archie Hahn remains the only sprinter to have retained a 100 metre title, although the Athens competition was only two years after St Louis and could not be described as a genuine Olympic Games.

Happy with his success, Hahn decided to retire from the amateur track world, turn professional and earn some money from his talents until he gave up competition at the advanced age of 38. He ran in pro races all over the USA and performed stunts at fairs, including a famous occasion when he outran a racehorse over 50 yards in Wisconsin. He also began to coach at colleges up and down the country, including Brown University, his alma mater at Michigan and Princeton, before he was appointed head coach at the University of Virginia, where he moulded some of the best track and football teams to come out of the state. During these years, Hahn majored in track and football, but he dabbled in just about every other sport, including a stint as a boxing coach during World War II.

Earlier in his career he put together a book on training for the track, called *How To Sprint*, which was the first major work of its kind and remains a classic text on the sport.

It contains dozens of photographs and drawings and describes in detail every facet of sprinting, from the basic techniques to fast starting and finishing, with important tips on how to dig the right holes in the cinder tracks, choosing the best running shoes and even the correct diet. After a lifetime in coaching, during which he became something of a legendary figure on the college coaching circuit, Hahn finally decided to hang up his coach's cap and retire in 1951, at the grand old age of 70. Sadly, he died from cancer in 1955, following a long battle against the illness, but his name lives on and he remains the most outstanding sprinter of the early Olympic era – a view shared by the modern-day athletic powers who elected him to the national track and field Hall of Fame, in Indianapolis, where the giant trophy he won during the 'renegade' Games of 1906 is on permanent display.

The American dominance in the sprints was expected to continue when the Games came to Edwardian London and the newly created White City Stadium in 1908. They had originally been assigned to Rome, but the Italians informed the IOC that they could not handle such a big event and a late switch was made to London. Sadly, the Olympics were beset with problems from start to finish, earning them the unfortunate title of 'The Battle of Shepherds Bush' due to international bickering and bad feeling.

In the sprinting world, it was James Rector, an American student from the University of Virginia, who was the favourite to take the 100 metre laurels back to the United States. Another strong runner was the Irish-born Canadian star Bobby Kerr, so it seemed inevitable that the medals would return again to North America – or so the sports writers believed. However, they had not taken into consideration one of the most unlikely heroes yet thrown up by the Olympics, a waif-like 19-year-old clerk from South Africa – Reg Walker.

There could be few people who looked less like an athlete than Walker, who, at just 5ft 7in tall and tipping the scales at barely nine stone, gave the impression that a light breeze would blow him over, yet when he ran he was a different person. As a teenager his only sporting experience had been as a fleet-footed winger on his local lacrosse team in Durban, which regularly drew big crowds. It was the team's managers who persuaded him to take up sprinting. He ran well in competitions on gravel tracks in Natal province, but when the elder statesmen of the South African Olympic Committee selected the team for London they considered the 19-year-old Walker too young to make the trip. His coach and friends at the Natal Athletic Association managed to raise the £100 needed to pay his return boat fare and keep him in modest accommodation in London. Consequently, Walker was able to travel to the Olympics with the four-strong South African track team.

He arrived in London in mid June about a month before the opening of the Games, in order to get acclimatized to the European conditions and test himself against some of the likely opposition in a few races in the intervening weeks. A week after arriving in Britain, Walker lined up in the AAAs championships in London, and lost by a decisive margin to the Canadian Kerr. However, watching from the trackside was the man who would enable Walker to make the jump from also-ran to Olympic champion. Mussabini was an old-fashioned coach from the halcyon days of professional sprinting who had been the motivating force behind the great Harry Hutchens. He was impressed with Walker's natural sprinting talent but blamed his less than average starting prowess as the main reason for his inability to win at the highest level.

A few years later, Walker published a training

Stamford Bridge 1908. H.A. Mears, the owner of the stadium, poses with the South African sprint sensation, teenager Reg Walker, and his coach Sam Mussabini during a training session

Coach Sam Mussabini puts his protégé Reg Walker through a gruelling training session geared to improving the slightly-built South African's starting ability

handbook in which he paid tribute to the influence of Mussabini who had taught him all the tricks learned during his coaching career. Mussabini even introduced him to the top pro of Walker's day, the Australian Arthur Postle, and they practised together in the build-up to the Olympics. Apart from rebuilding Walker's start, Mussabini ensured that the youngster maintained an almost regimental training schedule in the manner of the old pros, and ate a healthy diet. The regime clearly had an electric effect on the quiet and modest Walker and he took the 100 metre competition by storm. The heats began shortly after King Edward VII opened the Games, on 13 July, an appearance that heralded almost continuous rain for the remainder of the competition.

What made the sprints even more exciting than usual was the 'sudden death' nature of the heats, as only the winner of each race was guaranteed to continue in the competition. As predicted, James Rector looked the most impressive runner on view and tied the Olympic record in the heats with a run of 10.8, equalling the performance in the semi-finals, but Walker also tied the record in

his semi. A few years later, Walker wrote: 'I was practising my starts with unfailing regularity, but in the second round of the competition when Rector showed faster than I did, I realised even then I was not fast enough and during the morning of the final I went down to Stamford Bridge and did some more practising. The result was that when the final was decided in the afternoon, I was quicker away than the other competitors.'

Walker felt that the chief requisite for a top sprinter was an abundance of what he referred to as nervous energy and the ability to channel that energy into running. He also kept to a strict diet, which included boiled lamb chops, rusks and weak tea for breakfast; roast beef and vegetables, stale bread and milk puddings for dinner; and fish, toast and stewed fruit for late tea! So with his starting perfected and his diet in trim, Walker lined up in the final, alongside Rector, Kerr and the 1904 silver medallist, Nat Cartmell. The race was due to start at 4.15pm on Wednesday, 22 July, and because there were no Englishmen in the final the home crowd were all rooting for Walker and a colonial victory to wrest the title from the Americans.

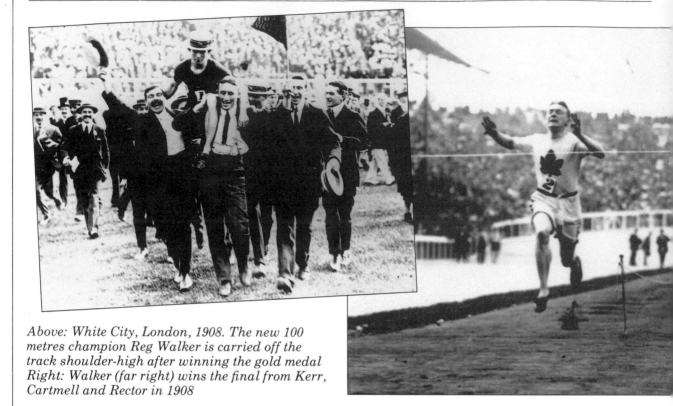

Above: White City, London, 1908. The new 100 metres champion Reg Walker is carried off the track shoulder-high after winning the gold medal Right: Walker (far right) wins the final from Kerr, Cartmell and Rector in 1908

However, everyone was still predicting a win for the speedy Rector, including the morning papers, despite the American's strange windmill arm action which seemed to propel him along the track. In the corner of the stand was an American 'compound' packed with noisy fans from the United States, yelling and chanting for Rector, waving huge banners and flags and playing regular fanfares on their bugles. But as the four men crouched into their starting holes a hush fell over the stadium, followed by a huge roar as the pistol cracked and the sprinters sped away. Walker, vivid in his emerald green, showed first and then Rector passed him at 30 metres. Walker drew level at about halfway and they ran neck and neck until about 20 metres from the finishing line when the young South African seemed to find another gear and flew past the American, hitting the tape a good half yard in front, with Rector just snatching second place from the fast-finishing Kerr.

Walker had again equalled the Olympic record, although two of the five stopwatches recorded a new world record of 10.7 seconds. As he crossed the line, the whole stadium erupted and the 50,000-strong crowd went wild, hurling their hats and programmes into the air, jumping on their seats and flooding on to the track. To his obvious embarrassment, Walker was swept up by the crowd and carried shoulder high around the track, and, with a giant South African flag waving at his side, he was paraded all the way to the dressing-room, even receiving a huge ovation from the American 'compound' as he passed. After changing and catching his breath, he was presented to the royal box for special congratulations.

The following morning, his unexpected success knocked even the Suffragettes off the front pages of the British newspapers, while the South African press, when the news finally reached them, reacted with wild enthusiasm about the nation's first ever gold-medal winner. There were calls for Walker to be given a top job for life when he came home and even Natal's Prime Minister sent a telegram of congratulation, while in his native Durban an unofficial Reg Walker Day was declared, with schools and offices closing early and celebrations in the streets. Walker's victory was one of the outstanding performances of the Games and even rivalled the famous marathon incident when the little Italian Dorando was picked up by officials as he staggered towards the finish and helped across the line. When Walker finally returned home to South Africa, he was treated like royalty and was acclaimed as one of the nation's greatest heroes, even by the Government, but when all the fanfares, parties, parades and hero worship eventually died away there was, of course, no top job for life. In fact, there was no

job at all and Walker could not make any money running as an amateur.

However, he managed to survive for the next couple of years, living on handouts and backing from various athletic associations, and winning titles both in South Africa and Britain, including the British AAAs 100 yards championship in 1909. By the end of the 1910 season, Walker decided that he was going to make his fortune as a professional sprinter, despite protests from South Africa who wanted him to run in the 1912 Olympics. But he had trained like a professional and beaten the pros in practice runs, so he thought that he could earn a good living. His stepson, Bill Walker, who still lives in Durban, relates a story of how the South African millionaire R. Edgar Walker offered him the staggering sum of £250,000 to stay as an amateur, run in the 1912 Olympics and not turn pro, but Walker could be a stubborn and headstrong man and never changed his mind once he had made a decision. Walker Junior believes that his stepfather probably made about £1,000 out of pro racing, despite the big purses, with the rest of the money going to managers, coaches, promoters and hangers-on, whereas when the old millionaire died he left his £6½ million estate to various cats' and dogs' charities.

For a few years Walker certainly made a decent living as a pro, racing against the top sprinters on the circuit, including his old friend Postle and Jack Donaldson, both from Australia, where pro sprinting was big business and purses for each race could be as much as £500. However, his career was relatively short and after World War I his health began to fail and he was forced to retire from the track, settling down in Manchester and returning to his job as a clerk, this time for a rug, mat and canvas company.

During his stay in England his Olympic gold medal was stolen and never seen again, although some years later a bizarre advertisement appeared in a British newspaper suggesting that the medal might be returned if he went home to South Africa. Eventually he did go home, where he dabbled in a little coaching, including his nephew Reg Kitchin, a good hurdler, who still credits his uncle for giving him an extra six yards. Walker died in his native Durban in 1952, but even today he is revered as one of his country's finest sportsmen and as one of only five South African athletes ever to win an Olympic gold medal. He is certainly one of the star names in the country's Sports Hall of Fame in Pretoria, where some of his track kit is on show.

So with Reg Walker plying his trade on the world's professional sprinting circuit, the way looked clear for the Americans to move in and reclaim their lost sprint title when the Olympics reconvened in Stockholm in 1912. The United

States team looked an awesome athletic force and included three exceptional sprinters, Ralph Craig, Howard Drew and Don Lippincott, with any one of them capable of winning the gold medal. The favourite had been Detroit's Ralph Craig, a tall, 23-year-old from Michigan University who had to be cajoled into making the trip to Sweden at all. He had twice equalled Bernie Wefers' 1896 record in the 220 yards of 21.2, and in 1910 had added the national collegiate 100 yards title to his collection of trophies. But Howard Drew, the first top-class black sprinter to run in the Olympics, had beaten him in the 100 metres during the final US trials, so the forecasters were having difficulty predicting the winner.

Craig had been coached at Michigan by Archie Hahn's old mentor, Keene Fitzpatrick, and the multi-medal winner from the 1900 Olympics, Alvin Kraenzlein, but when he graduated in 1911 he was ready to give up the sport. Although a close friend persuaded him to carry on running, Craig was still anxious about competing in the Olympics. He had just become engaged to be married and started a new job, so he did not have time to devote to training. His friend convinced him that he could make the necessary arrangements and even won over Craig's new employers to give him time off, with full pay, so that he could concentrate on his training, go to Sweden and bring back gold medals for the United States. Craig was finally persuaded and he joined the Detroit YMCA's track club and began training to get back into running shape.

Of course there were other sprinters capable of snatching a medal other than the Americans, including the talented German Richard Rau, who held the unofficial world record of 10.5, and Britain's Willie Applegarth, a top performer at both sprint distances.

Stockholm, bathed in July sunshine, was a breath of fresh air for the Olympic movement after the feuding and fighting of London; there were even calls during the intervening years to abandon the Olympics altogether because they were damaging international harmony rather than promoting it. De Coubertin needed Stockholm to succeed or the entire movement was in serious danger of collapse, and fortunately the 1912 Games remain one of the greatest in sporting history.

Stockholm had no Olympic village, so the teams were scattered around the city in various hotels, while the Americans preferred to stay on board their steamer in the harbour. This time 28 countries took part, with nearly 4,000 athletes competing in a new purpose-built stadium with the aid of an early form of electronic timing, being tested at the Olympics for the first time. The Games were opened formally on Saturday, 6 July, by King Gustav V before a crowd of almost 100,000 people, and most of them stayed to watch the first heats of the 100 metres competition. As expected, the Americans made it comfortably through their respective preliminaries to qualify

Ralph Craig, the United States double sprint gold medallist at the 1912 Olympics in Stockholm. Craig had to be cajoled into training for the Games after getting engaged to be married and considering giving up his athletics career

for the semi-finals and the final held on the following day. Here it was Don Lippincott who served warning to his rivals that he could not be taken for granted when he ran a superb 10.6 seconds to smash the Olympic record, although both Craig and Drew looked impressive in their semis. There were, in fact, six 'semi-finals' with just the winner of each qualifying for a place in the final later in the afternoon, so the Americans looked odds-on for a 1-2-3 sweep in the race when all five of their sprinters won their 'semis' with room to spare, and only the South African George Patching gave the final anything resembling an international flavour.

As the time of the final approached the runners began to go through their usual warm-up routine on the track, but a buzz started to run through the crowd when Drew, the man favoured by most of the American newspapers, limped off the track, his face contorted in pain. It was discovered some hours later that he had been injured during one of the preliminary rounds but had fought on bravely through the competition, winning his 'semi' despite an intensely painful strained thigh muscle. He had decided to go out onto the track at the start of the final in the vain hope that his leg might have recovered sufficiently to run just once more, but he suffered so badly in the warm-up that he was forced to give up and had to be helped off the track and back to the dressing-room.

So with the Massachusets student injured, both Craig and Lippincott were now clear favourites to take medals for the United States, but the final

Below: Howard Drew, the first world-class black sprinter to emerge in the United States, beats Ralph Craig, the future Olympic gold medallist, in the 1912 US Olympic trials at Harvard Stadium. However, injury robbed him of the chance to compete in the Olympic final

Below: after no less than seven false starts, Ralph Craig turns his head to see that he is clear of the field and wins the 1912 Olympic 100 metres little ahead of his competitors, Meyer and Lippincott, in 10.8 seconds

was marred by no less than seven false starts, including one in which Craig and Lippincott, so intent on beating each other, sprinted the entire distance on their own without hearing the recall. Eventually, at the eighth attempt, the anxious starter managed to get the field away and it was the speedy South African Patching who made the early break and led all the way to the halfway mark, but then the slow-starting Americans Craig, Lippincott and Alvah Meyer got into their stride and drew level. As the tape neared, Craig edged ahead and the rest of the field seemed to cross the line in a split second, so much so that the crowd could not tell who had won or who had come second and third. It did not take the judges long to award the gold to Craig, whose strength over the last 20 metres had brought him home first by about two feet in a time of 10.8 seconds, with the unfancied Meyer nipping Lippincott for the silver. The Americans revelled at the sight of three United States flags rising on the stadium's flagpoles – only the second time it had happened in Olympic history.

A few days later, Craig and Lippincott lined up for the final of the 200 metres, this time with the German Rau and the British hope Applegarth alongside them, but the elegant Craig proved his superiority a second time as he powered his way past the entire field after another slow start to win in 21.7, with Lippincott second and Applegarth just holding off Rau for the bronze. So Craig finished the competition with two gold medals and naturally became the toast of the American team, although the real hero of the Games was the brilliant all-round athlete Jim Thorpe, an American Indian who took the gold in both the pentathlon and decathlon. Even though he was stripped of both titles in January of the following year, because he had once been paid $60 for playing baseball, Thorpe remains one of the greatest stars ever seen at the Olympics.

When Ralph Craig returned home to Detroit he was without doubt the hero of the city and for the rest of his life he wore a diamond ring presented to him by the Mayor in honour of his success in Sweden. In the two years that followed the Games, before the outbreak of World War I, both Drew and Lippincott equalled the world 100 yards record of 9.6, whereas Applegarth equalled the official world 100 metres mark of 10.6. A few months after the Games all three of them equalled Craig's world 220 yards record of 21.2.

However Craig had won the two races that really mattered and while his old rivals were travelling the world trying to make up for their Olympic disappointments, Craig was at home in quiet retirement from the track, enjoying his new job and family life, with his two gold medals safely tucked away. In the 1920s he left his native Detroit and moved to New York, where he worked as an administrator in the State unemployment insurance office, a job he held until his retirement in the early 1950s. At the same time, Craig worked tirelessly in the Olympic Council, furthering the movement in the United States and promoting both athletics and watersports, the latter being something of a passion which he had enjoyed since childhood. He had sailed and rowed for the Detroit Boat Club as a young man and as he got older his interest and expertise grew until he was generally recognised as being one of the most proficient yachtsmen in the country, writing papers for the North American Yacht Racing Union and compiling the *History of Yachting in the Olympic Games*, which remained one of his proudest achievements. His work over three decades in the Olympic Council and his eminence in the yachting field earned him selection as a reserve skipper for the US yachting team, in the American Dragon Class, for the 1948 Olympics in London. But a greater honour still was kept a closely guarded secret until a few hours before the US team's ship docked in England, and that was his selection as the man to carry the US flag in the opening ceremony parade, an honour announced in front of the whole team by AOC chief Avery Brundage, who had been with Craig in the 1912 Games. The *New York Times* reporter at the scene described the 59-year-old Craig as 'a tall, distinguished looking gentleman, with a full head of grey hair and close cropped moustache'. Understandably, the thrill of carrying the Stars and Stripes around the giant Wembley Stadium, filled with around 100,000 people, remained one of his greatest moments and more than made up for the disappointment of not being needed to actually take part in the yachting competition.

During the 1950s, especially after his official retirement, Craig spent a great deal of time writing, particularly for the *Detroit News*, where he specialized in Olympic matters, but he also became something of an expert on the breeding and keeping of spaniels, writing a number of articles and a book on the subject. He died in July 1972, at the grand old age of 83, at his home in Ticonderoga, New York, but his exploits are kept alive at the National Track and Field Hall of Fame and he remains not only one of the finest sprinters of his era, but also the only gold medallist ever to return to the Olympic Games in a completely different sport, an achievement that is unlikely to be matched.

THE ROARING TWENTIES

1920 Charley Paddock

'*The first great entertainer in the world of track and field . . . one of the giants in the history of sprinting*'

1924 Harold Abrahams

'*Immortalized in the film Chariots of Fire . . . a lifetime built on just one Olympic victory*'

1928 Percy Williams

'*Hitch-hiked to his country's Olympic trials . . a reluctant hero with a tragic life story*'

1920 Charley Paddock

One of the most famous pictures in Olympic history. American Morris Kirksey (extreme right) turns his head in anguished realisation that his team-mate Charley Paddock (hands spread wide) has leaped past him at the tape to win the 1920 Olympics 100 metres title in Antwerp

By the time the 1920 Olympics arrived in the war-torn city of Antwerp the world had been starved of international athletic competition for eight years. The only major meeting held during this time was the Inter Allied Games, staged in Paris, where servicemen from all the Allied forces gathered to compete in what contemporary newsmen described as the 'Military Olympics'. One of the big stars of these Games and the man everyone would fear on the track a year later in Antwerp was the brash, confident American speedster Charley Paddock, a striking muscular athlete from California, who would not only become a dominant force in the sprints for the next decade but also the world's first real track superstar – a genuine showman who delighted in entertaining

the crowds with a trail-blazing series of athletic stunts and gimmicks. When Charley was on the track he made sure that every pair of eyes was firmly focused on him alone, and his life, both on and off the track, was always controversial, highly colourful, guaranteed to entertain but sadly very short.

He was born in August 1900 in Gainesville, Texas, but the family moved to the healthier climate of California when doctors said they were worried about his lack of weight, just seven pounds when he was seven months old, and suggested that it was the hot, humid Texan climate that was to blame. The move was clearly beneficial and Charley was soon developing into a powerful, barrel-chested young man. Although his parents tried to encourage him to play sports as a child, the only pastime that seemed to interest him was throwing rocks at the older boys and then running away to see if they could catch

him. Fortunately for him he was always too fast for them or a glittering career on the track may have ended there and then.

As a teenager, he began to take an interest in athletics and was encouraged both by his father, who was a keen miler in his day, and by a local track star called Forrest Stanton, who trained on the beach close to the Paddock's summer home at Hermosa. Young Charley used to sit and watch him train and as a result Stanton took him under his wing, even inviting him to his house and letting Charley take home some of his medals. Paddock vowed that some day he would win medals of his own. His first competitive races were over cross-country courses, and then he took up miling before eventually converting to the sprints, where he immediately began to win school titles at all ages, including the California high school title while still only 15. However, he abandoned his senior year at high school, just a

few months short of graduation, and enlisted in the army, joining a field artillery camp in Kentucky. By the time he was 18, he had attained the rank of 2nd Lieutenant.

US Army life clearly did not have an adverse effect on his running, and early in 1919 he ran an impressive 9.8 for 100 yards, a time that earned him an invitation to compete for a place in the American forces team which was shortly to leave for the Inter Allied Games. Again he ran impressively and was picked for both sprints and the relay in Paris where, despite the chaos that ruled throughout Europe, many of the world's top athletes were on show. These Games provided Paddock with his first major competitive test – one that he passed with flying colours by winning both the 100 and 200 metres, plus a further gold in the relay. Among the spectators was Nicholas I, the King of Motenegro, who was becoming increasingly alarmed at the way in which the small band of athletes representing his tiny Balkan state was performing and he decided to 'adopt' some of the stars of the Games by knighting them in the stadium. So it was that Paddock became Sir Charley of Montenegro, although it was a title he seldom used in later life!

When Paddock returned to the United States news of his success had gone before him and he was already becoming something of a celebrity. He loved to entertain and the fans enjoyed his stagey appearances, which often included multi-colour track suits and exotic silk running shorts. In addition to this kind of showmanship, he had a number of other gimmicks with which the crowds could readily identify, including a superstitious routine before each race, during which he would walk around the track looking for a piece of 'friendly' wood, more often than not a hurdle, knock on it three times, cross his hands and return to his marks. Apart from being a crowd-pleasing act, this also served as perhaps the first piece of psychological one-upmanship seen on the track.

His capacity for drawing crowds and his ability for self-promotion was something he carried off from head to toe, quite literally, as his son Charley Junior, who still lives in the family's home town of Pasadena recalled: 'He certainly was a showman and he really enjoyed running. Apart from his track outfits he insisted on having specially made running shoes, in deer or elk skin, so that when they got wet they would shrink and conform exactly to his feet, like they were glued to them. He wouldn't wear anything else.' But Charley reserved his theatrical *pièce de résistance* for the end of a race, when he performed his

A classic example of the famous Charley Paddock leap as he finishes yards clear of an international field in a 1920 European meeting

famous jump finish, taking off from the track some ten or twelve feet from the tape and hurling himself through it in midair. Track purists were horrified by this stunt and always felt it was the reason that he lost so many races that he really ought to have won, but Charley always maintained that this finish gave him about an extra fifth of a second over his rivals at the tape. He also realised that it would catch the eyes of the judges, who would see nothing but the flying figure of Charley Paddock at the end of a close race.

Athletics historian, Tom McNab, rates Paddock as one of the track's first great personalities. 'He was certainly the first star of amateur sprinting and undoubtedly one of the first great "shamateurs." He wandered all over America setting all sorts of weird and wonderful records in the type of races no-one but him would tackle. But he saw the value in doing it and similarly he saw the value in the jump finish, which from a coaching point of view was a complete waste of time, but it was a great grandstand ploy and people flocked from all over America to see Charley Paddock run.'

However, before these barnstorming race days began came the challenge of the Olympic Games and Charley had already won a scholarship to the University of Southern California, where he came under the influence of the famous US coach Dean Cromwell, who began to hone his skills in readiness for Antwerp. Paddock was hardly the ideal build for a sprinter – in fact, he looked like a small shot-putter, standing about 5ft 8ins tall, stockily built and muscular, with short, powerful legs. Cromwell began correcting a poor start, a short stride and altered Charley's habit of using just his shoulders and arms to run, although he remained essentially a power runner, with one of the highest knee lifts of any athlete on the track.

After winning the Far West sprint title he qualified automatically for the US Olympic team, joining an impressive line-up which included Loren Murchison, Morris Kirksey and Jackson Scholz. They were all aboard the steamship *Princess Matoika* when it eventually set sail from New York. This vessel would become infamous in newspapers around the world by the time it reached Europe, as the US team carried out a 'mutiny' on board with some of the athletes threatening not to compete in the Games when they arrived.

The 'Mutiny on the Matoika' is now long forgotten and the American track authorities certainly prefer it to be so, although the original protest petition still survives and contains the names of the mutineering athletes, a document organized and delivered by a seven-man committee, which included Charley Paddock. It was the first but by no means the last time that he would run foul of the US track powers. It was probably the most widely publicized of all the events in which he was involved, and so it was no small wonder that under such pressure he went on to achieve what he did at the Games after creating such a furore. The story surrounding the mutiny began when the US Olympic Committee realized that they had failed to organise passage for the team on conventional trans-Atlantic liners, as the effects of the war were still causing chaos to shipping and all the luxury steamers were booked solid for months ahead. So they went cap in hand to the US Government which decided that the army could lend a hand by providing a ship to transport the team to Europe at no cost, a scheme that pleased the cash-conscious USOC immensely as it saved the organisers the $70,000 needed for the conventional passage.

The ship selected was the modern transport steamer *Northern Pacific*, which was as fast as the top commercial liners of the time and could make

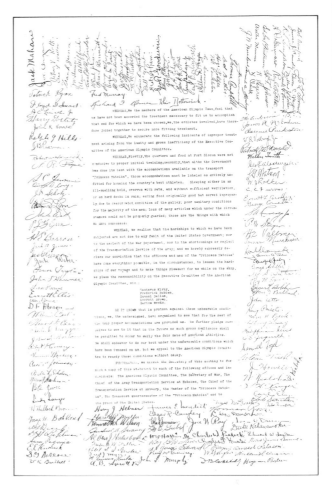

The infamous 'Mutiny' petition drawn up on board the Princess Matoika *in protest at the appalling conditions of the US athletes*

the crossing in seven or eight days, so arrangements were made for the ship to leave New York just after the final Olympic trials in Boston, in order to arrive in Antwerp about a fortnight before the competition began. Then disaster struck. The *Northern Pacific* loosened a huge plate on her hull, below the waterline, and had to be hauled into dry dock, leaving the Army and the USOC in a quandary and the entire US team stranded in New York, barracked *pro tem* in a basic army camp outside the city.

After lengthy negotiations, another ship was found, but there was little choice and the one finally chosen, the *Princess Matoika*, was certainly not in the same class as the *Northern Pacific*; it was old, slow and had few of the comforts to which the team were accustomed. The few cabins and staterooms that did exist were quickly snapped up by the officials and their wives, while the team had to make do with what were essentially troopship quarters. Discontent among the athletes was already simmering over the poor conditions on board, but the straw that finally broke the camel's back came when a wire from Europe was intercepted on the ship by a member of the team indicating that their situation on the *Matoika* was a garden party compared to what awaited them when they arrived in Antwerp.

A meeting was held deep in the bowels of the ship and a huge petition was drawn up and signed demanding that the USOC take some action. The signatures of all the athletes were written in a large circle just like the old-style mutiny papers so that the authorities could not identify a ringleader. It listed all their grievances, which ranged from general complaints about the awful conditions to specific examples of appalling food, over-crowding, poor sanitation and the fact that many athletes were sleeping in an ill-smelling hold which was over-run with rats. They wanted action and a promise that such a situation would never be allowed to happen again, or they would not compete in the Olympics. Fortunately for the officials, common sense finally prevailed among the team members, and the USOC pacified and eventually persuaded them that the return journey would be much better and that the emergency measures they were enduring would never be repeated.

But when the team arrived in Antwerp the 'Mutiny on the *Matoika*' almost turned into the 'Revolt of Antwerp.' The team were barracked in an old school, with hardly any food during a Belgian public holiday, with insufficient beds or proper facilities and no-one available to solve their problems until the end of the holiday. Charley Paddock, by this time, had suffered enough and he and his close friend Loren Murchison took an apartment a short distance away where they could eat properly and avoid the mayhem caused by the USOC's patent lack of planning. Instead of the proposed two weeks' preparation, the team had been delayed in New York, took twice as long as anticipated to cross the Atlantic and had just a few days in Antwerp before the Games opened.

The 100 metres competition began the day after the opening ceremony and thus the four American sprinters were not allowed to march in the procession behind their flag, but were forced to conserve their energy and watch from the stands. Some 30,000 people packed into the impressive white walled stadium, which had been built in just under a year by the Belgians despite the difficult circumstances created by the war. Apart from the four US stars there was tough compe-

tition in the sprint from Britain's Harry Edward and the Frenchman Emile Ali Khan, and all six breezed into the semi-finals.

The semis were run early the following day on the morning of Monday, 16 August, with the final later in the afternoon. The first semi was won by Edward in 10.8, while Paddock took the second in the same time, but all six favourites for the final had made it. The hours that passed between the end of the semis and the final itself must have felt like an eternity to the six athletes. Murchison spent the entire time wandering around in a dream muttering to himself that he was going to win and trying to summon up his nervous energy, whereas the rest of the field sat around and pretended to ignore him. Finally, when it was time to go out on the track and take up positions, Lawson Robertson, the American team's sprint coach, said to the four American runners: 'What you fellas need to warm you up is a glass of sherry and a raw egg'. The athletes looked at him in total disbelief, but Morris Kirksey leapt at the idea, seeing a possible psychological advantage if the others did not follow suit.

'It would make me sick,' moaned Murchison. 'I never could drink and raw eggs turn my stomach inside out.'

Jackson Scholz looked similarly unimpressed with the plan. Robertson turned to Charley and asked him if he wanted a glass. 'What's Kirksey going to do?' asked Paddock.

'He's on his way to the sherry and egg,' said Robertson.

That did it: Paddock saw what Morris was trying to do and decided to do likewise. In his book, *The Fastest Human*, published at the tail end of his running career, he recalled: 'Though I was considerably upset as to what a stimulant might do to me, I realised the tremendous moral advantage Kirksey would have on the rest of the field if he were the only one to follow "Robbie's" advice. I am not sure Kirksey was keen on the idea himself, but he probably thought the rest of us would not follow suit and he was always willing to gamble on anything. When he drank his sherry and egg he had three companions and it did warm us up and bring back the punch and pep we sorely needed.'

Paddock began to go into his good luck routine at the start and found himself a piece of 'friendly' wood, crossed his hands and prepared for the gun. He also had a habit, when called to his mark, of putting his hands way over the starting line and then drawing them back slowly as the second command of 'get set' was given. He was in the process of doing just that when the starter, unaware of this ritual, told him in French to pull his hands back. He then called 'prêt', the French for 'get set', and off went the gun. However, both Murchison and Edward misinterpreted what had happened and thought they were being ordered to stand up, so both had relaxed when the gun went off and were left trailing yards behind. Kirksey went off like a bullet and took an early lead, but by the halfway mark it was Scholz with a two-feet advantage, with the fast finishing Edward, who was making up for his bad start, closing quickly. Kirksey began to overtake the field, but Paddock was right on his shoulder, using his power to surge past everyone on the boggy cinder track. The race was almost over.

'Then I saw the thin white string stretched to

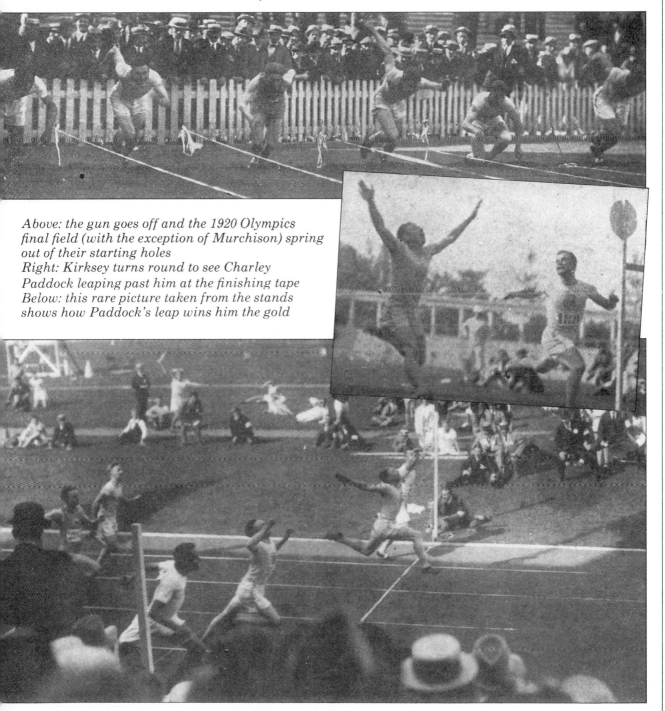

Above: the gun goes off and the 1920 Olympics final field (with the exception of Murchison) spring out of their starting holes
Right: Kirksey turns round to see Charley Paddock leaping past him at the finishing tape
Below: this rare picture taken from the stands shows how Paddock's leap wins him the gold

breaking point in front of me,' wrote Paddock, and I drove my spikes into the soft cinders and felt my foot give way as I sprang forward in a final jump for the tape, and just as my feet left the ground Kirksey turned his head towards me and for a single instant lost his forward drive.'

Paddock's description of the closing split second of the race is shown perfectly in the photograph taken at the finish, one of the most famous in Olympic history, with Paddock, arms spread wide, crashing through the tape, while Kirksey has turned his head in an apparent anguished realisation of defeat. That fatal mistake cost Kirksey the race and made Charley Paddock the champion.

'Nothing else mattered,' wrote Charley, 'my dream had come true and I thrilled to the greatest moment I felt I should ever know. The hands so eager to shake mine now might be doubled against me tomorrow and the autographs burned or forgotten. The real pleasure had been in the anticipation and in that single moment of glorious realisation.' Britain's Harry Edward was awarded third place although the photographs taken from the side of the track clearly show Scholz ahead of him.

By comparison to his triumph in the 100 metres, Paddock's silver medal in the 200 metres was somewhat disappointing, losing almost on the line to fellow American Allen Woodring, a shy young may from Syracuse University, who only made the race as a late replacement for the

exhausted Jackson Scholz. Paddock was also very tired but he dearly wanted a crack at winning the sprint double, something he looked odds-on to achieve as he charged into the lead in the final and came out of the turn almost five metres clear of the field. However, he had gone off far too quickly and, as the finish neared, Woodring closed on Paddock's shoulder and the two seemed to hit the tape together. The judges rightly awarded the gold to the boy from Syracuse who had just sneaked past Paddock on the line as he made his customary leap for victory. The long-legged Woodring, who had borrowed a pair of spikes before the race because his own had split, was so surprised at coming out of the reserves to win that he had to be convinced by Paddock that the 100m champion had not sportingly allowed him to do so by slowing up in the last 25 metres.

After leading-off the impressive US sprint relay team to another gold and a world record of 42.2 seconds, Charley returned home with three medals to a hero's welcome and a solid reputation on which to build and promote his future both on and off the track. He had never shunned publicity – in fact he openly courted and encouraged it, finding journalists and the media fascinating and generally easy to exploit. He had enjoyed writing since his play-producing days at school, adapting the classic works in the 8th grade, and had been working for a newspaper in Pasadena since he was 14 years old, so it came as little surprise to anyone who knew him that writing would play a major part in his future career. He contributed articles to newspapers and magazines, commented on people and events, wrote speeches for his lecture tours, and travelled the world covering athletics meetings. However, all this activity

Paddock (centre) speeds around the turn in the Olympic 200 metres final, but his team-mate Woodring will catch him right on the line, with second-placed Charley taking the silver medal

took a back seat in the spring of 1921 when he embarked on a wholesale assault on the world's sprint records as well as inventing some new ones of his own.

Charley was driven compulsively to win and break records, and by the end of his career he had established no less than 17 different world marks, ranging from the more traditional sprint distances to the typically Paddock-style runs of 90 yards, 110 yards, 135 yards, 250 metres, 300 metres and so on. In April 1921, he became the first man to claim the world 100 metre mark of 10.4, which remained unbroken for nine years. He next equalled Arthur Duffy's 1902 100 yard record of 9.6 during a meeting in California. Immediately after the race he was due to run a 220 yards but he was so tired that he could barely drag his feet back to the start. Urged on by the crowd he decided to run the race and surprised everyone, including himself, by eclipsing the 25-year-old world record of 21.2, set by Bernie Wefers, with an astonishing 20.8. Other incredible performances during this time included a 10.2 seconds for the 110 yards, a longer distance than 100 metres and a time that Paddock always felt was better than his 100 metre mark, although for some bizarre bureaucratic reason it was never officially recognised as a world record over the metric distance.

Such was his passion for breaking records and his ability for showmanship that on one memorable day he attempted to beat three world records in one race, by ordering the judges to stretch three tapes across the track at 75, 80 and 100 yards, with timekeepers at each distance! Contemporary reports suggest that he did beat all three records, but they were never accepted by the disbelieving authorities, and perhaps it is true that Paddock was often a victim of his own flamboyance, although it is unlikely that it ever bothered him unduly. As the next Olympic Games, this time in Paris, loomed on the horizon, Paddock was out on his own as the world's premier sprinter and was already dubbed the 'world's fastest human', a title invented by a West Coast sports writer and adopted enthusiastically by Charley. However in some ways the title could also be a millstone round his neck and early in 1923 he seriously considered retirement, feeling that he had little to gain and a lot to lose from appearing on the track, with every sprinter gunning for him. It was left to one of Paddock's close friends, the great movie star Douglas Fairbanks, to persuade him to continue competing until at least after the next Olympics, although Charley's single-minded contempt for the US track powers almost cost him a place on the team.

It was during 1923 that he received and accepted an invitation to run in a student games competition in Paris, despite threats from the AAU that he might lose his amateur status if he took part, as the Americans had decided not to permit any athlete to compete abroad in the year preceding the Olympics. However, they did allow a Harvard and Yale team to race against Oxford and Cambridge in England. True to form, Paddock treated the AAU with his customary disregard and told the authorities, via one of his newspaper columns, that he would go where he pleased because he was 'over the age of 21, free and white.'

He travelled to Paris, won all three sprint events in the competition, including a world record equalling run in the 150 metres, and promptly returned home to face the music. The furious AAU wished to suspend him and ban him from forthcoming Olympics, but Paddock found an ally in the other major US athletic force, the National Collegiate Athletic Association (NCAA) and a huge power battle ensued, fought for the most part in the pages of some of the big American newspapers. Paddock was finally reinstated, but not before he dropped a bombshell on the AAU by suggesting that they were aware of professionalism creeping into the sport and that some athletes were being paid secretly. Whether his revelations disturbed their cosy world is unclear, but it was not long after his disclosures were made that the Paris affair was quickly settled. In the years that followed, the AAU never missed an opportunity to snipe at Paddock.

So Charley was in the US sprint team that travelled to Europe for the Olympics, alongside Scholz and Murchison, plus newcomer Chester Bowman. Never before had there been such a red-hot favourite for a gold medal than Charley Paddock. However, when he arrived in Paris self doubt began to creep in, especially when he began running poorly in the heats, while the rising British star Harold Abrahams ran exceptionally well. Nor did it help when Bellin de Coteau, an eminent French doctor who had examined Charley before the Games, proclaimed: 'Paddock's freak. He's fat, has curvature of the spine and shoulder blades that stick out, his nasal respiration needs attention and when he runs he looks like a calf with two heads.' High praise indeed!

Paddock had travelled to Paris with 14-year-old Douglas Fairbanks Junior and his mother, who was a good friend. This was a trip that young Douglas would never forget. 'I remember Charley as a jolly, chunky fellow, though it was always a mystery to me how he could be such a speed demon on the track built like he was. He was a great one with the girls and I remember being terribly envious.

'We were on our way to Paris on the same ship as the team, which included Charley, the other great sprinter Loren Murchison and swimmer Johnny Weissmuller. I remember working out with them on the ship and I hero-worshipped them. When we landed on the other side they let me train with them. Charley trained every day and he would give me a 60 yard start in a 100 yard race and still beat me easily.'

Sadly for Charley, the races in the Olympics were not quite as easy and the best he could do was a poor fifth place in the 100 metres. 'It's no use, I just haven't got it anymore,' Charley told Fairbanks. 'My legs tie up, my speed is gone. I'm an old man sure enough this time.' Fairbanks tried to cheer him up and he was wined and dined by the movie star clan, including Mary Pickford and the French star Maurice Chevalier, who livened up the proceedings by doing outrageous impressions of the Games' two big stars, Paavo Nurmi and Harold Abrahams. The break from the competition clearly did Charley some good and he went back into the fray in much better shape, managing another silver medal in the 200 metres, and finishing just six inches behind Jackson Scholz, but he strained a thigh muscle as he made his desperate jump for the tape and that ruled him out of the relay team which duly went out and won its customary gold medal.

After a short but successful post-Olympic tour of Europe, which redeemed some of Charley's lost prestige, he returned home to the United States. While in Europe, he met the founder of the Olympic movement, Baron de Coubertin, who saw Paddock's value as a persuasive promoter and publicist and suggested a plan for both Charley and Loren Murchison to embark on a massive world tour, which the Baron described as 'Sprinting Around The World', in order to spread the gospel of track, sportsmanship and the Olympic ideal. The idea appealed to Charley, and early in 1925 he and Murchison left on an epic four-month trip that took them to the athletic outposts of Japan, China, the Middle East and finally to Europe. In every country that they visited, the two sprinters raced, spoke at meetings and banquets, met civic leaders and were generally hailed as great sporting ambassadors.

However, nothing that Charley did, it seemed, could ever go completely smoothly, and when he returned to the United States he discovered that allegations of expense fiddling had been levelled against himself and Murchison. There were alle-

gations that they had been pocketing large amounts of money from the countries that they had visited – far in excess of their genuine expenses. Both athletes were flabbergasted and vehemently denied the charges, but only after a lengthy and much publicized investigation by Charley's old friends, the AAU, were they cleared.

In the latter part of 1925, Charley was again considering hanging up his spikes and concentrating on his writing career, but an inner voice kept nagging him to break a few more records and he wanted to try and make up for the disappointment of Paris by making the US Olympic team for

a third time in Amsterdam. He even turned down a monumental offer from the top sports promoter C.C. Pyle to turn pro and run a series of races for a minimum fee of $30,000, a sizeable sum in those days. But he had other irons in the fire and after sidestepping yet another row with the AAU, when he bucked amateur rules by appearing in a gasoline advertisement, he decided to take up Douglas Fairbanks' suggestion and try his luck in the fastest growing and most lucrative business in California – the movies. They had been growing in a small Los Angeles outpost just a stone's throw from Charley's Pasadena home, a place called Hollywood.

Apart from the premier movie stars, Charley was just about the most famous face on the West Coast and *Paramount Pictures* decided to invest in that fame by casting him alongside one of their top stars, Bebe Daniels, in one of the first co-ed, college life comedies, in which he played himself as a coach at the college. The five reel silent *Campus Flirt* was moderately successful at the box office, but all the headlines were reserved for the off-screen relationship between the two stars. Rumours circulated about a possible real-life romance during the shooting of the movie, which was released in the late summer of 1926, and the Hollywood gossip columnists, including the legendary Louella Parsons, had a field day speculating on a possible wedding, even though Daniels had apparently broken off an earlier

Left: silent screen hero Charley Paddock gets tough in one of his western B-movie roles
Right: Charley in training with Paramount star Bebe Daniels for the 1927 film Campus Flirt
Below: Charley (second right) poses for a publicity shot on the set of Thief of Baghdad

engagement with fighter Jack Dempsey. 'Bebe Daniels to Wed Sprinter King', 'Charley Paddock Captures Film Star's Heart in Five Weeks' and 'Yes Sir She's My Bebe' crowed the papers, and the couple were seen around Hollywood for about 18 months, although there is no evidence to suggest that they were ever engaged, and the romance, if it existed at all, appeared to die a natural death.

Paddock's movie career continued and he starred, often as himself, in a number of sports based films and a few B westerns, where he got a reputation as something of a daredevil stuntman. He also produced a few minor pictures of his own and finally starred in a movie based loosely on his own life called *The All American*, in which he played a sprinter called Charley Patterson. His attempts to promote it during the Olympic year of 1928, landed him in even more hot water with the AAU and there were the inevitable calls, from other countries too this time, for him to be barred from the Games. However, again he managed to ride the storm.

In May 1926, he decided to run one more race against the up-and-coming West Coast sprinter Charlie Borah over 100 yards at the Los Angeles Coliseum. Before the confrontation, he billed the meeting as his farewell performance, but after he beat the young pretender and smashed the world record in 9.5, he reversed his decision yet again and returned to serious training in readiness for the 1928 Olympics. Sadly, the record was never ratified officially as in those days records had to be broken by two-tenths of a second to qualify.

As the Games approached Charley's form again began to fall away and another youngster from California, Frank Wykoff, who was soon to be the first man to register a 9.4 for 100 yards, beat him in two races over both sprint distances, so the writing was clearly on the wall. Charley was chosen for the US team, for the 200 metres eventually, and he was beaten in the semi-finals.

'After 1928 he saw people coming along that he no longer had the stamina to race against,' says stepson Prisk Paddock. 'He had been in the sport a long time and he wrote about the track scene and went to a lot of meetings, so he saw what people were doing and how they were coming along. So he decided it was time to retire.'

This time there would be no comebacks so, with his track career over and work in the movie business at an end, he wrote a book about his running life and then settled down to pursue his newspaper career. In 1930 he met and married divorcee Neva Prisk Malaby and took over the job of business manager of the *Press-Telegram* newspaper, in Long Beach, California, and then the *Star-*

Charley Paddock pictured posing for a photograph during a training session at the University of Southern California towards the end of his sprinting career. He subsequently became a successful West Coast businessman, managing several newspapers

Marine Captain Charley Paddock (left) poses with Major-General William Upshur and stepson Prisk Paddock at the United States Pacific Headquarters in San Francisco. It is one of the last pictures taken before Paddock's death

News, in Pasadena – both family concerns. He became an increasingly successful and influential figure on the West Coast, managing these two newspapers, and writing features, articles and editorials. Gradually he became more interested in politics and his editorial messages become increasingly political and more widely read. It was, says his family, for this reason that a local political rival, who was on the draft board, felt that Paddock was getting a little too influential and tried to get him drafted during World War II, despite the fact that Charley was bumping the upper age limit at 42-years-old. Paddock saw what was happening and decided to beat his rival to the punch by joining the marines, where his prior service and long association with the reserves enabled him to enter as a captain. He was assigned as an aide to Major-General William Upshur, first as a public relations man and then as morale officer, based at the Pacific HQ in San Francisco. It was on the final leg of a tour of the Pacific war front, in July 1943, that Charley was killed in a plane crash, over Alaska, along with Major-General Upshur and four others.

He was buried at Sitka in Alaska and not brought back to Pasadena, in accordance with family wishes, and a few months after his death a commercial freighter was named after him, along with a sportsfield in Pasadena. The news of his death made front page news in the *New York Times* and most of the other major American newspapers. Had he not been killed it is likely that Paddock would have returned home and become an even more successful publisher and probably a successful politician. Charles W. Paddock, the 'California Comet', not only goes down in athletic history as one of the greatest sprinters of all time, but also as the flamboyant personality who did an immense amount to raise the level of awareness and popularity of track sprinting all over the world. He may have been guilty of ignoring the authorities on occasions, but that was because he was highly individualistic and held his own opinions on how the sport ought to be run, but he attracted the crowds and certainly gave the sport a much higher profile than it might otherwise have received. For these reasons alone, Paddock must rank as a giant amongst the sprinters of the last one hundred years.

1924 Harold Abrahams

When the 1920 Olympic Games ended, the elder statesmen of British athletics returned home vowing never to send another team. British Olympic records (those that survive) show that there were several reasons for their sudden disenchantment with the Games, although it was clear that they felt humiliated at collecting only four athletic gold medals, despite an excellent performance by the track team. Thus there was serious discussion about abandoning the Games and not sending a team to Paris in 1924. Both the British Olympic Association and the AAAs felt that everything had gone wrong in Antwerp. The general public, they said, were totally apathetic to the competition: the Games had become alien to British ideals; professionalism was creeping in; the organization of the Olympics needed a complete overhaul; and moreover, the athletic bodies still had to plead with potential sponsors just to raise the few thousand pounds needed to finance an Olympic trip.

All these problems were aired regularly during countless committee meetings in the years that followed Antwerp, but after much wrangling

Paris, 7.05pm, 7 July 1924. Harold Abrahams dips at the line to become the first European to win a gold medal in the Olympic 100 metres. He remains the only Englishman to win the title

common sense finally prevailed and, with assurances on at least some of their gripes, the 'old guard' decided to bite the bullet and go to Paris. Had they decided otherwise, one of Britain's most successful track teams might never have set foot in the Olympic Stadium and one of the country's most enduring athletic legends might never have snatched his moment of glory.

That man was Harold Abrahams, now immortalized in the hugely successful, if largely inaccurate, film, *Chariots of Fire*. For most people, the film version of Abrahams' story is the real one, but his family all agree that, for the most part, it is a fairy tale. As Harold's nephew Anthony Abrahams succinctly put it: 'They got three things right. Harold was Jewish, he went to Cambridge and he won the 100 metres. The rest you can just "enjoy". It was a good film in the *Boys' Own Paper* style.'

Abrahams' Olympic ambitions were fired just before the outbreak of World War I, when his two eldest brothers, Adolphe and Sidney, both top athletes, took him along to Stamford Bridge, London's premier athletics stadium of the time, to watch the 1914 AAA championships. Harold never forgot the experience and the huge impression made on him by the running of the then British sprint king Willie Applegarth, who had been a double medal winner in the 1912 Olympics.

Harold came from a privileged background, born in December 1899, the son of a wealthy City financier, a heavy drinking Lithuanian Jewish immigrant, a man prone to violent tempers and who could not even write his own name in English. Despite this disadvantage, he achieved great wealth and power in his adopted country.

Born prematurely, Harold weighed just over 2lb, and was not expected to survive. Consequently, he was spoiled by all the family. He was the youngest, by some years, of six children, four boys and two girls, and grew up in Bedford. He was acutely aware of the sporting achievements of brothers Adolphe, a good half-miler, and Sidney, who represented Britain in the long jump at the 1906 and 1912 Olympics. They were always pushing and bullying young Harold, and the need to be better than them was a constant spur to him.

'Harold told me,' recalls Anthony, 'that when he first started showing signs of being a good athlete, they would make him run everywhere. Their favourite game was to make him run around the houses in Bedford. They'd give him a time to beat and if he didn't make it they used to hit him over the head with rolled newspapers.' With such family support, it came as no surprise to the family when Harold made a successful racing debut at Stamford Bridge – at the age of ten.

By the outbreak of World War I, most of the family had grown up and left home, but Harold was just entering his teens, and when his parents split up, it was decided that he should be sent away to boarding school at Repton, a long established and expensive public school. In the film *Chariots of Fire*, Harold's prime motivation for running is his fight against anti-semitism which, claims the film, dogged him throughout his early life. However, there is little evidence for this view and if it did exist at any time in his life, then it was probably at Repton, where he spent some lonely years. Indeed, Harold does not appear to have been a dedicated Jew, as all the athletics meetings in those days were held on Saturdays – the Sabbath. 'What drove Harold,' says Anthony, 'was firstly the need to be better than his brothers; secondly, that throughout his life he was a perfectionist and wanted to succeed. He knew he had great athletic and intellectual powers. The family expected him to do well and that made him even more determined.'

By the end of the war he was already making a name for himself as a sprinter and long jumper, winning titles in the 1918 public schools championships and in the following year beating his former idol Willie Applegarth in an exhibition race, giving him a two yard start and – winning by six. Two months later, he followed the tradition of his brothers and sisters and went up to Cambridge, where he studied law at Caius College and quickly earned his athletic blue, although he never ran around the university quadrangle as depicted in *Chariots of Fire*: that was Lord Burghley some years later.

Less than a year after settling into college life, while still a freshman, he was selected for Britain's track squad for the 1920 Olympics. However, at this early stage of his athletics career Harold was not in the same class as the cream of the world's sprinters – the likes of the Americans Paddock and Scholz, or even Britain's Harry Edward – and although he won his first heat, he went out in the next round. But Harold was philosophical about the trip. 'I had a long distance view of Charley Paddock's large back,' he once said, 'and although my competing at Antwerp was far from distinguished, I benefited enormously from the experience and I'm sure it played a large part in my good fortune at Paris four years later.'

In those intervening years he enjoyed mixed fortunes on the track, including a world record in the rarely run 75 yards at Stamford Bridge, only for it to be disallowed when it was discovered that the track was eight inches too short. It was not until 1923 that things began to move forward quickly for Harold – a year that saw him leave Cambridge and join forces with the now legendary coach Sam Mussabini. Mussabini, half Arab, half French, a cycling and billiards expert, had coached both Willie Applegarth and Harry Edward, in addition to helping out on the professional circuit, which had not endeared him to the athletics establishment.

Nevertheless, Harold sought him out and trained with him relentlessly for almost a year before the 1924 Games. His single-minded desire for success in Paris set him apart from every other athlete in the country. The New Zealander Arthur Porritt, now 87-year-old Lord Porritt, was running at Oxford during this time and remembers the effect that Harold had on his contemporaries. 'His training methods were today's training methods. I was always very impressed with his effort. His methods were absolutely unknown at that time and I couldn't help admiring the way he trained, practised, dieted, did this, didn't do that, just to keep fit. This was entirely out of keeping with the spirit of the time. Harold was almost professional, though obviously not to the extent of getting any remuneration. For the rest of us, our training, by today's standards, would do nothing but make people laugh. A few hours on a Sunday morning, perhaps a few starts, a couple of hundred yards and some chatting. Whereas Harold was training long hours and three or four times a week.'

A highlight of the 1923 season and a measure of how far Harold needed to progress was to have been the AAA championships, in which he was destined to take on the rising Scottish star Eric Liddell, but a throat infection ruled him out and Liddell romped home in an impressive 100 yards of 9.7. The two never met on the track, another *faux pas* by the drama-seeking makers of *Chariots of Fire*, who showed them running in those championships. Mussabini took Harold's running apart, and together the coach and athlete worked at rebuilding every facet of his sprinting, aiming at just one goal – a gold medal in the Olympic 100 metres in Paris.

Wily old coach Sam Mussabini puts Harold through another session on his starting technique. It was a professional training regime that put the Englishman above his team-mates

Athletics historian Tom McNab, the historical consultant on *Chariots of Fire*, believes that Mussabini's influence cannot be overestimated. 'Abrahams was the first British athlete to be thoroughly trained in a very professional manner. The anti-semitism in the film was there for added drama, when in fact it didn't really exist, except possibly for a general level of anti-Jewish feeling which pervaded the twenties. But it may have been the grit in the oyster that produced the pearl of the 1924 Olympic winner, though he never made any point about it. Mussabini was far more important; he came from the traditions of professional running, the lore and mystique of the old "pro" racers of the nineteenth century. He knew the likes of Harry Hutchens and much of what he had learned came from that era.'

Harold himself wrote: 'Sam was "dead nuts" on the arm action, with the arms kept low, bent at the elbows. He maintained that the action of the arms controlled the poise of the body and the action of the legs. So my training sessions consisted largely of perfecting the start and practising the arm action over and over again.

'There were no starting blocks in those days, so we took meticulous care with the placing and digging of the starting holes and the accurate control of the first few strides. I always carried a piece of string the length of my first stride and marked the spot on the track, at which I would gaze intently on the word "set".'

Mussabini was a stickler for stride length and Harold always believed this gave him an extra yard and a half by not over-striding. To ensure he was running properly, Mussabini would place pieces of paper at strategic points along the track and Harold would have to run and pick them up on his spikes. After perfecting the stride length, Mussabini then taught Harold to adopt what became his famous 'drop' finish. So by the spring of 1924, Abrahams emerged as a completely different athlete to the one who had failed at the Olympics four years earlier. As if to prove his new standing, he ran a wind-assisted 9.6, which would have equalled the world record had it been officially ratified, and then raised his national long jump record to 24ft 2½in (7.38m), a mark that remained unbroken for 32 years. The Olympic Games were beckoning.

To his amazement, Harold was selected to run at the Games in the 100 metres, 200 metres, sprint relay and the long jump. An angry letter, published in the *Daily Express* a few days later, suggested that this was too much for one man and that he should be omitted from the long jump. It was signed by 'A Famous International Athlete'. Incredibly, the selectors took heed and Harold was duly dropped from the long jump. The author of the letter was, of course, Abrahams himself.

Although there was nothing like today's media interest in the Olympics, the British press latched onto Harold and reported his every movement and opinion, including his view that there was little chance of him winning the 100 metres. 'This wasn't mock modesty,' he wrote some years later, 'for I always (according to my friends) had far too high an opinion of my ability. But the Americans appeared to me to be in a different class from myself.'

Arthur Porritt was selected to run for New Zealand in the sprints. 'By and large we expected the Americans to more or less clean up the show, except for Harold. He was, if you like, the great white hope,' he said.

A glance at the quality of the opposition bore out Harold's pessimism, especially with the Americans in fighting mood after a poor performance, by their standards, in Antwerp. No expense had been spared to ensure that the United States team would return triumphant from these Games, and after the American trials, chief coach Lawson Robertson pronounced the team to be the greatest athletic force ever to leave the country. A huge amount of money had been raised to ensure that the team arrived in Europe at the peak of fitness, and the giant *SS America* was chartered specially to transport the team in the lap of luxury. The promenade deck was even fitted out with a 220-yards cork track so that the athletes could train during the week-long trip. When they arrived in Paris they were greeted by thousands of cheering fans and boarded a convoy of 70 cars taking them to their own US Olympic village, an estate in the countryside outside the capital, once used as a stately home by one of Napoleon's marshals. What a difference to the preparation of the British team. 'We went from Newhaven to Dieppe, then to Paris, because it was the cheapest as well as the longest route,' Harold once said, 'and we all stayed in a rather miserable little hotel.'

The Games opened on Saturday, 5 July, and the first heats of the 100 metres began on the following day, with no less than 75 athletes taking part. The first round soon sorted out the men from the boys and Harold cruised comfortably to victory in a sedate 11 seconds, although he needed to run faster in a much more competitive second round, where he won equalling the Olympic record time of 10.6. After an agonizing 24 hours wait, the semi-finals took place the following afternoon and Harold later admitted that he nearly failed to qualify for the final. Drawn in his heat were the Australian champion 'Slip' Carr and the Americans Paddock and Bowman.

'I did a very stupid thing that nearly cost me the race. Out of the corner of my eye I saw Carr move. Bang! The gun went and I was certain there would be a recall, but I was wrong and immediately running nearly two yards behind the others. A small voice inside me said, "Keep your form, don't panic" and gradually the gap closed and I dropped down for the tape and thought I broke it. I walked disconsolately back to the start. Had I won? Had I even qualified? To feel the tape break is no criterion. An agonizing few minutes, which seemed like hours, followed, then at last the loud speaker gave my number and time. I had qualified and equalled the Olympic record for the second time. The relief was tremendous and from that moment I felt certain that I would win the final.'

The final, the ultimate goal in the Abrahams masterplan, was to be run nearly four hours later and Harold admitted afterwards that he felt like a condemned man just before going to the scaffold. But he still found time to come to the aid of his fellow Empire athlete, Arthur Porritt, who against all the odds had battled his way through to the final as well. Porritt still remembers it clearly. 'Because Harold had been working for this one race for a solid year, he and Mussabini had arranged to have a special hut just outside the stadium. After the semi-final Harold came to me and said that as I was the only other Briton left against the four Americans, would I like to share his hut with him in those awful hours before the final. I thought this was a superb gesture, because here was a man who had devoted his whole life for a year to winning this race and it had now reached its most crucial stage, yet he was willing to take in somebody he only knew vaguely to let him share the peace and quiet of his hut at this very last stage.

'We mostly just lay on our backs, chatted a little, listened to Mussabini and had a rub down. It was very quiet and restful. I don't know what the Americans were doing but Harold and I were now in a totally different state of mind. Just before the race we were taken to a holding room, prior to going onto the track, and while we were there the Prince of Wales, the future King Edward VIII, came down to see the two British athletes and wish us well. It was quite a kick.'

The six finalists – Abrahams, Porritt, Charley Paddock, Jackson Scholz, Chester Bowman and Loren Murchison – began to assemble on the track just before seven o'clock. Harold had read a note from Mussabini saying that he would win, and old Sam's parting words were ringing in his ears: 'Only think of two things, the report of the pistol and the tape. When you hear the one, run like hell till you break the other.'

An eerie hush came over the packed grandstand at the Stade Colombes as the athletes took their marks, but a huge roar went up as the starter got the field away and by the halfway point Harold, 'scudding along like some great bird,' as one reporter put it, was leading, slightly up on Scholz and Bowman, with the favourite and world record holder Paddock nowhere near them. In the final 50 metres Harold managed to stretch his lead to about a yard and he hit the tape, with the newly adopted drop finish, in 10.6, ahead of Scholz in 10.7, and, incredibly, the fast-finishing Porritt in 10.8, beating the other three Americans out of a medal. The noise from the crowd was deafening.

'My victory was a great piece of luck,' he wrote later. 'I won't say it was only luck, for I trained solidly for over nine months. But it is luck just to find your very best form at the right moment. The start was a perfect one. I soon felt myself going a tiny bit faster than the others and in just over ten seconds I had achieved the ambition of a lifetime. One chance every four years and I was never to compete in the Games again. Ten seconds out of a lifetime.

'The smallest error, less than one per cent, and all would be lost. What is the good of being second in an Olympic final? For ever one's name

Left: the front page of the Daily Mirror *after Harold Abrahams' triumph in Paris – another splendid run for Britain! Below: an unusual view of the 1924 100 metres finish showing Harold (419) winning; American Scholz (274) second; and Porritt (689) third. Paddock (on the right) leaps but can only finish fifth*

appears on the roll of Olympic champions, while the second man is soon forgotten. The winner gets all the flowers; it may not be justice, but it is life.' Shortly before he died, at his home in Florida in 1986, Jackson Scholz, a retired pulp fiction author, was asked what he remembered of Abrahams. 'I remember his ass,' he said, with a wry smile.

Porritt also smiles when he talks about the race of his life. 'I got a good enough start, but a slow one, and halfway through the race I was exactly where I expected to be, running nicely last. Then something, which I've never understood to this day, bit me and I just started getting into high gear and I could feel myself going through the whole crowd, passing one after the other. Had there been another five yards I'd have been second, I was catching up so fast. But I'd never have caught Harold, he was a clear yard ahead.

'My reaction was complete disbelief, I'd won a medal in the final. Harold was obviously delighted, you could feel it. But being Harold it didn't show, not on the outside. There was no arm waving or great joy, he just smiled. On the other hand I could sense that all his tension had gone. He'd achieved what he'd set out to do. Harold did a lot after that race, but I think it was an apex in his life. The whole of his subsequent life depended on the fact that he'd won the Olympic 100 metres.'

Above: many of Abrahams' opponents were well acquainted with this view – his rear! It is one that the American Jackson Scholz remembers clearly from the 1924 Olympics final

Below: Abrahams (second right) finishes a tired last in the final of the 1924 Olympics 200 metres, which was won by Scholz from Paddock, with Scotsman Eric Liddell (obscured) in third place

Left: Abrahams performing at the long jump for which he held the national record for 32 years Above: the moment his career ended – a terrible fall at Stamford Bridge. An operation was inadvisable due to the risk of losing a leg

Harold had become the first European to win an Olympic sprint title and remains the only Englishman to have achieved it, the perfect example of an athlete who peaked at precisely the right moment. However, there was an interesting addition to the story many years later, when he revealed that he had been using a special tonic, called Easton Syrup. This tonic contained a small amount of strychnine, a stimulant which can be found on the current IAAF list of banned drugs. Had there been dope testing at the 1924 Olympics, Harold would probably have been disqualified.

The effort he put into winning the gold medal had clearly taken its toll and in the 200 metres that followed he managed to make the final but ran in a very tired-looking last. He always maintained that he ran the first 100 metres too slowly. Scholz took the gold from Paddock and Scotsman Liddell, who would go on to win a gold in the 400 metres. But Harold did win a silver medal in the sprint relay, behind the United States, alongside Walter Rangeley, Lancelot Royle and W.P. Nichol. Running the first leg, he was two yards down on the American lead-off runner Francis Hussey, a high school kid, at the changeover.

There were no medal ceremonies at the Games and the French authorities sent both his gold and silver medals through the post. They arrived about a month after the Games and because the

French had put insufficient stamps on the package Harold had to pay the excess postage. Sadly, some 50 years later, the gold medal was stolen from his home, although a replica was cast for him by the Olympic Committee.

With the Paris Olympics over, Harold set his sights on the next Games, in Amsterdam, where he decided to ignore the track and concentrate on the long jump. However, it was during a minor long jump competition, in May 1925, that his athletic career came to an abrupt and painful end. He was competing for Bedfordshire against his old London Athletic Club, at Stamford Bridge, when he missed the board on his second jump, twisted his foot as he jumped and landed on it, falling awkwardly sideways. Cambridge athlete Rex Alston, who would team up with Harold in later life as a BBC radio commentator, was in the stadium that day.

'I had already run that afternoon and was getting changed in the dressing-room when there was a great shout outside. A few minutes later the door opened and Harold was carried in by three ambulancemen.

'He looked absolutely ghastly, as white as a sheet and only barely conscious from the pain. I have never seen a man look so ill or in such terrible pain. As he fell into the pit the momentum of his body tore all the muscles and nerves of his leg and he said himself that he heard them ripping and rending like a piece of sailcloth. For a while it was feared he would never walk again and he never put his foot to the ground for six months. Of course, that was the end of his athletics career and for the rest of his life he walked with a limp.'

Harold was his usual philosophical self, saying: 'I wonder, if, in a sense, that it was not another piece of good-bad luck. How many people find it almost impossible to retire at the right time? Would I have gone downhill and tried to go on? That was the decision I never had to make. It was made for me. Rather painfully, but it was made.' The accident formed another watershed in his life and to son Alan marked the division between two distinct phases in his life: the first, a highly ambitious young man, driving to succeed, very aggressive, totally competitive and single-minded; the second, with the pressure removed, a much more relaxed, easy-going man.

His sudden departure from competitive athletics (although he did act as the non-playing captain of the British athletics team at the 1928 Olympics) prompted him to venture into other spheres of his beloved sport, notably journalism, broadcasting and administration. His standing in the sport earned him the post of athletics correspondent of the *Sunday Times*, a job he held from 1925 until he retired in 1967. When the BBC began to broadcast athletics it was to Abrahams, with his polished approach and in-depth knowledge, that they turned to get their early programmes off the ground and he became a cornerstone in the BBC sports department for more than 40 years.

He also wrote a popular athletics book, with brother Adolphe, which dealt primarily with training but also advocated the radical, by 1928 standards, idea of broken-time payments for athletes.

From 1926 he became interested in the administration of athletics and became a member of the AAA general committee. Until his death more than 50 years later, he held a variety of posts, his reputation as a great athlete guaranteeing him the respect necessary to climb the ladder to the

Harold peers out of one of the BBC's early athletics commentary boxes at a varsity meeting in the early 1930s. He would later become the 'voice of athletics' on British radio

front benches of the controlling bodies, his legal brain and keen intellect enabling him to manage the sport efficiently.

But as his career in administration burgeoned, alongside his work in journalism and broadcasting, his life at the Bar, at which he had quite a reasonable practice by the outbreak of World War II, took something of a back seat. However, he did find time to meet and marry divorcee Sybil Evers, a light opera singer he met in 1935 at a party thrown by a mutual friend, and certainly not, as depicted in *Chariots of Fire*, before the 1924 Olympics across a crowded theatre during a performance of Gilbert & Sullivan's *Mikado*. It was a happy marriage and they adopted two children, Alan and Sue. Harold was devastated when Sybil died in 1963.

After the war, during which he served in the Ministry of Economic Warfare as head of the statistics section, he joined the Ministry of Town and Country Planning and in 1950 became Secretary of the National Parks Commission, a post he held for 13 years and which earned him the CBE. However, his passion for athletics continued and as he got older his control over the sport in Britain grew. Together he and his colleague Jack Crump ruled athletics, and his powerful position drew him into two clear areas of controversy.

Tom McNab, a national coach from 1963, thinks that Abrahams was more interested in controlling the sport on his own terms and that he was deeply suspicious about the growing role of coaches. 'Abrahams was a poacher turned gamekeeper. In his athletic days he had a professional coach and often went against the mainstream of athletics thinking. But when he became part of the establishment he became a reactionary.'

This manifested itself when Britain's first national coach, Geoff Dyson, was appointed and began trying to modernize the sport and update the coaching methods. His theories were adopted by Eastern Bloc countries and are still valid today. But to Abrahams, Dyson constituted a threat.

'He was one of the main antagonists and was undermining everything Dyson was trying to do,' says McNab. 'He got on very well with many athletes, but he had a very imperious view of his own position. He felt he and his class ran the sport and that everything else had to relate to them. But times were changing and the balance of power had to change. People like Abrahams could not develop from the public school-Oxbridge ethos. He was not well liked by the coaching fraternity and he had little time for professional

Harold pictured with his wife Sybil, a light opera singer whom he met in 1935. They shared a passion for Gilbert & Sullivan operettas, although Harold certainly did not share his more talented wife's singing ability!

coaches, which was a little ironic. I always considered him to have a first class intelligence, but he carried with him the shadows and attitudes of the twenties. He looked upon coaches like Sam Mussabini as social inferiors, people who should speak when they were spoken to, instead of people who were going to help the sport develop to meet modern demands.'

There were yet others who thought that Harold and his colleagues at the British Board were actually holding back athletics, preventing athletes from competing abroad and halting the development of the sport in a truly international sense. Among those who experienced the rough side of Abrahams' policy was the top sprinter Peter Radford.

Radford, who would win a medal in the 1960 Rome Olympics, had broken the world 200 metres record in 20.5, but had never competed against anyone who had run under 21 seconds. He wrote to the Board asking if he could go to the US Olympic trials to see how he would fare against the top Americans. 'But that wasn't met at all favourably,' recalls Peter, 'and the answer I got was a firm no. They said my duty was to run in the Midland County Championships, which were on the same day, as I'd climbed the sport's ladder through the county, area and eventually the AAA championships. So I dutifully went to the Midland County Championships, on a soggy track, with no competition, won as I pleased and came away having learned absolutely nothing.' So, Radford went to Rome knowing nothing about world class 200 metres running and despite his vast natural talent and his world record, failed to reach the final.

Harold's son Alan, however, feels that his father has been much maligned and disagrees with suggestions that he was suffering from a degree of athletics megalomania. 'He appeared to me to be a born compromiser,' he says, 'and seemed to spend an enormous amount of time running around acting as a kind of "sweeper" to all the others, who seemed to be scoring own goals. He would try and take the heat out of situations and try and stop squabbling parties from getting their hands around each other's throats.'

However, Harold also antagonised the press. He was instrumental in drawing up many of the rules that governed the sport, including one forbidding athletes to write or broadcast about athletics without the permission of the Board, a body run by himself and Crump. Permission was rarely given, and the two of them monopolized the media market, with Harold working for BBC Radio, Times Newspapers, Thomson Newspapers and *World Sports* magazine; while Crump plied his trade with BBC TV, the *Daily Telegraph* and *L'Equipe*. Apart from annoying some of the athletes, who saw their 'elders' doing exactly what they were forbidden to do, the position of these two men gave them a unique insight into the sport and much privileged information, which caused understandable friction between them and other journalists on the 'outside'.

Among them was John Rodda, athletics correspondent of the *Guardian* since 1948. 'Overall, during his time he did much good, or what he thought was good. But my feeling, one that is shared by others, was that his position was an iniquitous one. Here was one of the senior officials in the BAAB, he held posts as treasurer and chairman, a man with great influence in the sport. Should he have been working for all these

Two of the pre-war 100 metres greats. Harold Abrahams talks to Jesse Owens, whom he greatly admired, during a break in the 1966 Commonwealth Games held in Kingston, Jamaica

media organisations?

'It's obvious to me now that he was holding things back, though perhaps not deliberately. I suppose some would say it's sour grapes, but in some cases it could be quite damaging. I remember when Harold attended the selection meeting for Britain's Olympic team for 1952. We were all to be told on Monday, the day after the meeting, so our stories would appear on Tuesday. Harold sat down after the meeting, wrote his story for Thomson Newspapers, popped it into their offices on Sunday night and it promptly appeared in all their provincial papers the next morning. He'd forgotten to put an embargo on.

Even the Press Association complained.'

Although Harold did not seem perturbed by the dissent, all these things failed to endear him to many people in and around the sport and, indeed, he was not an easy person to get along with; even his friends and family admit that he could be difficult. He could be condescending and arrogant, he could be very prickly and always said what he thought, at the moment he thought it and to the person of whom he thought it, a characteristic recognised by Lord Porritt, who himself had a distinguished career as surgeon to the Royal Household and later as Governor General of New Zealand, and remained a lifelong friend of Harold; they even met for dinner, with their wives, every year at the precise time of the 1924 final.

'There's no doubt he could be a prickly character. He said what he thought, he said it quite openly and he said it pretty hard. Perhaps he wasn't feeling enough, but I think that after going through all the pain and agony in those early days to win that medal, he felt he was boss.'

Harold's friends always talk of his intense loyalty, his modesty, his keen sense of humour, his skills as a great entertainer, and of an extremely kind-hearted and generous man. He was certainly a complex personality.

Throughout his life he always remained a somewhat eccentric character and one of his legendary quirks was his fascination with time. Naturally he took a keen interest in times on the track and spent hours documenting athletics statistics, but he took this hobby a stage further. Time governed his life. He always got up at six, went to bed at ten and wore three stopwatches.

'He was always timing things,' says son Alan. 'He did small things like timing an egg, catching a bus or even going to the toilet, but he also timed things like flying from London to Australia, not just the flight, but all the various stages, like how long it took to get to the airport, time in the air, time to land. He just had this mania to time things.'

As he got older and the sport began to change, Harold believed that professionalism in athletics would become inevitable, although he never came to terms with receiving money for races, and he loathed political interference. He was a strong believer in the theory that athletes should run as individuals without flags or countries. As a member of the sport's hierarchy he did much to rationalize the laws as athletics grew more complicated, and he served for many years on the IAAF, especially on the technical committee.

A close colleague for many years and someone who knows what Harold achieved was Sir Arthur Gold, now himself one of the so-called 'elder statesmen' of British athletics. 'Harold was the voice of British athletics for more than 40 years, especially in the days before television. He was the John Arlott of his sport. Some of the comments about him are fair, he certainly wasn't blameless, but some are completely unfair. Harold was a lawyer and had all the skills of a cross-examining counsel, but he often didn't remember when he was speaking to people that he wasn't cross-examining them in the witness box. It was unintentional, but it was unfortunate. He did not suffer fools gladly and many people found him intimidating.

'There was clearly a personality clash between Harold and Geoff Dyson and they argued who had responsibility. But that argument continues today. Harold would get Dyson to justify everything he said and there were problems between them.

'It was obvious there was criticism of Harold because of his position as an administrator and a journalist. When I took over from Jack Crump I took this criticism to heart and I never wrote another sentence. I don't think Harold abused the situation but I always felt it was unwise. He was a great loss to athletics because it was impossible to replace a man who had such a depth of knowledge about the sport. Remember, he attended every Olympics, with the exception of 1932, from 1920 until he died. He also contributed greatly to framing various rules in the sport and his clear legal mind helped minimize the ambiguities in the sports rules and regulations.'

Harold remains one of the greatest figures in British athletics this century, both on and off the track. When he died, in January 1978, hundreds turned up for his memorial service and plans were already in motion to make a film based on his exploits in Paris. It was certainly strange that he never received any public recognition for his work in athletics, something that clearly irked him, especially as his elder brothers were both knighted.

However, he dominated athletics in its three main areas: first as a competitor, where winning the gold medal changed his life dramatically and gave him the impetus to break into the two other areas of the sport, administration and the media, at a very early age. For Harold, winning the gold medal was crucial and he would have been the first to admit that he effectively lived off those 10 seconds of glory for the rest of his life. What a contrast there would be in the man who succeeded him as the 100 metres champion and 'Fastest Man on Earth' in 1928.

1928 Percy Williams

Percy Williams was always an unlikely, as well as an unwilling, sporting hero. The son of a tram conductor, he was born in May 1908 and grew up in Vancouver. His parents separated when he was quite young and he was brought up by his mother. Although they did not live in abject poverty, money was certainly scarce. Percy was always indifferent to sport as a child; his first recollections were of winning a junior cycle race, although there are records of him winning a school sports 100 yards race, at just 13 years old. But two years later he suffered a bout of rheumatic fever which damaged his heart so badly that the doctors told his mother he should never again be allowed to over-exert himself.

This ban on active sports did not bother young Percy unduly – his general indifference was supported by a poor physique, which was hardly in the sportsman mould. He was thin and frail with a delicate constitution, but his interest in sport was reawakened at high school, where after two years of inactivity he ignored doctors' orders and began winning prizes in shooting and tennis. The sports-minded principal of the school encouraged him and his classmates to compete in many different sports, including running, and it was he who convinced Percy that he should enter a sprint race against Vancouver champion Wally

Above: this picture, taken in the 1930s, captures perfectly the powerful start that Percy Williams gained from holes dug in the cinder track

Scott in 1926. 'You kinda got pushed into these things,' Percy said many years later. 'You were a bum if you didn't try out.'

The race brought Percy into contact with a man who would have a lasting effect on his life – track coach Bob Granger. Granger was coaching Scott and watched in complete disbelief as this skinny, almost ghost-like 18-year-old, ran his man to a dead heat. He later recalled: 'I think he violated every known principle in the running game during that race. He ran with his arms glued to his sides. It actually made me tired to watch him.' But Granger recognised young Percy's promise and immediately took him under his wing.

It is clear now that but for the fanatical support of Bob Granger, Percy would never have competed in the Olympic Games, or any other Games, a fact that he himself confirmed many years later. He bullied, cajoled and persuaded Percy to achieve success after success, in a sport for which the athlete clearly had little interest. His enthusiasm waned even further, if that were possible, when he learned that Granger had banned, his real sporting love – swimming.

The coach, by today's standards, had some bizarre ideas about training and technique. Granger maintained that Percy possessed 'precious energy' which should be preserved at all costs. If possible he would always avoid letting the frail Williams burn himself out in training.

He mapped out special training sessions and designed racing tactics geared to conserving the athlete's valuable energy reserves. On cold days Granger would rub him down with cocoa butter and keep him covered with layers of clothing, even blankets, to keep in his body heat and stop his muscles from getting cold. At one meeting, much to the amusement of the crowd, Percy emerged from the dressing-room wearing four tracksuits and three sweaters, looking like a visitor from another planet. Such was Granger's fascination with preserving Percy's 'precious energy' that he even organized groups of boys to demonstrate starts and arm actions so that Percy could watch, save his strength and practise later in front of a mirror.

Gradually his style and technique began to improve and Granger started entering him in local meets, setting records that would last in Canada for more than a quarter of a century. At a high school meet he set records for the 100 and 220 yards on a grass track, where the first 50 yards were run uphill and the last ten yards under water.

It was during the 1927 season that Percy had his first unhappy brush with officialdom, the first of many as it turned out, and the root of his bitterness toward athletics in his declining years. He won the British Columbia sprint title and this

Below: Percy Williams, an unknown from Vancouver before the Games, wins the 100 metres title in 10.8 seconds in the 1928 Olympics

qualified him to run in the Canadian champion-ships in Hamilton. In a rare interview with Vancouver sports columnist Jim Kearney, Percy recalled: 'The official here, who was supposed to look after my travel, had already gone east. He'd decided before I even ran that I wasn't good enough to go. So he went instead. Bob Brown, the baseball man, bought my ticket and sent me. But Bob Granger had to work his way there washing dishes on the railway diner.'

By the back door route both men duly arrived in Hamilton for the championships, but it was time for the Canadian officials to upset the young runner again. 'Tracks in those days had only six lanes, not eight,' said Percy, 'or at least they were supposed to have six. After the heats six of us qualified for the final of the 100. Then one of the officials suddenly discovered – I think he may have taken off one of his shoes and counted his toes to make sure – that the track had only five lanes, not six. But they had the solution. There were two runners from western Canada, Buster Brown, from Edmonton, and myself. So they tossed a coin to see which one of us would drop out. I lost and didn't get to run.'

The following year, a little older and wiser, Percy again won the state sprint title and headed east across Canada for the national champion-ships, which this time would be the Olympic trials. This time the officials paid his fare, but the Trans Canada Railway again had the pleasure of coach Granger's company as a dishwasher. Some of Canada's top sprinters were on show, many of whom had been training at US colleges, and Williams, still a relative unknown even in his own country, caused something of a stir by taking both the 100 metres (10.6) and the 200 metres (22.0) and booking his ticket for the Olympics in convincing style.

The Canadian assault on the 1928 Games was launched on a shoestring budget and once again there was no ticket for poor Granger and this time no trains across the Atlantic or dishes to pay the way. Seeing how this might affect Percy's performance, his mother Dot, a woman totally devoted to her only child, toured Vancouver rais-ing money to send Granger with her son. She managed to raise several hundred dollars, enough to keep him in the same hotel as the Canadian team, but Granger had to pay his fare. Once again the coach's ingenuity was not found to be wanting.

'The team sailed for Europe on a liner,' Percy remembered, 'but Granger had to work his way over on a cattle boat. It was headed for Amster-dam, he knew that, but he didn't know how many stops it would make before it got there, or even if he'd arrive on time. As it happened he got there only three days after we did and took over my training.'

Percy's room in the Canadian team's third-rate hotel, on the edge of Amsterdam's seedy red light district, was made the training headquarters and a mattress was pushed against a wall to use as a buffer for starting practice – much to the conster-nation of the management and the guests next door. Granger, who refused to leave his protégé in the hands of team coach Cap Cornelius, always maintained that these bedroom practice sessions gave Percy the rocket starts that marked his racing in Amsterdam.

The personal care that Granger gave Percy was certainly unique, and another member of the sprint team, Harry Warren, now a professor of geology at the University of British Columbia, has every reason to remember his role in his unusual training methods.

'Percy was a delicate boy,' he recalled, 'and Granger wouldn't let him out of his sight for a minute if he could help it. Percy had this habit at night of pulling the sheet over his head when he went to sleep and Granger was afraid he might suffocate.

'I was sleeping in the same room as Percy and I'd usually go over and check and pull the sheet down. But Granger was sleeping on a chair outside the door in the corridor and there would always be a note stuffed under the door asking if he was all right. I'd push a note back under the door saying yes he was.'

The Games opened on Saturday, 28 June, without the presence of their creator Baron de Coubertin, who was lying seriously ill in France. He sent a poignant message to the athletes say-ing: 'I should be wise to take this present opportu-nity of bidding you farewell.' Although it was another nine years before he died, he never saw another Olympics.

The day after the opening ceremony, on the Sunday afternoon, Percy and 86 other hopefuls began the 100 metres heats and he cantered easily through the first round, equalled the Olympic record of 10.6 in the second round and thus attracted the attention of the 40,000 spectators, who were clearly warming to this slightly-built 'unknown' from Canada. The semis were held on the following day, but Percy started badly and could only finish second to the big American Bob McAllister. However, it was enough to carry him safely into the final several hours later.

By now the Americans were worried and were making excuses about how and why Percy was

Percy Williams, on one knee in the centre, looks down the track as he and the other sprinters prepare for the 100 metres final

winning. The track had only been finished the day before the competition began and was very soft, so the US coaches and pressmen claimed that their runners were all 'pounders' and could not run in such conditions, whereas Percy was a floater and made light of the stodgy track. When he trounced the same US sprinters on the post-Olympic indoor circuit, one wry Canadian pressman observed that all the sprints must have been run on soft wood tracks!

Two hours before the final was due to start, Granger took Percy to the dressing-room and gave him a book to read, supervised a short warm-up and rubbed him down with cocoa butter, a large consignment of which had survived its trip on the cattle boat. The line-up for the final was impressive: towering over the diminutive Williams, as they dug their starting holes and warmed up, were the giant 6ft 2in British sprint star Jack London; the New York policeman McAllister, who had beaten Percy in the semis; the Californian pre-race favourite Frank Wykoff; the German Georg Lammers; and the white South African Wilfred Legg.

Percy was still the real underdog but after two false starts – by Legg and Wykoff – he tore out of his holes and led the field all the way to the tape, holding off late challenges from the fast finishing London and Wykoff, to win by a yard in 10.8. The crowd went wild with delight. They were surprised, Percy was surprised and so too were the Olympic officials – they could not find a Canadian flag or a record of the Canadian national anthem and so the medal ceremony had to be delayed while they searched frantically for both. Winning the title was the climax to nearly two years' hard

work for Percy but it also had its dark side. He wrote in his diary that night: 'So I'm supposed to be the world's 100 metres champion. Crushed apples. No more fun in running now.'

However, the victory also had its lighter side and many years later Percy remembered: 'People don't believe me when I tell them, but I didn't know any of those people I ran against. I didn't even know what they looked like until I saw them on the track. And certainly very few people over there could recongnize me. In the age of television people think this is impossible. But let me give you an example. A few hours after I won the 100, Doral Pilling, a Canadian javelin thrower, and I saw this big crowd outside our hotel. So we came out to see what it was all about. We joined the mob, looking over their shoulders. I asked a person in front of me why they were there and he said, "We're waiting for the Canadian runner Williams to come out of the hotel." I didn't tell him who I was. I stood around waiting for him too and talking to some of the people, it was much more fun.'

There was little time to relax and savour the moment as the heats in the 200 metres were already upon them and despite his gold in the 100 metres, Williams was again given little chance, especially against a field of fresh runners that included the American gold and silver medallists from the event four years earlier, Jackson Scholz and Charley Paddock. But again he proved the doubters wrong, easing into the final, whereas both Paddock and his highly fancied US team-mate Charlie Borah were edged out.

Coach Granger, still obsessed with Percy's well-being, was now beside himself, spending hours roaming the streets outside the hotel trying to quieten the rowdy taverns and clubs so that his charge could get some sleep. On the day, Granger once again marked Williams' card and perceived the German Helmut König as the danger man. He told Percy to stick with König coming out of the bend and to pull him in down the home straight. Sure enough, Percy was sitting a yard or so behind the German as they came out of the curve and, as they entered the straight, Percy changed gear and came home a yard clear, with Britain's Walter Rangeley overhauling König for the silver. The German dead-heated with the fast-finishing Scholz for third and the judges offered a re-run, but Scholz magnanimously declined and gave the bronze to König.

The stadium rose to cheer the first double-sprint champion since 1912, and the first man to reach him was the 1908 Canadian 200-metre champion Bobby Kerr, who heard the unassuming

Williams say simply: 'Won't Granger be pleased?' Even the great Charley Paddock was in awe of the new champion, telling reporters and anyone else who would listen: 'That boy doesn't run – he flies. He's a real thoroughbred. He starts a race as a pull runner, with his leg action in front of him and his knees high. But in the closing metres of a race he's not a pull runner, but a driver. In all my years of running and watching runners, I've never seen a sprinter who could employ two methods in one race.'

Percy failed to win a third gold when the Canadian sprint relay team was disqualified for running out of lane and the US team took first place and equalled the world record. However, there was one last award for the Canadian before he left Amsterdam and a rather surprising one. A massive medical survey had been conducted throughout the Games by a team of Dutch doctors and scientists to try and pinpoint the perfect Olympic athlete. Every one of the 3,000 athletes at the Games had to fill in forms and undergo medical tests, which included details about their height, weight and measurements, and tests on breathing, weight-lifting and chest expansion. At the end of this exhaustive study the researchers announced, to everyone's amazement, including the athlete in question, that the skinny looking 5ft 7in, 125lb pound Percy Williams was the most perfect athlete at the Olympics.

With the main show over, Percy and some of the Canadian team were despatched on a European tour by their official overlords, to earn back some of the money that they had spent on transporting them to the Games. They insisted, however, that Percy ran only relays so as to preserve his unbeaten record before returning to Canada. For this journey the officials delved deep into their pockets and came up with a ticket to get Granger home alongside Percy and the team, rather than the cattle. Almost overnight, Percy was transformed from a nobody in his own city into an international celebrity and therefore the trip back across Canada to Vancouver was just one long string of civic receptions, parties and celebrations. No other Canadian has taken the country by storm as Percy did during those few weeks. At each major city he was hauled off the train and taken to special welcoming receptions. At Winnipeg he was given a golden retriever, which sparked his lifelong interest in hunting dogs; and in Regina, his old friend and sprinter Harold Wright, who just missed the 1928 team but ran in 1932, dragged him off to the city theatre for a huge party. Wright, who became Canadian Olympic Association President, remained one of Williams' few close friends.

But the biggest welcome of all was reserved for his triumphant return to his home town Vancouver. 'City Goes Wild As Percy Comes Home' screamed the front page of the *Vancouver Sun* on the day that he finally arrived in mid-September. The city's schools were closed, the state Premier S.F. Tolmie and the City Mayor sat with Percy in an open-topped car as a vast motorcade snaked through the streets, while some 30,000 cheering people lined the route to show their appreciation of what he had achieved in Europe. He even got an escort from the Mounties. After all the speeches, congratulations, dinners and parties, Percy, now hailed as Vancouver's Lindbergh, was presented with a new Graham-Paige sports car, $500 in gold and, later, a $15,000 trust fund.

'If we received anything over $25 we were supposed to be professional,' recalled Percy. 'But the officials had an out. If they said it was OK, then it could be done.' By now several universities in the United States were vying with each other to enrol him, but he eventually accepted an offer of a place at the local University of British Columbia. Such were the demands on his time and his lack of enthusiasm for studying that he caused a furore by leaving college and running off to compete in the US indoor season. There were calls in the Canadian press for his trust fund to be withdrawn, but he managed to ride the storm. Throughout 1929 and 1930, Percy was simply the best sprinter in the world and ran his way across the United States, winning an astonishing 21 out of 22 races. His feat prompted US Olympic team manager General Douglas MacArthur to pronounce him: 'The greatest sprinter the world has ever seen.' Track fan and comic Will Rogers joined the complimentary bandwagon when he told a radio audience: 'The United States must annex Canada to acquire Williams.'

During this indoor success he posted a new 45-yard world record of 4.9 seconds, equalled three other world records and beat the rising US star Eddie Tolan, whose day would come during the 1932 Olympics. Years later Percy maintained that his indoor tour of the USA was the highpoint of his career, and not the 1928 Olympics. 'I think I came up with my best performances in the winter of 1929. I had never run indoors before, but I ran 22 races in 21 days and I came second in one and won all the others. Everyone remembers Amsterdam, but nobody remembers that. Louis D. Taylor, who was the Mayor of Vancouver, sent me a wire urging me to come home before I burned myself out. But I was enjoying myself. I was running so often I didn't have to train. I liked the indoor circuit better than outdoors. It had a real circus atmosphere. It was more fun.'

When the fun was finally over, he returned, early in 1930, to a Depression-hit Vancouver to look for a job. But memories were short and all the back-slapping businessmen of two years earlier could only apologise and tell him that times were hard and there just were not any suitable openings. So he continued to run and in August, at the Canadian national championships, set a new world record of 10.3 for the 100 metres – a mark that stood unbeaten for six years. 'I'm glad I don't have to run like that every day,' he told pressmen. Sadly his running days would come to an end sooner than he thought.

About 40 miles from Toronto, where he set his world mark, preparations were well underway in Hamilton for the staging of the first British Empire Games (now the Commonwealth Games). The day of the 100 yards final (the Empire had not yet gone metric) was cold and wet, so Bob Granger cocooned Percy in blankets until the very last moment and gave him his usual cocoa butter rub down. He was perfectly warmed up as the runners went down on the starting line and waited for the gun. Just as the starter raised his pistol a national anthem suddenly came blaring through the PA system. Some athletes from a previous event were receiving their medals on the podium and the organisers decided to delay the start of the race until it was over. By the the time the race was ready to start, the finalists, including Williams, were all shivering and soaking wet.

Percy took up the story: 'Forty yards from the tape I felt the muscle go. Two things can happen. The leg collapses and you fall down. Or it keeps flipping and you manage to finish the race. Mine kept flipping and I managed to win.' Old newsreel film of the race shows Williams' hand reacting at the precise moment of the tear and clutching at his left thigh. It was a miracle that he kept going, let alone winning, despite almost falling through the tape. 'The Canadian team didn't have a doctor there,' recalled Williams, 'and nobody seemed concerned except Bobby Robinson (who was promoting the Games) and his only concern was that he would be out of the $700 he'd been promised if he could deliver me to a meet in Chicago the following week.' The damage was a severe muscle tear high up on the thigh, in the groin area, and although he managed to resume training, the injury never healed properly and Percy never again scaled the heights of his early racing career.

But so outstanding was he, that despite this injury he still managed to qualify for Canada's

Percy Williams, despite tearing a thigh muscle, manages to finish and win the British Empire Games 100 yards in Hamilton, Canada, in 1930

sprint quartet at the Los Angeles Games in 1932, captaining the team. 'Before I went to LA I had a physical and the doctor told me that an operation right after the injury in Hamilton would have repaired the damage completely. But it was too late at this point.' He recalled bitterly how they were treated this time around by Canadian officialdom.

'After the team was named, a man from the Canadian National Railways arrived on my doorstep. He'd been authorized by the AAU in the east to offer me a one-way ticket to LA and $10 in expense money. I thanked him and told him I'd make other arrangements.

'Some of us ended up driving down with George Irvine, who owned a Seven-Up plant here in Vancouver. We kept track of all our expenses, divided them up among us and handed them in. A team official said we'd be reimbursed but couldn't say when, so we told him if it wasn't by opening day we wouldn't be running.

'We were angry. The team officials had come in by train from eastern Canada, travelling first class. One of the hurdlers told us the athletes from the east had been offered a choice. If they rode the day coach they could eat in the diner. But if they wanted a berth to sleep in they'd have to grab their food at the station sandwich counters whenever the train stopped.'

The LA experience was just another that soured Percy's memories of athletics. In addition to the problems with the officials, his injury meant elimination in the semis of the 100 metres and anchoring the Canadian relay team to fourth spot, just outside a medal place. It was the last track and field meeting in which he raced and the last he ever attended. After returning to Vancouver he made an abortive attempt to set up an indoor track meeting, which was thwarted by his old friends at the Canadian AAU, and then abandoned the sport forever and, in his own words, 'grabbed a pencil and started writing insurance.'

He was a keen aviator and acquired a commercial pilot's licence, which he put to good use during World War II by training navigators. After the war he returned to insurance and set up his own company, which he ran until a few years before his death. Throughout his life he enjoyed shooting, golf, dogs and horses, but never athletics.

When Vancouver opened its new athletics stadium in 1954, for that year's Empire Games, there was a suggestion that it should be named after Percy, as a few years earlier he had been voted the nation's outstanding track and field performer of the century. It was greeted unenthusiastically by officialdom, who felt that he had done little to encourage sport in the city since retiring from the track. But Percy was always candid about the motives behind his track career. Interviewed in the early 1950s he admitted: 'I never did like running. Anything I accomplished I did because of the determination of Bob Granger. I always thought it was a lot of hogwash to say that you ran for your flag and country. I was out there to beat the guy beside me.' But the Games organisers did manage to persuade him to 'turn the first sod' of the new stadium.

In 1972, he was voted Canada's all-time Olympic athlete and should have played a role in the massive publicity drive aimed at successfully launching the Montreal Olympics of 1976. This was orchestrated by the COA President Harold Wright, his great friend, but Percy refused to take part. 'I was one of his few good friends and I'd known him for years,' says Wright, 'but he wouldn't even do it for me. He wouldn't do anything that would put him in the limelight.'

In 1978, on the 50th anniversary of his Olympic feat, he was given the Vancouver Civic Recognition Award and two years later he received the Order of Canada, one of the nation's highest awards, although he refused to travel to Ottawa to receive it, so Governor General Edward Shreyer came to Vancouver to perform the ceremony.

Wright agrees that especially towards the end of Percy's life he became a sad figure. 'He was a real reluctant hero. I suppose he was just a terribly shy, introverted and lonesome guy. The only way he would come out was if my wife would call and tell him we were picking him up at a certain time. Even then he'd be waiting in the street outside his front door. We'd never go in. He felt people had taken advantage of him during his athletic career and I suppose that was true. But he was a true friend and he didn't have many close friends because of his shyness. But he really was a nice person.'

Columnist Jim Kearney, probably the last journalist to conduct an in-depth interview with Williams, agrees that he was a deeply embittered man. 'He felt very bitter about the treatment of athletes in his time, especially compared to the ritzy lifestyles of some of the officials. He lived with his mother until she died during the sixties and from then on lived alone. I think he had a bit of a drink problem and he avoided all publicity. I know he suffered terribly from arthritis and swallowed a dozen aspirins a day to ease the pain in his knees and ankles.'

After his heart condition worsened and he had suffered two strokes, Percy sought a quick end to his pain and committed suicide in November 1982.

Over 200 people attended his memorial service nearly 50 years after his double Olympic triumph; the Rev Dr Gerard Hobbs told the gathering: 'Percy Williams proved a difficult hero. Shy by disposition, he found himself uncomfortable in the spotlight, reluctant to exploit the opportunities for glory that fame threw his way. When injury brought an end to his brief running career, he withdrew to a quiet life of friends, of work, of the sport he could still enjoy without fanfare, hesitatingly accepting the honours that continued to come his way.'

For the few who managed to get close to him, Percy was a kind and honest friend, but to those who did not, who were many, he could be a difficult, introverted and bitter man, who put nothing back into the sport that had made him famous. But Percy's dilemma was that he had never wanted to be famous. He had always been acutely shy, almost to the point of being a recluse. Everyone knew Percy Williams the legend, but few knew the man. The harsh and sad facts were that the man was not as endearing as the legend.

BLACK POWER

1932 Eddie Tolan

'*I want so much to send the American flag to the top of the winner's staff . . . I know if I can win the two dash events . . . some brightness will return to our lives*'

1936 Jesse Owens

'*He was the smoothest runner I have ever seen and the most physically co-ordinated. When he ran it was like water flowing downhill*'

1948 Harrison Dillard

'*I remember the race vividly . . . I was able to stay relaxed and kept driving and praying for the tape to just hurry up and get there*'

1932 Eddie Tolan

As the 1930s began, a new crop of sprinters arrived on the scene ready to replace the recently injured Olympic champion Percy Williams and prepare for the next Games in Los Angeles in 1932. For the first time, an increasing number of black American athletes were emerging, especially among the new wave of sprinting talent, alongside some of the more established white track stars. A few black Olympic athletes, rare though they were, had been selected for USA teams since the Games began, but the American college system, particularly in the east, was now waking up to the fact that black students and black athletes were just as talented as their white counterparts. Progress was beginning to be made towards offering them more in terms of sports scholarships and educational opportunities, but these were still the early days and opportunities were extremely limited. Two men who managed to take advantage of this small move forward were

People still disagree about the finish of the 1932 Olympic 100 metres final. Tolan and Metcalfe appeared to hit the tape together, and afterwards both claimed to have won the race

the black sprinters Ralph Metcalfe and Eddie Tolan, a pair who would go on to dominate the sprint events at the Olympics.

Metcalfe, a tall, powerful athlete, famed for his slow start and astonishing finish, ran for Marquette University in Milwaukee, whereas Tolan, a tiny, bespectacled figure, hailed from America's traditional 'school of sprint champions', the University of Michigan, where Olympic sprint champions Archie Hahn and Ralph Craig were produced. They were challenged in the United States by the improving Frank Wykoff, who had made the 1928 Olympic final at just eighteen, and the Ohio State star George Simpson, who had claimed a new world record of 9.4 in the 100 yards in 1929 only to see it rejected by the IAAF because he had used an illegal piece of equipment to help give him a better start – namely, starting blocks. The only competition for the superior US sprinting force came from the tough German Arthur Jonath, South African Daniel Joubert and the 24-year-old Australian James Carlton, who ran an incredible 20.6 for the 220 yards in Sydney during January of the Olympic year only to see it ignored by the authorities because the judges ruled that there was a following wind, although eye witness reports maintained that there was no wind and that Carlton had won by about 15 yards. So incensed was Carlton about the decision that he promptly quit athletics, did not go to Los Angeles, became a monk and entered a monastery.

So the scene was set for a high standard of sprint competition in Los Angeles and although Metcalfe was a clear favourite in everyone's books, it was generally agreed that the race would be close. However, no-one could have foreseen just how close it would actually be nor predicted that the result of both sprint finals would still be causing doubt and controversy

even in today's athletic circles. To the day he died, a respected Chicago Congressman in the late 1970s, Metcalfe insisted that he did not lose the 100 metres, a view that seems to be backed by the official black and white film of the event, although the camera itself was not directly in line with the tape. The athlete actually declared the winner of the contest was Detroit's Eddie Tolan who, at just 5ft 4½in, remains the smallest ever Olympic sprint champion. With his horn-rimmed glasses and a bandage around his left knee to protect an old football injury, a more unlikely looking champion would be difficult to find. But if the tale of Percy Williams was a sad one, then Tolan's life story was one of similar misfortune and despite triumphing against all the odds to take his place in Olympic history, his life was dogged by bad luck, misery, setbacks and illness.

Eddie was born in Denver, Colorado, in September 1908, and grew up with his family in Salt Lake City, realising at an early age that he was faster than most of his friends when the angry farmers near his home could not catch him when he stole their watermelons. His parents, an hotel cook and a washerwoman, found that work was scarce, and in 1924 they moved the family north to Detroit, where a year later Eddie started attending the local Cass Tech High School. Despite his obvious talent for running, his first love was football, but he maintained that his older brother Hart was the real athlete of the family. Eddie always looked up to Hart and when his big brother became the first athlete to win six school letters in the state of Utah – in their Salt Lake City days – he knew that sport was where his own future lay. When the two boys enrolled at Cass Tech, Eddie started his football career as a reserve for his brother on the school team, but when the track coach saw his speed he convinced him to try out for the track.

Eddie was a worker and trained hard, and while Hart did not have the necessary application to make it to the top, Eddie always delighted in relating a story about how a short time after graduating from college he was due to run in a big track meeting in Detroit but fell ill. Hart, who had been out of competition for about five years, put on a pair of spikes and went out and won the 100 yards to keep up the family name. During his three years at Cass Tech, Eddie won 17 out of the 18 state indoor and outdoor competitions he

entered and his bedroom was plastered with the countless medals and ribbons that he had won, including those he was given for winning the national interscholastic meeting in both the sprint distances.

In 1928 he chose to attend the University of Michigan, despite great interest from six other top colleagues, hoping to play football for the great coach Fielding Yost. He managed to pick up a scholarship for the college, but it did not cover all his fees, and so his mother had to work around the clock, doing mostly menial jobs, to pay his way through college. But Eddie was not destined to become the great football player he had always dreamed about, although he always considered the six touchdowns he scored as a quarterback for Cass Tech as his greatest sporting thrill, rather than his Olympic success in 1932.

It was football that almost cost him his future in sport when he ripped the ligaments in his left

Eddie Tolan, nicknamed the 'Midnight Express', poses for a picture after another successful run for the University of Michigan. His left knee was always bandaged to protect an old football injury

knee during a junior game and was told that probably he would never run again. Of course he did, but it was always with that famous elasticated bandage protecting the damaged knee and he walked with a limp from that day. 'It was a surgical miracle,' he once told a Detroit sportswriter, 'I didn't think I'd be able to walk properly again, much less run.' It was for precisely that reason when he joined Michigan that head track coach Steve Farrell managed to persuade the college powers to have him barred from football so that he could concentrate his efforts on running – a decision that deeply upset the young athlete. But Farrell managed to convince Tolan that he was doing the right thing, and many years later Eddie admitted: 'The track team did a lot more travelling then so I saw the opportunity to travel on a Pullman and see the country. People would say on the streets of Chicago when they saw me, "That's Eddie Tolan of Michigan".

'That was something because I wouldn't have been allowed in a lot of hotels and places if I hadn't been with the Michigan team.' Had he continued to play football in addition to his track running, he would never have reached the 1932 Olympic team, let alone the winner's rostrum.

As a freshman at Michigan he was dubbed the 'Midnight Express', for obvious reasons, a nickname that stuck with him throughout his running career, although some of his college friends liked to call him 'Twinkle Toes' because of his amazing leg speed. Eddie did have a crack at making the 1928 Olympic team but he still was not ready for the major league. His opportunity came in the following summer after an indifferent start to his intercollegiate racing, when he took his first top-class title by winning the 100 yards at the Big Ten Championship, at the Dyche Stadium, at Evanston, Illinois, sprinting to a new world record of 9.5 *and* beating the highly rated George Simpson. The trip also revealed the realities of how different it was being a black athlete on the road, even if it was with a top college.

'It was my first Big Ten meet and there was one other coloured fellow on the team, a weight man called Booker Brooks,' Eddie revealed during a rare newspaper interview in the 1950s. 'We went to three hotels before one would take us. Then they told us we would have to eat in the kitchen. I wanted to go back to Ann Arbor and told Farrell I was quitting. I remember what he told me. "You are the only coloured boys on any Michigan team. If you quit you will hurt your people." I called friends in Detroit and they told me to stay, so during the meet we ate our three meals each day at the YMCA, a coloured YMCA.'

Later that year he won both sprints at the national AAU meeting, a success that earned him a place on a small US track team to tour Europe, where he twice equalled the world 100 metre record of 10.4 and earned rave reviews from sports writers throughout the Continent. Even though he worked hard, Eddie did not enjoy training, and if he could win a race without turning on the gas, then he would do it. A track official who held watches on races in Michigan for 40 years, Phil Diamond, remembered: 'If someone else could run 100 yards in 9.6 seconds, Eddie would beat him by a foot. If the competition could do only 10.1, Eddie would still only win by a foot.' Diamond remembered some of the stunts that coach Farrell used to get Tolan to train harder. 'Farrell knew all the gadgets and stunts used in the professional races in England. One morning he offered theatre tickets as prizes for the winners at different distances, but Tolan wasn't interested.

'He knew he could beat all the other sprinters so why bother? Finally Farrell called over Roddy Cox, a big hammer thrower and football player. He put another man on Cox's back and then bet Tolan he couldn't run 100 yards faster than Cox could run and carry his rider 50 yards. Tolan bit at that. The suggestion that he couldn't beat a slow man with a heavy load, even with a 50 yard head start was too much. But Farrell knew what he was doing. Tolan couldn't win no matter how much he tried. Farrell knew from experience that one man would carry another 50 yards in 9.1 or 9.2 seconds. Tolan was the fastest sprinter in the world but even if he equalled his own world record of 9.5 he was still going to lose.'

When the 1930 track season began, Eddie was already established as one of the world's top sprinters, if not the top sprinter, but by his standards it was a poor season, with only one major title, the AAU 100 yards, plus a win at a bizarre meet in Canada to show for his efforts. His trip to Vancouver was for the Dominion Day competiton and on a warm July afternoon he amazed the crowd and the judges by clocking an astonishing 10.2 for the 100 metres, on a track that was proven to be slightly uphill. He then followed that performance by taking second place behind Simpson, by a whisker, in the 200 metres where both athletes clocked a world record equalling 20.6. For some reason the wind conditions were not known and the records were never officially ratified by the IAAF. A month later Percy Williams set a new world mark of 10.3, and an official 10.2 would not be set for another six years.

After that disappointment Eddie continued his

mixed fortunes on the track, losing some races, winning others, and in 1931, the year in which he graduated from Michigan, he was rated the best 220 yards man in the world, with both the NCAA and IC4A titles, but he had little success in the shorter sprint. Although he had graduated and set his sights on becoming a doctor and studying at medical school, he put the plans on ice so that he could concentrate on making the 1932 Olympic team and took a job as a teacher, working at the West Virginia Institute, near Charleston. The job did not pay much but what little he earned was sent back home where his entire family were out of work and suffering like so many others in the Great Depression. When he eventually returned to Detroit in the spring of 1932 ready to start training for the Games, he did not have enough money to make the daily trips out to Ann Arbor to run on the University of Michigan track – a necessity because Detroit did not possess a track and his coach Steve Farrell was based there.

At first he had to be content with barricading some of the streets around the Tolans' west side home so he could practise on the road, but an old Cass Tech friend, then a chauffeur, drove him back and forth to the track so he could qualify for the Mid West trials. He attended the Chicago trials thanks to a donation from a member of the Michigan Olympic Committee, but his benefactor was unable to help when it came to travelling to the final Olympic trials out in Palo Alto, California. Eddie had decided the only way to reach the trials was to hitch-hike the 1800 or so miles, when another benefactor, former Governor Alex Gorsebeck, rallied to his aid, signing a cheque for his fare and living expenses in California.

But in the trials he was dominated by the rising star from Marquette University, Ralph Metcalfe, who eclipsed him in both the 100 and 200 metres, with Eddie placing second and George Simpson assuring himself of a place in both sprints by nipping third. While Eddie had been the number one US sprinter in the pre-Olympic year, Metcalfe had breezed through the 1932 season undefeated and his awesome form made him the out and out favourite to beat the apparently fading Tolan in Los Angeles.

Naturally the Americans were heralding the Games as the greatest leap forward in Olympic history and despite concern that they would fail because of the global depression, they were carried off in some style by the organisers, with more than 1500 athletes, from 34 nations, arriving to compete and in excess of 1,250,000 spectators paying to sit and watch the Games unfold. They would become one of the most successful in Olym-

pic history, the first to boast a healthy cash surplus at the end, which ran to almost $1 million, and one in which 16 new world records were set, two were equalled and 33 new Olympic marks were made.

On Saturday, 30 July, with a mammoth crowd of nearly 105,000 packed into the stadium, the Vice President Charles Curtis declared the Games open in the absence of President Herbert Hoover who was too busy campaigning in the forth-coming presidential elections, which he then lost, to spare time for the Olympics.

The 100 metres competition, which began soon after the opening, was a record breaking affair from start to finish, with German Arthur Jonath shaving a tenth of a second off the Olympic record in running 10.5 in his heat, only to see Eddie Tolan lower the record to 10.4 in the second round. In the first semi-final, Tolan was awarded first place in 10.7 ahead of the South African Joubert, while the Japanese star Takayoshi Yoshioka edged out the reigning champion Percy Williams for a place in the final. However, photographic evidence over-ruled the official verdict as Joubert actually won ahead of Yoshioka, with Tolan only third, two feet ahead of Williams.

In the second semi, Metcalfe was still steamrollering everyone before him and cantered to victory in 10.6, with team-mate Simpson second and Jonath in third. These six sprinters made up the field for probably the most talked about Olympic sprint final in history, a final that was held under clear blue skies and high temperatures on Monday, 1 August. The American fans were keen to re-establish their supremacy in an event that they had not won for 12 years, and a hush fell across the crowd as the lane announcements were made, putting Tolan out in lane six, by the stands, with Jonath inside him, while Metcalfe drew lane three. All attention was on the six runners as they stripped off their track suits and limbered up, dug their starting holes and got to their marks. At the gun, the visibly nervous Joubert got a flyer and the athletes were called back for another start, but this time they were away cleanly and it was the Japanese star Yoshioka who shot out of his holes the fastest and held the lead for the first 40 metres. But then Eddie began to assert himself, and at about 50 metres he had a definite lead. As the rest of the field drew level with the fading Japanese sprinter it was Ralph Metcalfe who began to put on his famed finishing burst and from 80 metres onwards there was almost nothing to separate the two runners; Eddie's piston-like leg speed keeping him level with the fluent power of Metcalfe until they both seemed to hit the tape

Above: this picture of the finish of the 1932 Olympic 100 metres final supports the view that Metcalfe may well have hit the tape first and won Left: however, the judges awarded the gold to Tolan, with Metcalfe receiving the silver and Germany's Arthur Jonath the bronze medal

together in a dead heat.

Eddie, with his spectacles taped to his temples to prevent them falling off during the race, pulled up just past the tape, while Metcalfe eased off the power and cantered around the bottom turn before turning and walking back to the finish line. Although it was uncertain as to who had won the race, it was clear that Jonath had pipped Simpson for the bronze. Metcalfe went straight over to Eddie and shook his hand, then arm-in-arm they walked to the start, photographers clustered around them, talking animatedly. It was some time before the announcement came booming over the public address system that Eddie had been named the winner, just two inches in front of Metcalfe, in a new Olympic record of 10.3, which also equalled Williams' world record. Metcalfe was given the same time, but a silver medal, a fact that haunted him for the rest of his life. Shortly before he died he said: 'I have never been convinced I was defeated. It should have been a tie. The judges took a lot longer than they normally did and they awarded me the same time as Eddie Tolan.'

He took it sportingly at the time but a close look at the photographs and the film of the event adds credence to Metcalfe's claim for a dead heat. In fact, had the race been run a year later he probably would have won because the rules were changed as a result of the controversy over the finish. Shortly after the Games the AAU changed the rules so that crossing the line determined the winner of the race, not just breasting the tape, which is how Eddie just edged out Metcalfe. The AAU convention voted retroactively and awarded the 100 metres title to both Tolan and Metcalfe, but not the gold medal – the Olympic organisers never accepted their vote as binding, and Eddie's name stands alone in the record books.

Metcalfe, however, had his best event at Los Angeles to come, where his speed and power in the 200 metres would count and again he was everyone's favourite to win. The final was held on Wednesday, 3 August, after some fierce heats where yet more records had fallen, with the old Olympic mark of 21.6 broken no less than four times, first by Metcalfe and Tolan who brought it down to 21.5, and then by German sports writer Jonath and the Argentinian Carlos Bianchi Luti, who lowered it to 21.4. In the first semi, Metcalfe won easily, but in the second Eddie Tolan just managed to hold off the fast-finishing Canadian Harold Wright to take third place and qualify for the final.

In the final, Luti had the faster start, but as the runners came out of the turn and into the home straight Simpson was about a yard in front, with Eddie closing fast. The gum-chewing Detroiter caught and passed Simpson with 50 metres to go and won by a clear margin of about six feet. Eddie's time was clocked at 21.2 by electronic timing – an official world record for the distance and a new Olympic record. The crowd cheered another American victory, but were puzzled about what had happened to pre-race favourite Metcalfe. His bad luck story had continued, and even today some doubt remains over his part in the race because a study of films of the 200 metres revealed that he had started three or four feet behind his proper mark. He was offered a re-run by the officials, but rejected it because he did not want to jeopardize the clean sweep of the event by the Americans, with Simpson taking the silver and Metcalfe performing miracles to finish third.

There is a counter-theory to this suggesting that the film is an optical illusion created by the fact that Metcalfe dug his holes on the inside of his lane, whereas Simpson, in the next lane out, dug his on the outside, giving the impression that they were too far apart. However, the long lane measurement was the more likely theory and just one more reason why Metcalfe felt so frustrated after the Games.

Eddie Tolan was now the athletic toast of America, the only man to win two gold medals on the track at the Games, and his homecoming to Detroit was eagerly awaited. Their hero returned to the city's main station with two gold medals in his pocket, but he was soon forced to face the realities of the Depression – he was black, unemployed and penniless.

He was looking forward to seeing his mother at the station as they were very close and wrote regularly to each other during the Games. He asked her permission to forget the family's plight during these few days so that he could concentrate on racing and wrote: 'I want so much to send the American flag to the top of the winner's staff. I want to see our name head the list when the result is announced for I know if I can win the two dash events our worries will be lessened and some brightness will return to our lives.' On his

Eddie Tolan unexpectedly wins the Olympic 200 metres final, in world record time, by a good six feet from the fast-finishing Simpson and Metcalfe. However, controversy surrounded even this result

return he found that nothing had changed. There may have been thousands of people cheering him at the station and a seemingly endless supply of glib, smiling politicians eager to shake his hand, but he did not have a job, his father had not worked for two years and his two brothers were also out of work and likewise his two sisters. Only his mother was working and keeping the family from starving. Just before Eddie arrived home his mother received a phone call from the Governor of Michigan who made an elegant speech about her son's achievement. She thanked him politely but told him about the family's real problems, and he vowed to do something to get them all work. So it was that on the very day that Eddie returned home, his brother Fred was working outside the station picking up the waste paper dropped by the crowd who had come to pay tribute to him. The rest of the family were still out of work.

In December of 1932, the Mayor of the city presented him with the official thanks of the city, in the form of a beautifully crafted leather bound resolution, after which Eddie made a short speech intimating that something a little more tangible would have been preferred. More promises were made by the councillors who all agreed that the Tolan family could not eat a resolution. One of the many offers, most of them bogus, that were made to Eddie on his return was from dancer Bill 'Bojangles' Robinson, who invited him to tour with him on the vaudeville circuit relating stories about his running career and his success at the Olympics. Eddie saw this as a way of providing much needed money for his family and helping him pay his way through medical school, so he jumped at the chance. He was booked for a 103-shows tour at $1500 dollars a week and it seemed that all their problems were over. However, the Depression forced the cancellation of the show after just one week and Eddie returned home broke and conscious that his dream of becoming a doctor was gone forever. Early in 1933, he finally got the job the city had been promising him – as a filing clerk in the city's Registry of Deeds – and he stayed there for nine years, with a short break during 1935 when he travelled to Australia to take part in the professional sprint circuit.

He took part in a four-race tournament against some of the top pro sprinters of the day, including the Australians, Austin Robertson and Tom Roberts, and Scotsman Willie MacFarlane. Eddie won three of the four races and took the world pro title, running on grass at night under floodlights, and although it was all a million miles from the Olympics he managed to return home with a suitcase full of trophies and medals and a wallet full

Eddie Tolan and Jesse Owens arrive in New York in 1954 to attend a banquet at the Waldorf Astoria honouring the United States all-time track and field team

of foreign currency which went straight into the family's still empty coffers.

During World War II he worked as a stock control officer in the giant Packard car plant and later ran a petrol station for eight years before giving up and selling burial insurance. Eventually he returned to teaching and became a substitute physical education teacher on the Detroit schools books, working for the city right up to his death in 1967, at the age of 57. Two years earlier he had suffered kidney failure which needed constant attention and this finally prompted the heart attack from which he died.

Eddie's Olympic feats are remembered in several Track & Field Halls of Fame, and shortly after his death a playing field in Detroit was named after him. He once said: 'Most people think a tall man has a better chance of winning because his feet are in the air over a longer stretch. But height is not a factor. A small man's ability to get speed can be compared to the pistons of an automobile. His pistons generate a lot of power if he has the legs and the heart.'

Eddie Tolan, a lifelong bachelor, certainly had plenty of heart, and throughout his life, despite all the setbacks that he suffered, he remained a kindly and affable man, shrugging his shoulders at his misfortunes. His epitaph should read: Eddie Tolan tried hard, but he deserved better.

1936 Jesse Owens

Jesse Owens, nicknamed the 'Ebony Antelope', triumphs in the final of the 100 metres in Berlin at the 1936 Olympics. This was to be the first of his record-breaking four medals at the Games

After the deep disappointment of his defeats in the 1932 Olympics and with Eddie Tolan now retired, Ralph Metcalfe emerged as the world's premier sprinter, taking both sprint titles in the American championships in 1933 and 1934. However, his lack of good fortune dogged him yet again, because in 1935, just a year before the next Olympic Games in Berlin, his complete dominance was challenged by two newcomers to the sprinting scene. The first was Eulace Peacock, the Philadelphia flyer from Temple University, who took Metcalfe's national 100 metre title in 1935, beating him into second place. The other was the athlete who finished third in that particular race but would go on to become one of

the greatest names in athletics history and arguably the greatest sprinter of all time – Jesse Owens.

More than 50 years after his Olympic achievements his name is still known throughout the world, while his influence on the track scene, particularly on the sprints and the athletes who followed him, is incalculable. But like most legends his is founded in part fact and part fiction, and as the years went by it became increasingly difficult to differentiate between the two and his life followed a roller coaster of ups and downs.

The public image of Jesse Owens was not always the real man, and the genuine story of his life and times, stripped of some of the publicity hype and gloss, is perhaps not one with which his fans are well acquainted. Owens first burst on to the track scene as an 18-year-old trying out for a place in the 1932 Olympics, but despite a brave showing he was knocked out in the preliminary heats. However, he was still hailed as a future track star in Cleveland, the city to which he and his family had moved just after World War I to escape the poverty and racism that abounded in rural Alabama, in the Deep South. Jesse was born in 1913, the youngest of 10 children, and, as a child, he suffered a serious bronchial illness which threatened his life on several occasions. But he recovered and on arriving in Cleveland he

was packed off to the local elementary school where he earned his famous name. He had been christened James Cleveland and when his new teacher asked his name he drawled, in southern fashion 'J.C. Owens, ma'am.' The teacher, misunderstanding him, wrote down Jesse Owens, and the eager-to-please newcomer did not have the heart to correct her. From that day onwards, he adopted the new name.

His athletic talents were spotted at junior high school by the part-time Irish coach Charles Riley, a wily old mathematics professor, who recognised Jesse's natural ability, but had difficulty in convincing him to take track and field seriously. Eventually he persuaded Jesse to train with him for an hour before school every morning, and during this time Riley built in excellent habits, making him watch how effortlessly horses ran and coaching him to run as if he were treading on hot coals, which produced the aesthetic running style that is marvelled at even today. Jesse began to win a handful of junior high competitions, but his eyes were not set on the Olympic Games until a visit to his school by the 1920 sprint king Charley Paddock, during one of his famed lecture tours in 1928. Paddock's persuasive speaking convinced Owens that he wanted to follow in his footsteps, and from that day Charley became his idol and the Olympics his ultimate goal.

In September 1930, Owens joined East Tech High School, but asked Riley to continue coaching him, which he did gladly, working for the next two years to make Jesse the brightest track prospect in Ohio. After failing to qualify for the 1932 Games, Jesse became even more determined and, the following year, won three titles in the national interscholastic meeting in Chicago, taking the long jump and the 220 yards, and equalling the world record in the 100 yards in 9.4. His performance enabled East Tech to win the event and, for the first time, Jesse became something of a hero in Cleveland, with the Mayor even organising a parade to City Hall in his honour. His fame spread and when the time came for him to leave East Tech and select a college, there were countless offers to sign him up, and his decision and the reasons for it became the subject of hot local debate. After much haggling over the incentives that each college was prepared to offer, including a stipulation that his unemployed father was offered a job, Jesse chose Ohio State University, despite the fact that racism was quite prevalent on campus and he was barred from using the men's dorm because of his colour. He was not even allowed to live on the campus, and shared a boarding-house with the small number of

Jesse Owens' first mentor, Charles Riley, is among the scores of people to congratulate him on his return home to America from Berlin

other black students at Ohio State, about a quarter of a mile away.

At this time, the percentage of black students in American colleges was small, and sports scholarships, as we know them today, extremely rare, especially in track, so Jesse only received a partial scholarship and had to make up the rest of the money by working before and after school. One of the most celebrated of these part-time jobs was operating a lift in the State office building in Columbus – a simple enough job which paid a reasonable wage, but illustrated further the deep divide between black and white students even in 'modern' Ohio. Whereas Jesse had to operate the freight lift at the back of the building and was not permitted to be seen at the front, the white students manned the main lifts for the employees and visitors.

Although he was a great athlete, Jesse was not the greatest scholar, and after his freshman year at Ohio State he was placed on academic probation because of his poor grades. A bright and alert man, he would never acquit himself well in the classroom. His main ability, off the track, was his passion for public speaking and he could hold an audience spellbound with a well rehearsed speech, something at which he was already earning money even in these early pre-Olympic days, touring schools and clubs for $50 a time. He also spent some of his time helping out needy organisations for no reward, and he soon realised that the speaking circuit was something he could develop in the future.

Ohio state coach Larry Snyder trains Owens to keep low after his start by using a high jump bar to ensure that his head remains down

In the spring of 1934, he reached another landmark in his track career when his coach, Riley, handed over his 'rough diamond' to the young, ambitious new track coach at Ohio State, Larry Snyder, whose job would be to hone Jesse's natural talent and polish his technique. Snyder entered Jesse in many meetings when his college track career began in 1935, and such was his popularity that 12,000 people turned out to watch him compete in a dual meet between Ohio State and Notre Dame, in which Jesse won all three of his events. This local popularity turned to international fame at the Big Ten Championhip at Ann Arbor, on 25 May, when to the astonishment of the crowd and everyone connected with track and field, Jesse broke three world records and equalled a fourth in less than one hour, a feat that is still unparalleled in track and field history and regarded by many people as greater than his performances in the Olympics a little over a year later. 'The Days of Days', as it became known, was held on a warm, clear afternoon, but there

was one athlete who was not looking forward to the event at all. Owens felt awful – he was still aching from falling down a flight of stairs while horsing around with a college friend five days earlier and had not been able to train all week. As he made his way to the stadium he was so sore that Snyder and several athletes had to assist him into the rumble seat of a car, help him out and almost carry him to the locker-room, where he sat for half an hour in a steaming hot bath.

Jesse remembered some years later: 'Some of my team mates had to help me get on my running gear. Our trainer put a big swab of hot liniment on my back and they had to help me get on my sweatsuit to keep me warm. I got out to the track and hoped I would feel better after I did my usual warm-up of jogging a 440 and then stretching, but I couldn't even jog, let alone stretch.'

Jesse propped himself up against a flagpole at one end of the stadium and watched the other athletes darting up and down the cinder track as Coach Snyder tried to persuade him to pull out of the competition. But Owens decided to have a go at the first race – the 100 yards – and slowly pulled himself to his feet and walked gingerly to the start. Little did he know that he was about to step into the history books.

At 3.15pm, the starter called the field to their marks and suddenly the pain in Jesse's back, which had even hindered him digging his starting holes, disappeared. 'It was completely gone. I couldn't feel anything. I didn't know why then and I don't to this day,' he once said. At the gun he sprang out of the holes and burst smoothly down the track to equal the world record of 9.4, a clear tenth of a second ahead of the second placed man. Ten minutes later he moved across to the long jump pit, which had been dug recently in front of the stands, and a white handkerchief was placed on the 26ft 2¼in (7.98m) world mark of Japan's Chuhei Nambu, set in 1931. As a hush fell over the crowd, Owens took off down the runway and got tremendous lift off the board, landing six inches beyond the handkerchief and smashing the record. His mark of 26ft 8¼in (8.13m) would not be beaten for more than 25 years. It was the only jump that Jesse made that day and he enjoyed the thundering applause of the crowd, the officials and the other athletes in the stadium for a full five minutes.

At 3.45pm, he stepped up for the 220 yards and was well clear of the field after just 10 yards, cruising down the straight and breaking the tape in a remarkable 20.3, knocking three-tenths of a second off Ralph Metcalfe's record. At 4pm he tackled the 220 yards low hurdles, and though he was not a technically good hurdler he tore the opposition apart, winning by a clear second from the next placed man and breaking the world record by four-tenths of a second in 22.6, even though two of the three timers clocked him in 22.4. In the two furlong races, Jesse had also set metric world marks, and thus in effect he had broken five world records and tied a sixth in less than 60 minutes, despite his back injury. Afterwards he had to be helped into the shower and then into a car to get home.

It was a subject that Jesse liked to talk about and he later revealed: 'Actually all I thought àbout was the next event. I never thought about records, I just wanted to get through what was next and do my best. I wanted to do well in my first Big Ten meet but I never expected anything like close to what happened. Afterwards, the only real pressure I felt was that I was a target for other people, the guy to knock off. The records were a launching pad for the Olympics, the Big

Jesse Owens, a supreme 100 metres sprinter, was not renowned as a hurdler, but he was still good enough to break the 220 yards hurdles world record by four-tenths of a second in 1935

Ten was the starting point where I first knew I could compete against top class athletes and achieve things. But the Games were the ultimate, the biggest competition against the very best.' After touring the country, performing in various meetings, he returned home in July 1935 and married his childhood sweetheart, Ruth Solomons, who he had met at junior high. But the marriage seemed to have an adverse effect on his track performances, and these coincided with the rise to prominence of Eulace Peacock, a tall, powerful athlete in the mould of Metcalfe, and on the 10 occasions that they met in the sprints or in the long jump during 1935, Peacock beat Owens seven times – so much so that Charley Paddock publicly put his money on Peacock to beat Jesse in Berlin.

Eulace, now 74 and still active in athletics as an official in New York, is modest about his achievements and what might have been even though Jesse himself admitted that he was the only man he ever feared on the track. Eulace recalls: 'I remember he once said to me "you know, I never could beat you, I didn't know how to handle you". I was like Metcalfe, but Jesse was so smooth he could run all by himself in world record time. But Metcalfe and I knew if we came out even with him, or just a yard behind, we could overtake him, because in the last 20 or 30 metres we'd close right down on him.'

Peacock's victory over both Metcalfe and Owens in the 1935 AAUs in Lincoln, Nebraska, made him the favourite for the Olympic team, but then tragedy struck and during an anchor leg in the Penn Relays he pulled a hamstring so badly that it put him out of the reckoning. 'I went to the final trials and gave it a go but it pulled again,' he says, 'and that was that. But I never got down in the dumps about it, I never worried about what might have happened. There would have been some interesting races in Berlin with Owens, Metcalfe and myself, because with the three of us it was a case of who felt right on the day.'

There are those who suggest that had Peacock travelled to Berlin in full health he would have taken at least two of the four gold medals that Jesse eventually went on to win. No-one will ever know, but with Peacock out of the way, Owens knew that his only real competition in the sprints came from his team-mate Metcalfe, but his form had dipped slightly since his almost invincible years of 1932, 1933 and 1934.

However, like all black athletes of the day, Owens had to face other pressures as well as athletic competition – overt racism often made life on and off the track a misery. It ranged from a poisonous remark to being refused entry to res-

taurants and hotels and being forced to ride in the back of a bus. Peacock suffered just like Jesse and remembers: 'It was pretty rough at times, but you tried to adjust yourself to it. It was part of America and you had to take those knocks. Jesse, Metcalfe and me all had these problems and we had to handle it, though there was never a question of fighting. We would go into restaurants to eat and get thrown out, hotels would refuse to let in the black members of our team and we'd eat in kitchens.

'I remember one time on our way to the AAUs in 1935 when the train we were on was re-routed because of a storm. It stopped and a conductor got on and said to the guy on our train, "I understand you've got some niggers on the train, what are you going to do about it?" We were in bed, but we were all awake and heard the guy on our train say we were fellas from the top colleges in the east and we weren't causing a problem. He told the conductor, "If you want to throw them off the train, you do it," but no-one bothered us. You can imagine how we felt, here we were on our way to the national championships and this happens, but we played it cool and kept quiet.

'We always felt we could do more by actions on the track rather than fighting and knocking somebody down. Our attitude towards these people was if that's the type of person he is, then fine, just walk away.' It was an attitude shared by Jesse and one that would get him involved in

Eulace Peacock, of Temple University (extreme left), beats Jesse Owens (far left) and Ralph Metcalfe (centre) to win the 1935 100 metres AAU title in Lincoln, Nebraska

trouble later in his life, because for all the changes that followed he remained very much a man of the thirties.

It was not until early in 1936 that Jesse began to return to his Big Ten form running a new world mark of 10.2 for 100 metres in Chicago in June, a record that would last for 20 years, so by the time the *SS Manhattan* sailed for Europe he was already being touted as a favourite for three gold medals, in the 100 and 200 metres and the long jump. Just before the team left for Europe, America's other big black sports hero, heavyweight boxer Joe Louis, was beaten in humiliating fashion by Adolf Hitler's favourite, Max Schmeling, and although Louis would be back it was left to Jesse Owens to shoulder the nation's sporting hopes in Germany.

The awarding of the Games to Berlin had been made prior to the arrival of the Nazis, and as the Olympic year grew closer there were calls to boycott them because of the human rights violations in Germany – protests that grew more vociferous when Jews were banned from German sports clubs. By then Hitler had grasped the propaganda value of staging the Olympics and performed an amazing bluff on the Olympic

Committees from around the world by convincing them that the stories that visitors had heard about persecution and violence were pure invention. In fact, those who attended the Games returned home enormously impressed with their organisation and with Germany itself, thanks to a massive cover-up operation mounted by the Nazis. The 1936 Olympic Games would be the first, but not the last, to be exploited for political gain, and more than 50 years later it is difficult to understand how the rest of the world fell for Hitler's deception. The leading advocate of US participation was AOC President Avery Brundage, a hard-line right-winger who persuaded the committee to vote for participation after a spurious fact-finding mission to Berlin as the guest of the Nazis. Despite protests about the treatment of Jews and blacks in Germany, the AOC finally voted to compete, as did Britain, which was slower to mobilize opposition than the USA. The decisions were backed by the IOC, which argued blindly that politics had no part to play in sport. For Hitler, the Games were a political and moral fillip because the world had come to Berlin and, with very few exceptions, had left the city liking what they had seen. Had the Games not been held, maybe the world would have been prompted to examine what was really happening in Germany and what Hitler's true motives were. Berlin was completely transformed for the Games, decorated from top to bottom, with all racist grafitti and offensive newspapers removed and giant swastika posters and flags draped from every building. Some 4,000 athletes and officials were billeted in the Olympic village, along with nearly 3,000 press men.

On board the *SS Manhattan*, Ralph Metcalfe, one of the older athletes, spoke to his black colleagues urging them to resist emotional involvement in the political atmosphere, a move that seemed to calm some of the athletes' anxieties about what they might expect in Berlin. The Games opened, under cloudy skies, on Saturday, 1 August, in the spectacular new Olympic stadium, before 100,000 clamorous spectators, and as the US team swept into view they whipped off their straw boaters and clasped them to their chests. In the team was the young Jewish sprinter Marty Glickman, now one of the elder statesmen of American broadcasting and a consultant with the Home Box Office Cable TV channel. 'We kind of shuffled into the stadium, the US team never really marched, and it was the first time we were going to see Adolf Hitler and company. We were among the last to enter the stadium and as we walked down the track in front of Hitler's box,

flanked by all the Nazi bigwigs, Goering, Goebels, Hess and all that gang, he looked sternly down at us and we looked up at him and you could hear the comment go through our ranks, in fact I said it as well – he looks just like Charlie Chaplin, and that's the way we felt about him. He was like some two-bit South American dictator who might last a few months, he was not to be taken seriously. Little did we know about what was to take place.' Despite the political differences, the German people made everyone, particularly the American team, feel very welcome, and Jesse Owens became their hero, although there were racial overtones from some sections of the Nazi media which accused the United States of relying on 'black auxiliaries' to win their medals – a race that the Nazis regarded as sub-human.

Jesse himself once recalled: 'We all knew about the racial thing but we couldn't read German so we couldn't read what was being written about us, being animals and all that. But the German people were tremendous. Every day we got a standing ovation from the multitude of people. They were looking at you, not as a black man, but in terms of the ability you displayed. This was the Olympics and there was spillover into your own country. You made headlines here and people saw them and they had second thoughts about you and about blacks, instead of making just a categorization.'

There was no doubt that Jesse was the focus of the public's attention in Berlin, and everywhere he went in the city he was pursued by fans clutching autograph books; they even pushed photos and autograph books through his bedroom window at night while he tried to sleep. Glickman recalls: 'His popularity was such that in order to get him safely in and out of the stadium each day he had to use a secret tunnel entrance and exit, otherwise he would have been mobbed by the adulating crowd.'

This adulation grew still further when the competition began, and from the first day he appeared on the track a deafening chant of "Oh-vens, Oh-vens, Oh-vens" would go up every time the crowd spotted him. The competition itself was not a great challenge for Jesse, and when his first event – the 100 metres – began the day after the opening ceremony he had little trouble in living up to German expectations, and in the first round tied the Olympic record of 10.3. In the second round, he ran a wind-aided 10.2 and then eased off to win his semi-final in a sedate 10.4, while Metcalfe strolled the other in 10.5. In the final, it was a one-horse race from the start, with Owens leading from the gun to build a two yard lead by

A perfect illustration of Jesse Owens' efficient start during the 1936 Berlin Olympics – eyes on the tape and legs driving away from the start holes

the halfway mark which was enough to thwart Metcalfe's strong finish and still win the race by a yard at the tape, with Holland's Martin Osendarp third, Frank Wykoff fourth, and Hitler's favourite, Erich Borchmeyer, back in fifth. Round one of the Jesse Owens' Olympic show was complete. Of course, one of the most famous stories surrounding Jesse Owens was his supposed snub by Hitler, who refused to shake his hand after his 100 metres victory, or so the story goes. It was pure invention by the American press and if there was any snub at all, which is doubtful, then it certainly did not involve Owens.

On the first afternoon of competition, when Jesse was running just heats, Hitler sat in his box and watched with glee as two German athletes won gold medals, summoning them immediately to his box for personal congratulations. Later the same afternoon, he did likewise for a Finnish athlete, but when Owens' friend, the black high-jumper Cornelius Johnson, won the gold medal, Hitler decided that it was getting late and left the stadium before Johnson was awarded his medal. He was not invited to the box because Hitler was not there. The official explanation was that the Führer had left at a prearranged time and that no snub was intended, but before the Games reconvened the following day (when Owens would run in the 100 metres final), the IOC officials informed Hitler that he would have to congratulate every winner in his box or none at all. Hitler agreed and, apart from the first day, he received no other athlete for the duration of the Olympics. When Jesse won his gold medal there was no invitation to Hitler's box, nor should there have been, but the American press decided to build themselves a story, running headlines like 'Hitler Snubs Jesse' all over the country. When he returned home, at

first Jesse tried to put the record straight, but he later found that continually denying the tale was increasingly tedious, so he began agreeing with it and later even embellishing it.

He had little time to savour his win in the 100 metres, which equalled the Olympic record of 10.3, despite a heavy track soaked by a sudden downpour just before the race. The following day, he was plunged straight into the 200 metre heats and the long jump competition, the latter being where his stiffest competition lay, in the blonde, blue-eyed German Luz Long, a model of Hitler's supposed Aryan supremacy. For the first time in the Games, Jesse felt a little nervous and, still in his tracksuit, took a practice run down the runway and into the pit. To his surprise, the German officials counted it as his first jump and he was so rattled by this that he fouled his second and had only one jump remaining to make the final or he would go out of the competition. At this point, Jesse was approached by the Germanic looking Long who introduced himself in perfect English. 'Glad to meet you,' said Jesse, 'How are you?' 'I'm fine,' replied Long. 'The question is how are you?' 'What do you mean?' said Owens. 'Something must be eating you,' said Long, demonstrating his knowledge of American slang. 'You should be able to qualify with your eyes closed.'

Jesse Owens (right) wraps himself in blankets for protection against the rain and cold of Berlin before a 100 metres heat. From left to right, Frank Wykoff, Paul Hanni and Ralph Metcalfe

While more than 100,000 pairs of eyes, including those of Hitler and the other top Nazis, gazed down on them, Owens and Long chatted in the middle of the stadium. Long joked about how much he looked like the typical Aryan model, a theory in which he did not believe, and then suggested that Owens should jump just before he touched the board to ensure that he did not foul. Jesse made the qualifying distance by just one-sixteenth of an inch on his final jump. In the final held the same afternoon, Jesse started the competition with a new Olympic record of 25ft 5½in and then followed up with 25ft 9¾in. However, in the penultimate of the six rounds Luz Long brought the huge crowd to their feet by matching Owens' leap exactly. Inspired by Long's challenge, Jesse then jumped 26ft ¾in and then went on to better that with his last jump of 26ft 5½in to clinch the gold. The first person to offer his congratulations was Long, and Owens wrote later: 'You can melt down all the medals and cups I have and they would be a plating on the 24-carat friendship I felt for Luz Long at that moment'. Sadly, Long was killed while fighting in the German Army at the Battle of St Pierre in 1943, but Jesse continued to correspond with his family for many years.

On day three of the competition, having qualified easily for the 200 metres final, Jesse eased his way around the damp, red clay track to his third gold medal in a new Olympic record of 20.7, beating Mack Robinson, the older brother of Brooklyn Dodgers star Jackie, by an incredible four yards, with Osendarp taking another bronze. Despite the light rain that fell all day making the track even heavier, Jesse looked absolutely effortless, while the athletes behind him strained and grimaced their way to the tape. He had become the first athlete to win three track and field golds since the Games of 1900. 'He was markedly better than anyone,' recalled Marty Glickman. 'He was also the smoothest runner I have ever seen and the most physically co-ordinated. When he ran it was like water flowing downhill.

'The sprint team used to practise on the cinder track and we would all dig up the cinders where we ran – except Jesse. When we looked at his lane all you would see were six spike marks for each step where his spikes had gone into the cinders and come out clean. It was as if he was running six inches off the ground.'

Jesse's Olympics ought to have ended after he received his gold medal for winning the 200 metres and 18-year-old Marty Glickman's should have begun because, as with US tradition, such was the strength of American sprinting that the first seven past the post in the 100m trials made up the sprint team in Berlin, with the first three, Owens, Metcalfe and Wykoff, running in the individual race, and the next four home, Foy Fraper, Glickman, Sam Stoller and Mack Robinson, making up the 4 × 100m relay team. But here unfolded the really sinister story of the Berlin Olympics, certainly as far as the Americans were concerned. The first change to the team, an understandable one, came when Robinson qualified for the 200 metres final and decided not to run in the relay. He was replaced by Wykoff who had something of a relay pedigree, having been in the last two US Olympic teams that had won gold medals on both occasions.

The track team was run by two men, Lawson Robertson and Dean Cromwell, and shortly after the 200 metres Robertson was quoted as saying: 'Owens has had enough glory and collected enough gold medals to last him a while. We want to give the other boys a chance. Marty Glickman, Sam Stoller and Frank Wykoff are assured places on the relay team. The fourth choice rests between Foy Draper and Ralph Metcalfe.' Two days later, however, the situation had changed and, despite a time trial held in Berlin, where Stoller won, Glickman placed second and Draper third, it seemed that the two Jewish boys were going to be kicked off the team. Newspapers were full of the coach's indecisiveness and the whole affair smacked of backroom politics. The athletes involved are, with the exception of Glickman, all deceased, but much of what they had to say at the time and since is still on record.

Glickman explains: 'The relay team was composed of Wykoff and Draper, both of the University of Southern California, Sam Stoller, the only other Jew on the US track team, and me. We'd practised passing the baton the several weeks we were in Berlin. The morning of the day we were supposed to run we were called into a meeting by Lawson Robertson, the head track coach and Dean Cromwell, the assistant head, and we were told that because of a rumour that the Germans had been hiding their best sprinters and saving them to upset the American team in the relay, that Sam and I would be replaced by Jesse and Ralph Metcalfe. Now there's no question that Owens and Metcalfe were faster than Sam and I, a yard faster at least, but we'd been practising. In fact, years later Wykoff said we probably would have run faster because of our superior baton passing.

'I was a brash kid and I said, "But coach, that's silly, you can't develop world class sprinters unless you run in world class competition".' Metcalfe and Wykoff always maintained that Owens was to blame for selfishly campaigning to be permitted a crack at a fourth gold medal, but Glickman's account differs greatly and he stresses that Metcalfe uttered not one word of protest. 'I said we'll win by 15 yards no matter who runs, but they said, "You'll do as you're told and that's the way the team's going to be". Owens, to his everlasting credit, and to my undying gratitude, said, "Coach, let Marty and Sam run. I've already won my three gold medals. I'm tired, I've had it, let them run, they deserve it".

'At that, Cromwell pointed his finger at him and said, "You'll do as you're told," and in those days black athletes did as they were told. So Sam and I watched the race from the stands. In the entire history of the Games, as far as I know, no American athlete, physically able, has ever been there and has not competed except for Sam and myself.

'Mere coincidence, was it, that we were both Jewish or out and out anti-semitism? As it turned out later, Avery Brundage, head of the AOC, and

Cromwell, turned out to be America Firsters, which was the group that was sympathetic to the Nazi cause. Brundage was one of the founders so there was no question about his sympathies.'

The suggestion was that Brundage and Cromwell had pulled out the Jewish pair to spare any embarrassment on Hitler's part at seeing them on the winner's rostrum. Naturally, the relay was won by the US squad in world record time, with Owens leading off and handing to Metcalfe, by which time they were so far ahead that the two white members of the team, Draper and Wykoff, could have run in backwards and still won.

Clearly, there were several motives behind the relay debacle and probably some of them will never be known, although anti-semitic feelings loomed large. However, it was unforgiveable for the US organisers to have brought two young athletes halfway across the world only to dash their hopes at the last moment. Besides, had they been serious about improving the quality of the US relay teams they would have been better served working on the 4 × 400 squad, where medal winners Archie Williams, Jimmy LuValle and Glenn Hardin were all left out and the original quartet promptly lost to the British foursome by more than 12 yards. There was one touching moment to the miserable affair and that came when the relay team received their medals and Owens insisted that Ralph Metcalfe, an Olympic bridesmaid, should stand at the top of the winner's rostrum.

Jesse won four gold medals and the achievement made him a household name all over the world – even the Southern newspapers in the USA carried reports and pictures about him – so when the AAU began a barnstorming tour of Europe with some of their star athletes, to try and make up their expenses on the Olympic trip, he was the man whom everyone wanted to see. But he was exhausted and just wanted to go home and, as he dragged himself from meeting to meeting around Eastern Europe and finally to London, his performances deteriorated and his desire to return to the States grew stronger. Both he and his coach, Larry Snyder, were made aware of a number of lucrative offers from show business which had arrrived by telegram from the States and that made matters worse, as he was not being paid for running. The last straw came when he learnt that the tour was to go to Sweden, Norway and Finland before heading home. Jesse decided that he had had enough, and wanted to go home and seek his fortune and earn the dollars that were being waved in his direction. He ran the third leg of a relay at a packed White City Stadium in London, before jumping on a ship bound for New York. It was to be his last ever race as an amateur.

Brundage and the AAU were furious when they realised that their star attraction had gone home – they were guaranteed 15 per cent of the gate money with Jesse appearing in the team and only 10 per cent without him. In typically cavalier fashion, Brundage and his colleagues suspended Jesse for life for refusing to compete, even though he was an amateur and had never signed a contract to run in Scandinavia. As Jesse said at the time: 'The suspension is very unfair to me. There's nothing I can gain out of this trip. All we athletes get out of this Olympic business is a view out of the plane or train window. It gets tiresome, it really does.'

So just two weeks after taking the athletics world by storm and winning four gold medals for the United States, his country's athletics chiefs effectively kicked him out of the sport. He returned home to a hero's welcome in the streets of New York, and later in Cleveland and Columbus too, but most of the attractive offers made earlier soon began to turn to dust. A $40,000 offer to appear on the Eddie Cantor radio show proved to be false, as did most of the showbusiness offers, and the only concrete ones he received were to appear on stage with Bill 'Bojangles' Robinson, who had hired Eddie Tolan, or to coach track at Ohio's premier black college, Wilberforce. Jesse chose the dancing, but before he signed a contract he had a change of heart and asked to be reinstated as an amateur. The AAU refused, and to most people it seemed that he had thrown away his athletics career for a pile of empty promises. Two weeks after returning home as a hero, he was still looking for the job that would set him up for life, but it never came. 'One day he was riding at the head of the parade,' recalled Marty Glickman, 'and the next he was just another black man in America, once again riding in the back of the bus, and he had a very difficult time for several years after the Games.'

Jesse himself, talking some years later about his dilemma, said: 'I was taught at a very early age by my coaches that even though ours was a social structure which prohibited people from mingling and eating and living and riding together, that eventually things would change through deeds. I thought then about those things because when I came back after all the stories about Hitler and his snub, I came back to my native country and I couldn't ride in the front of the bus, I had to go to the back door, I couldn't live where I wanted. Now what's the difference? I

The professional runner: Jesse Owens prepares to take on a race-horse in Havana, Cuba, on Boxing Day, 1936. Jesse beat the horse by running 100 yards in 9.9 seconds and earned himself $2,000

wasn't invited to shake hands with Hitler, but I wasn't invited to the White House to shake hands with the President either.' Of course, Jesse was right and nothing had changed for the better – President Roosevelt never even sent a message of congratulations.

However, Professor William Baker, who spent five years researching Jesse's life story for a biography, maintains that the hardship was something of a myth. 'The suggestion is that when Owens came back he couldn't get a job and he couldn't make any money, so he had to race against horses, motor cycles and automobiles and that sort of degrading activity. The truth is that he came home from Berlin and did find some of the offers he received were bogus, but in fact he made a lot of money. He gave his name to the Democratic Presidential candidate, Alf Landon, and made $10,000 for that, he did a lot of public appearances and late in the year he did race a horse, in Cuba, but was paid $2,000 for that, which was a lot of money for 1936.

'The fact is between '36 and '39 he held more than a dozen jobs, made a lot of money and didn't spend it wisely. He had a dry-cleaning business go bankrupt, he lost money on a touring basketball team and a softball team, but every year he

bought a brand new Buick and kept a fabulous wardrobe for himself and his wife. He made a lot of money and he spent a lot.'

But only a year after the Berlin Games, Jesse Owens' fame was waning, and until after World War II he became something of a forgotten man, working during the war as the personnel director of black workers at Ford Motor Company. He resigned and went back on the road, touring as a special attraction alongside the Harlem Globetrotters and working in dead-end jobs, never seeming to be able to break out of the racial stranglehold under which the majority of blacks suffered in America at the time. Athletically, Jesse was still a force, and in 1948 he produced an exhibition long jump of 25ft 11in and was reputed to have run 100 yards in 9.8 seconds as late as 1955. The turn around for Jesse, one that saw a renaissance of interest in him and his name, came in the early 1950s and from then on he never looked back. In 1950, Associated Press voted him the greatest athlete of the half century and he began to get involved in youth work. In 1953 he was appointed secretary of the Illinois State Athletic Commission and started working in radio and television.

Professor Baker has an interesting theory to account for his sudden re-emergence into the public consciousness. 'I am convinced that were it not for the Cold War Jesse Owens would have been forgotten. America desperately needed to have some black, visible hero who had made it in American society, because the race question was the achilles heel of US propaganda. The only other candidates were Paul Robeson, a communist living in Paris, Jackie Robinson, who was too outspoken, and Joe Louis, whose career was on the down.

'Jesse Owens was a wonderful spokesman for Americanism. He had made it, he was enthusiastic, he had a work ethic about him and he was very patriotic.'

Owens became something of a roving ambassador to President Eisenhower, visiting Third World countries in Ike's People to People programme and attending Olympic Games, starting in 1956, as the official Presidential representative. Alongside such other celebrities as Bob Hope, Jesse Owens had finally made the big league in the fame stakes and he never let it slip away again. Despite his overt patriotism he still managed to fall under the scrutiny of the FBI during the fanatical 'reds under the beds' purges led by J. Edgar Hoover. A file existed on him, following a three-year investigation, which was headed 'Foreign Inspired Agitation Among the American Negroes', prompted by his once having sent a greeting to the National Negro Congress, but eventually he was exonerated and it was probably the only time in his life that Jesse Owens was ever described as a radical.

At about the same time he became something of a corporate figure, endorsing multi-national companies and working as a "front man" for them, making speeches to employees, attending meetings, making commercials and generally representing their interests. These included Ford, ARCO, Greyhound, Paramount and Lincoln Mercury, plus a selection of smaller concerns. Jesse was an inspirational speaker and throughout his career used just six basic speeches, each one lasting about half an hour and intended to be motivational, thoughtful and entertaining, which they all were. He told one interviewer: 'I'm not in the entertainment field, my business is primarily to be able and willing to talk to people from a motivating and inspirational standpoint. I talk about

people who have succeeded with a great deal of handicaps.'

On top of his corporate commitments, Jesse had more than 100 requests each year to make speeches to various groups, of which about 30 were accepted, at around $2,000 a time, although he also worked on charitable and civic groups for nothing, at well as hospitals, boys clubs and the Salvation Army.

As the sixties arrived, he was caught up in the racial tension that swept America and some critics maintain that he should have presented a much higher profile in the civil rights movement. He was condemned by some radicals for staying on the side of the establishment, but they forgot that Owens was still a man of the thirties, and although they considered him a poor role model, to others he was someone with whom they could identify as an athlete and as a man who had made it against all the odds.

After escaping a four-year prison term for non-payment of taxes in 1965, he was caught in the middle of the black power rows during the Mexico Olympic Games and alienated himself still further from the angry young blacks when he tried to intervene on behalf of the US Olympic Committee after the famous black power salutes of John Carlos and Tommie Smith. He was attacked as an "Uncle Tom" figure and a tool of the white establishment. 'I just tried to get them to realise nobody owes you anything in this country,' he once said. 'Whatever you want is there for the taking, if you have the ability and desire to take it.'

New York Times athletics correspondent Frank Litsky remembers: 'The US Olympic Committee were aghast at what was happening and they looked for help, for someone to reason with the black athletes. They asked Jesse and he tried to intervene but I don't think he really understood the thinking of the modern black athlete and he was not treated with huge respect by these people, they weren't listening to him and I think he was hurt very much by it.'

'To these angry young blacks, Jesse Owens was frankly something of a fossil,' says Professor Baker. 'He was a man of the thirties and had been taught to smile and turn the other cheek and to say "yessir". Blacks in the sixties were no longer willing to do that, so to them Owens seemed utterly outdated. There was even conflict at home with his three daughters who were into the civil rights movement.'

He returned home from Mexico and penned the book *Blackthink*, in which he attacked the black power movement as pro-negro bigots. It was

Jesse Owens captures the attention of a group of Chicago children during a campaign for vaccination against polio in the mid-fifties

powerful material and got a mixed reaction in the black press, so much so that two years later he published another book called *I Have Changed*, in which he watered down some of his previous statements and philosophy. Throughout the seventies, Jesse became an Olympic elder statesman, raising funds, attending banquets, making speeches, becoming what one writer described as a 'professional good example, a combination of nineteenth century spellbinder and twentieth century PR man'. He received dozens of awards, including America's highest civilian decoration – the Medal of Freedom Award.

In 1971, he suffered a severe attack of pneumonia, which almost killed him, and he was forced to give up his daily packet of cigarettes, something he had enjoyed since his teens, for a more characteristic pipe. In 1978, he had a jolt when his old rival Ralph Metcalfe died from a heart attack, and less than a year later Jesse himself fell ill while filming an American Express commercial and was rushed to hospital, where doctors diagnosed lung cancer, almost certainly caused by cigarette smoking. The condition was inoperable and so he returned to his home in Phoenix, Arizona, where he died in hospital in March 1980, still vehemently opposing President Carter's planned boycott of the Moscow Olympics. Amid heavy snowfalls, more than 2,000 people turned out for his funeral at the Rockefeller Chapel at the University of Chicago, and the most poignant line was reserved for one speaker who said: 'No doubt the first man to meet him at the pearly gates will be Ralph Metcalfe,

saying "I beat you this time".'

There are dozens of monuments and memories of Jesse Owens scattered around the world – even the street leading to the Berlin Olympic Stadium was renamed after him, and a foundation geared to aiding young athletes was established in his name and continues to thrive. There are many different points of view about him, some complimentary and others not, but ask anyone who knew him well and they find it difficult to say anything unflattering about him without a smile. As Frank Litsky says: 'Jesse was a nice human being. He was warm, he'd put his arm around you, he'd tell you a story, he was full of stories and they were nice stories, they were inspiring. When you left him you had a feeling that something good had happened and you smiled. Your day had been made and he did that for a lot of people.'

Others who did not know him so well or not at all found it easier to be uncharitable. Professor Baker feels that he was a plastic man who sold his name and fame, whereas many people regard him as a man with a turn of speed and a commanding presence who lived a lifetime off the legend he created in those few far-off days in Berlin.

Jesse was not an intellectual and he never did get his degree from Ohio State – although he was awarded an honorary doctorate in 1972 – but he survived on his wits and his charm. 'He was articulate, he was well mannered, he was very handsome, he was the life of the party,' says Marty Glickman, who remained a friend until Owens' death. 'He was a terrific guy. But he was no Albert Einstein. He lived out his life as the figure he was in 1936. He was always Jesse Owens, 1936 quadruple Olympic champion.'

But for all his frailties, Jesse Owens was a good man, an athlete of unrivalled talents who saw an opportunity to make a better life for himself and his family and took it. In today's athletics market he would be a millionaire, but back in the 1930s and 1940s he did what was necessary to survive and after some years it paid off. His name will live forever in Olympic history and will always be synonymous with speed, while his influence on thousands of young athletes is impossible to measure – almost all subsequent Olympic sprint champions admit that they owe him a debt. 'You learn to play the game of life according to the society in which we live,' he once said. 'If you remember these things and try to live them day by day, then I think there are people you talk to day after day who won't forget the things you did. Therefore, you walk the streets of your home 10 feet tall because you never know how many kids wish to emulate what you have done.'

1948 Harrison Dillard

Among the thousands who packed the streets of Cleveland to see Jesse Owens' triumphant return home from the Berlin Olympics was a young 13-years-old from the lower east side of the city called Harrison Dillard. He and some of his friends had been permitted by their parents to go and watch the parade and had to run over a mile from their homes to the centre of the city's black district where Owens was due to pass.

They forced their way through the crowd and were standing on the edge of the kerb as Owens, dressed immaculately in suit and tie and sitting in the back of a huge convertible car, glided slowly by. Owens spotted them looking up at him, gave a big smile and a wink and shouted out, 'Hi kids, how are ya?' Of course they thought that this was the greatest thing that had ever happened – their hero had actually spoken to them – and Harrison ran all the way home, burst into the kitchen, almost pulling the door off its hinges, and breathlessly told his mother, 'I've just seen Jesse Owens and I'm going to be just like him.' She just smiled, like mothers do, and said, 'Yes son, I'm sure you will be.' She may have had her own private

Harrison Dillard (extreme left) wins the 1948 100 metres Olympic title at Wembley Stadium, London. Team-mate Barney Ewell, wearing vest number 70, thinks he has won the race, but gets only the silver with Panama's Lloyd La Beach (dark vest) receiving the bronze medal

doubts, but for Harrison his Olympic dream began that very afternoon.

Mrs Dillard, however, had other more pressing things on her mind, like feeding the family; times were tough during the Depression and Cleveland had been hard hit. Harrison's father, who sold ice and coal door-to-door from a horse-drawn wagon, suffered like everyone else and for some years the Dillard family existed from hand to mouth in great poverty. Despite the hardship of his childhood years, young Harrison's love of running began on the back streets of the city and at a very early age he realised that he had a talent for running fast, something he especially enjoyed when it meant beating the older children. He also watched the young Jesse Owens running and jumping at the local high school, only a mile from the Dillard home, but his first memory of Owens was as a high jumper. His other heroes were the fighters Joe Louis and Henry Armstrong, although he chose to follow in the footsteps of his track idol as he always ended up with a bloody nose in boxing!

What was particularly interesting about his early development as an athlete was his passion for hurdling, an event to which he had a very bizarre introduction, thanks to a friend who ran on a local high school track team. 'His name was Jimmy White, I'll always remember him,' says Harrison. 'He was the only kid in the neighbourhood who had a pair of running spikes and we thought they were marvellous. There was an alley behind our street and Jimmy would set up obstacles for us. We took the seats out of old cars, set them on fire to burn off the fabric, so there was just the springs remaining, then used them as hurdles. They were light so you didn't hurt yourself if you hit one and they were low enough for us to jump over.'

So from the tender age of eight, using burned-out car seats as hurdles, Harrison began to acquire a technique for hurdling that would one day make him not only the greatest of his time, but also one of the best in history. With that early training and the guiding light of Mr Owens to motivate him, it was not long before he was making a name for himself in athletic circles, although more often than not it was not his real

name! When he was just six-years-old he acquired the nickname 'Boney Babe' because he was so thin, a name that was then shortened to just 'Boney' and later to 'Bones.' The latter stuck and to this day close friends who have known him for 30 or 40 years still call him 'Bones.'

In 1941, it was Owens who took a special interest in the 18-year-old Harrison's exploits at East Tech High School, although the famous story about how he got a pair of the great man's track shoes is not absolutely true. 'It's a little apocryphal,' admits Harrison. 'We were at school and he went into the locker room and brought out a brand new pair of shoes, suggesting I give them a try. Though they were his shoes he hadn't actually worn them himself, but he'd given them to me so of course I wore them till they just disintegrated!'

After high school, Harrison enrolled at Baldwin-Wallace College in the Cleveland suburbs. His training was more sophisticated than leaping car seats in alleys, but only just. 'We had a small gym that enabled me to set up one hurdle and run the 15 yards to it, get over it, hit the ground and have just enough room to stop by going through a door on the opposite side of the building. That's how small it was.' To perfect his timing outdoors, he placed matchboxes on top of the hurdles and attempted to knock them off cleanly with his spikes to ensure that he was clearing them by the barest margin.

In the summer of 1942, Harrison took part in his first national championships, albeit in the junior section, finishing a creditable second in the low hurdles and fourth in the high hurdles, but it was not long before the war took an active role in his life and in the following spring, during his second year as a business student at Baldwin-Wallace College, he was drafted into the US Army. Although he did not enjoy combat, he matured physically as an infantryman in Italy, marching across mountain ranges. It was May of 1945, when the war was drawing to a close, before he was able to start running again and he competed in a number of army meetings in cities all over Italy, where he was stationed. Then he travelled to Frankfurt, Germany, for his first taste of real international competition, the 'GI Olympics', where Allied troops from all over Europe and the Mediterranean theatre competed. Harrison took them by storm emerging with no less than four gold medals. There was a special spectator among the crowd that day, General Patton, and the American reporters asked him what he thought of this young private winning all the medals. Pausing for a moment, Patton finally declared in his inimitable style, 'He's the best goddam athlete I've seen in my life,' which Harrison considered a great compliment.

In the winter of 1945, he returned home to Baldwin-Wallace to start training with coach Eddie Finnigan, but already his sights were set firmly on the forthcoming 1948 Olympic Games in London. His confidence was strengthened further in the summer of 1946 when he won two major US hurdle titles and broke Jesse Owens' 220 yards low hurdles record with a run of 22.5.

But it was not until 1947 that he won universal recognition in the US when he began an awesome series of straight wins that would take him to the very brink of the Olympic Games, a run that lasted for 82 consecutive finals, in sprints and hurdles, indoor and outdoor, at home and abroad. It included two more world records, the first in June 1947, during the NCAA championships in Salt Lake City, where he lowered his own 220 yards low hurdles mark to 22.3, a record that would stand for nine years. In the following spring, at the Kansas Relays, he clipped a tenth of a second off the 120 yards high hurdles record with an electrifying run of 13.6 seconds – but it could have been faster!

Ted Theodore, a close friend and team-mate of Harrison, now Alumni Director at Baldwin-Wallace, explained: 'He'd run a tremendous race in the preliminaries and looked so free and easy. In the final I was at the finish line and saw him run one of the most amazing races I had ever witnessed. I was really excited because Bill Porter, who was second, was just coming off the last hurdle when Harrison was crossing the finish line. The three starters were looking in amazement at their watches and as I peered over their shoulders I saw two watches at 13.5 clean and the other one at 13.6. I said hurray he's got a 13.5, but no, lo and behold they were reluctant to award such a fine time and gave him a 13.6. He was cheated out of a tenth of a second.'

This incredible winning streak established him as the world's premier hurdler, but it was finally broken when he lost four races in quick succession during the run-up to the Olympics. It started with defeat over 100 metres at the AAU Championships at the hands of Barney Ewell, who along with Harold Davies, the great Californian sprinter, would probably have challenged for the 1944 sprint title had it been held. Less than an hour later, he lost the 110 metres hurdles to fellow American Bill Porter and suddenly the man whom everyone thought invincible, and the favourite for a gold medal in London, was looking decidedly shaky.

Coach Eddie Finnigan gives his young protégé Harrison Dillard some helpful tips about his starting technique during a training session at Baldwin-Wallace College, Ohio

Incredibly, the next two races he lost were in the final US Olympic trials themselves. First, he was beaten into third place in the 100 metres, a race won in a world record-equalling 10.2 seconds by the in-form Ewell. Mel Patton, who had smashed the world 100 yards record a few months earlier, took second place. But a third spot meant a guaranteed place in the US 100 metres team for London and a run in the sprint relay. In the 110 metres hurdles trial, Harrison, despite the recent setbacks, was still odds-on favourite – he was still faster than anyone in the world and no-one could match his incredible speed between the hurdles or his silky technique over them. It would take a disaster to rob him of a gold medal said the press, and a disaster they got.

'All I had to do was finish third and I was in the team,' says Harrison, 'but on that particular day, as history shows, I finished dead last. I hit the first hurdle, got over the second and then hit every other hurdle in succession, stopping completely at the eighth. I had totally lost the rhythm of the race and my timing was so completely destroyed I just stopped and didn't even finish. Here I was the world record holder and American champion and it all went for nought because under the

American system you qualify on that day or you don't make it at all.'

The 25,000 crowd at the stadium in Evanston, Illinois, were stunned by his spectacular failure and the race made headlines all over the country, but thanks to his scraping a place in the sprint Harrison avoided missing the Games altogether, so he was not totally crushed by the hurdles catastrophe. There was the inevitable inquest between the athlete and his coach Eddie Finnigan into what went wrong and Harrison says: 'We came to the conclusion I simply wasn't getting my lead leg up, because I was running so fast my timing was just a fraction off, but it was enough to make my lead heel catch the hurdles.'

So he had to be satisfied with a crack at the sprints, joining Barney Ewell and Mel Patton on the sprint team, and in July the US squad set sail for austere London, a city in turmoil after the horrors of German bombing during the war and still living with strict food and clothes rationing. Despite the fact that great areas of the city still lay in rubble, the awarding of the Games to London was acclaimed universally and 59 countries, with more than 4,500 athletes, flooded into Britain. 'There's no atmosphere like the Olympic Games,' recalled Harrison, 'nothing like it anywhere in sport in the world. In America, we have the World Series, the Super Bowl and the Kentucky Derby, but they're nothing like The Olympics.' The site for the athletics was Wembley Stadium, the traditional home of British soccer, with the athletes themselves barracked in school buildings and service camps at RAF Uxbridge and Richmond Park. The British public responded in magnificent style, packing the stadium throughout the competition and even the weather managed to smile on the proceedings.

'We certainly had everything we wanted at Uxbridge,' Harrison remembers, 'including good training facilities, a laundry, a bank, even a motion picture theatre. But our food was flown in from the States, even the meat, vegetables and milk, because of the rationing in Britain and because we all liked to eat the type of food we were accustomed to, so we also brought our own cooks to prepare the food once it arrived. The British people were very friendly, I think they were glad to have something to celebrate after the years of bombing, so we had an excellent time sightseeing or renewing old acquaintances.'

As was common practice, the 100 metres competition was among the first track events to be held so Dillard was confined to the Olympic village during the opening ceremony and listened to it on the radio. When the sprint heats got underway, all eyes were on the American pair Patton and Ewell, plus the Panamanian student Lloyd La Beach, who had also equalled the world record of 10.2 a few months before the Games. The American track coach Dean Cromwell had been widely quoted in the press, saying that he felt Patton would win both sprint events, but there seemed nothing to choose between the three favourites. One name was not mentioned at all during the pre-race hype and that was Harrison Dillard, but he was not worried about all the publicity surrounding the big names because he knew that he was going to win! He looked impressive in the heats and in the semi-final beat his friend and rival Barney Ewell, but even that victory could

not persuade the experts that he had a medal chance in the final.

The six men who lined up for the final, held in blazing sunshine, on Saturday, 31 July, were Dillard, the British duo of McDonald Bailey and Alistair McCorquodale, La Beach, Ewell and Patton; all taking special care with their starting blocks, which were being used for the first time in an Olympic Games.

'I just knew I was going to win,' says Harrison. 'The only unknown quantity in the race was McCorquodale because none of us knew anything about him. But a few days before the final I had what amounted to a vision and I saw myself crossing the line first. Barney Ewell and I were sharing

Above: the electronic photo clearly shows Harrison to be the winner in the 100 metres final, equalling the Olympic record of 10.3 seconds

Left: a more unusual view of the final at the 1948 Olympics

a room and we were sitting on his bunk when I turned to him and said, "Barney, I'm gonna beat you, I just know I'm gonna win on Saturday". He just smiled and laughed it off, saying, "Yeah, big deal," probably thinking I was trying to psyche him out but I really could see myself winning that race.'

On the eve of the final few of the masses of international press men would rate him in the company of the real sprinting 'heavyweights', and opinion seemed to be divided between Patton and Ewell. 'I was so relaxed between the semi and the final, I managed to get a nap for 20 minutes on the dressing-room table, but Barney was so highly strung before a race you daren't talk to him or he'd snap your head off, while Mel got so nervous he'd throw up before most competitions.'

Harrison had been drawn on the outside lane, with the 31-year-old Ewell in lane two and Patton on the inside. After a Bailey false start, the pistol cracked and Harrison flew off his blocks like a bolt of lightning. By the second stride he was already ahead and he led all the way and seemed to hit the tape first, with Ewell a fraction behind him, but it was a real photo finish. Naturally Ewell could not see Dillard in the outside lane and he thought that he had won and began to dance and jump around the track with his hands in the air. Even Mel Patton, who finished a disappointing fifth after a poor start, came over to Ewell to offer his congratulations as the crowd of 83,000 cheered wildly. However, when the judges studied the photo-finish picture, it was clear that Harrison had won by a couple of feet, in an Olympic record equalling 10.3, with Ewell second in 10.4 and La Beach third.

When the result was finally announced after a few minutes' wait, Ewell sportingly accepted it immediately and impressed the crowd by going straight over to Harrison to offer his congratulations. 'By the time I got to the finish Dillard was halfway to Cleveland,' laughs Ewell today. 'I knew that winning hinged on the start I got,' says Harrison, 'and I spent the entire time between the US trials and the Games working on nothing but starts. For a hurdler I was a pretty good starter, but that still wasn't good enough for the sprints, so I worked on them for three weeks and I lost about five pounds in weight – and there wasn't much to lose – just practising.

'I remember the race vividly. I was right up against the stands, which was the worst possible lane in normal circumstances, but this year they were using the electric photo, so it wasn't so bad. I remember hitting the middle of the race and I was definitely in front, no question about it, so the problem was to keep running fast without tying up. But I was able to stay relaxed and keep driving and praying for the tape to just hurry up and get there.

'I remember lunging for the tape and out of the corner of my eye I saw another white American jersey, which was Barney Ewell and he thought he'd won and started that victory dance. But I remember Lloyd La Beach, who finished third in the lane next to Barney saying to him, "Man, you no win, Bones win". That reassured me because I thought I'd won too.'

The gold medal more than compensated the dis-

A packed Wembley Stadium watches as Barney Ewell congratulates the winner of the 100 metres sprint. Ewell was so convinced he had won that he broke into a victory dance on the track

appointment of not making the team in the hurdles and his performance earned rave reviews in the press, particularly the American newspapers, where it was headline news. Coach Finnigan was the proudest man in the stadium and raced from his seat in the stands and tried to leap the rail and get on to the track. It was not the first time that he had done so – that was back in 1942 when Harrison was placed fifth in his first senior AAU championship in New York. On that occasion, Finnigan raced down the stands and as he attempted to jump on to the track he was stopped by a big Irish New York policeman.

'Where d'you think you're going?' he demanded.

'That's my youngster out there, I wanna go out and congratulate him,' replied Finnigan in his strong Irish accent.

The policeman asked: 'What would your name be?'

'Finnigan,' replied the coach.

'Go right ahead, my boy,' said the policeman.

Back at Wembley, the same thing happened again and this time he was stopped by a British bobby and they went through the same routine. Finally the policeman asked his name.

'Finnigan,' he replied.

'Get back in the stands, you bloody Irishman!' came the answer.

Harrison loves to tell the story, but Finnigan was a resourceful man and did find his way on to the track eventually, lifting his charge off his feet, tears streaming down his face. Overcome with emotion, he returned to his hotel room and left a note for Harrison's close friend Jack Clowser of the *Cleveland Press*, which said: 'This is the day we waited for so long. To think it came not in the hurdles but in the event we all thought Dillard couldn't win. Fate is strange and wonderful. I'm going out to find a church somewhere. My heart is bursting.'

The unhappiest man in the stadium must have been Mel Patton. Many reasons were given for his disappointing performance, although he blamed the lack of training and top-class races, whereas coach Cromwell attributed his failure to the humidity and the chewed-up inside lane of the track. It has also been suggested that he was too nervous before the race, got off to a bad start and seized up trying to catch a fast field. The real answer is probably a combination of all these factors. Fortunately he came back with a vengeance in the 200 metres and won the gold by a clear yard from Ewell and La Beach. Harrison did not run in the 200 metres and he watched the 110 metres hurdles with mixed feelings as Bill Porter won the gold and the United States went 1-2-3 in

an event that he could have won easily. But he was selected for the sprint relay, a competition that proved to be one of the most controversial in the Games with the US team boasting the gold and silver medallists in the 100 metres and the winner of the 200 metres, Dillard, Ewell and Patton, and the talented long jumper Lorenzo Wright. They made the final with ease.

There was little competition and, as expected, the US squad took first place with relative ease, Ewell leading off, handing to Wright and then Harrison blazing around the bend, leaving Patton to canter down the home straight practically unopposed to win by about six yards. However, then the alarm bells rang as one of the judges claimed that Ewell had run beyond his restraining line as he passed the baton to Wright, and the US team was disqualified, much to their amazement. Barney Ewell was so upset about the decision, insisting that he had not run out of the zone, that he asked the coaches to make an official complaint. The strength of Ewell's protest convinced the US team managers to lodge the complaint, but it could not prevent the medal ceremony from taking place, with the British team receiving the gold medal while the Americans looked on in disbelief.

It was three days later at a jury of appeal that the film of the race was studied and it became clear that the judge was wrong. 'The moving pictures showed Barney had another four or five feet before he crossed the line,' says Harrison. 'We discovered that the judge who made the decision was a Scottish Presbyterian Minister, so nobody could question his honesty, it was just a simple mistake. Coming into that first turn there was a proliferation of lines and he just got confused and watched the wrong line.'

So Harrison received his second gold medal and became one of the heroes of the Games, no mean achievement when you consider that these were the Olympics of Emil Zatopek, Fanny Blankers-Koen and the 17-year-old decathlete Bob Mathias. Harrison was in great demand when the US team embarked on their usual European tour and it was some weeks after the closing ceremony when he finally arrived home in Cleveland for the sort of welcome he had seen Jesse Owens receive all those years before. It really was the stuff that dreams were made of.

But when the dust had finally settled there was still the matter of winning the gold medal he had always wanted, the 110 metres hurdles. He was still the world record holder and he had spent most of his time training for the event. He felt that he could not retire without having one more crack at it, even though it would mean another four years in competition before he could make the team for the 1952 Olympics in Helsinki.

He took a job as a public relations officer for the Cleveland Indians baseball team, where the general manager Hank Greenberg, a baseball Hall of Famer, gave him plenty of time to train.

He did a lot of running indoors, and in the run-up to the 1952 Games he was allowed to disappear to the warm climate of California for special training, and the Indians even sent his pay cheques out to him. He decided not to defend his 100 metres title, feeling that at 29 years old with many up-and-coming younger track stars, it would be too tough a task.

In the summer of 1952, Harrison made no mistakes in the national championships or the Olympic trials, winning the hurdles in both, but although he was the favourite to win the gold medal in Finland there was no room for complacency as fellow American Jack Davis was beginning to run him very close. Once in Helsinki, Harrison began to look good, equalling the Olympic record of 13.9 in the semi-finals while easing up, so he went into the final itself in very good shape.

From the start, it was a two-horse race, with big Jack Davis, who dwarfed Harrison at 6ft 3in and 190lb, on the inside, but it was Harrison who got away quicker and led to about the sixth hurdle. 'Then I saw a big foot on my left, then a head and then the whole of Jack's body,' he recalls. 'I knew I just had to clear the last few hurdles and if I could hit the ground off the last one just ahead or even with Jack I knew I would win because I could run faster than him. Jack knew he had to be in front so he was trying hard to get even and in doing so clipped one of the hurdles and I hit the ground running after the last hurdle well in front and I guess I won the race by a couple of feet.' The time was a new Olympic record of 13.7.

Harrison had finally achieved his ultimate goal, at the age of 29, winning the gold medal that he had worked so hard for all his life. Jack Davis, at 21, would live to race another day and would go on to win another silver medal in the 1956 high hurdles. Harrison's joy was completed in Helsinki with another gold medal, the fourth of his collection, in the sprint relay – this time on the second leg around the first turn. Although he continued to run and even made an unsuccessful attempt to make the US Olympic team for Melbourne in 1956, his performances in Helsinki were the peak of his athletics career and thereafter it was all downhill. When he finished sixth in the trials in 1956, just a week before his thirty third birthday,

Helsinki, 1952. Harrison Dillard leads in the semi-final of the 110 metres hurdles and is well on his way to winning that elusive gold medal

he decided to quit and he never raced competitively again.

Jesse Owens' old coach, Larry Snyder, once said of Harrison that if he had abandoned the hurdles and concentrated on the sprints he could have been one of the all-time greats, and it is a theory that he does not dismiss. 'There's no question that I could have been a better sprinter. The fact that I won the Olympics without concentrating on it throughout my career would certainly indicate that, but I enjoyed running the hurdles, they were a distinct challenge and when people asked me about the two events I would tell them that sprinters were a dime a dozen! I've always maintained that hurdling is one of the high arts in track and field. When you run outdoor hurdles you have 10 obstacles to negotiate cleanly and clearly – that's 10 opportunities you have to fail. Now that's quite a challenge.'

He was still working with the Indians after the 1956 trials but by the end of 1958 the ownership of the club had changed hands and, struggling with financial problems, it had to make economies and

Harrison was among the first people to be laid off. He moved from job to job, working full-time in radio and television, and then after a spell of selling life insurance, went back into radio work before finally, in the mid 1960s, joining the Cleveland Board of Education, in what was called a Manpower Training Programme, which helped people who had dropped out of high school and were lacking basic skills.

Dillard recalls: 'I had a friend who had been looking for a job and one day he told me he'd applied for this job but said he couldn't get it because he didn't have a college degree. He said I should apply, so almost as a lark I did. I was hired a couple of days later and I've been here ever since.' He stayed on that programme for five years before moving downtown after promotion to executive level in the city's business department within the Board. Meanwhile, he was continuing his media career with a regular chat show on Cleveland's WABQ Radio and a weekly column in the *Cleveland Press*.

The Board of Education has been his career now for more than 20 years and after successive promotions he is now the Business Chief of the department, responsible for the maintenance of all the city's schools and the acquisition of books and supplies – a demanding post that he took over amid apparent political controversy and one that regularly hits the headlines. However, he does it in the same self-effacing manner that typified his track career, and that has earned him the high regard of his staff. Despite his busy working schedule, Harrison still maintains a keen interest in today's track and field and works as a consultant to the Mobil Corporation on their massive Grand Prix programme, a job that ensures he stays close to the sport and the people in it. He is also involved with the city's youth, following the lead of his hero Jesse Owens by encouraging youngsters and helping them as much as possible.

Baldwin-Wallace's Ted Theodore says: 'I've seen Harrison around athletes, men and women, and he never turns his back on them. He's always ready to give them advice, to give them encouragement, to suggest ways they could improve. We're really proud of the fact that he cares about his own roots and is helping others, hopefully, to aspire to the same kind of greatness.'

Although he admits that track and field and the Olympic Games have changed, Harrison still enjoys the sport and he would love to be out there running today. 'I was just born 40 years too early,' he smiles. 'Look at the money some of these guys are earning.'

Ask anyone involved in track in the USA about Harrison and the answer will always be prefaced by a smile of affection or a kindly remark or anecdote. He is held in high regard for his ability, modesty and humour by everyone who meets him. Today, at 65, he is a contented man, still living in his native Cleveland with his wife, Joy, whom he met in Jamaica after the 400 metres star Herb McKenley introduced them, although his daughter Terri, now 27, lives in Los Angeles and he does not manage to see her very often. He still gets a little starry eyed when there is talk of Jesse Owens and rates him as probably the greatest sprinter of all time although he admires Bob Hayes and admits that Ben Johnson is clearly the fastest.

Winning the gold medals during his track career has had a positive effect on his life. 'There's every chance I would not be in the position I am today had I not been a gold medal winner,' he admits candidly. 'It opened a lot of doors, but once you go in those doors you have to produce the goods. In life in general there are places I can go where I am still recognized and it's still a good feeling. But just competing in sport gave me a great deal of self confidence and enabled me to travel and meet people and made me an all round better individual.'

Harrison Dillard, quietly spoken and mild mannered, remains one of the great post-war athletes and the only man ever to win an Olympic gold in both the sprint and the high hurdles, a record that is unlikely to be matched. At one period he held no less than eleven world, Olympic or American records, and his run of 82 straight wins stood for 35 years. His list of titles could fill several pages, but the most impressive include eight AAU indoor hurdles titles, seven of them in succession, and victory in nine successive years in the Millrose Games hurdles. He is a member of four national track and field halls of fame and his achievements form the bulk of a museum at his alma mater Baldwin-Wallace College, where an impressive indoor track was recently opened and named after him.

'I think it's great just to see the photographs and the history,' says Harrison, looking around the museum. 'It makes me feel good that I'm part of it. Occasionally I'll run into somebody who will say I saw you at Baldwin-Wallace and they didn't know who I was, so that's nice.'

The most fitting tribute to Dillard comes from his long-time friend Ted Theodore, who says simply: 'Harrison would have been a champion even if he'd never put on a pair of track shoes. He's a champion's champion, he's proven himself both as an athlete and as a human being.'

WHITE HEAT

1952 Lindy Remigino

'*I thought Herb had won it so I shook his hand . . . my name went up and I just jumped for joy. That moment has stayed with me for the rest of my life*'

1956 Bobby Morrow

'*He had great strength and he was unbelievably disciplined . . . We said he had ice water in his veins . . . If he ran on the tracks we have today there's no telling what he could do*'

1960 Armin Hary

'*He had everything, marvellous reactions and he was so well motivated . . . he had tremendous natural talent, he allied that to hard work in training – he was just a genius*'

1952 Lindy Remigino

Every Olympic Games throws up a romantic story of triumph against all the odds, but few could match the tale of a young American sprinter who came from nowhere to win the Olympic title at Helsinki in 1952. Little Lindy Remigino was not regarded as a world-class sprinter; he was not even considered as American class; in fact, he was only rated as the third best sprinter on his college team. However, fate decided to smile on the young New Yorker, and while the strongly fancied athletes fell by the wayside, for a variety of reasons, Lindy just kept on running – right into the pages of Olympic history.

The story of 'Cinderella' Lindy, had it been written as a movie script would have been thrown out by a Hollywood producer for being too unbelievable. But being an Olympic sprint champion is much more than being the best in the world; it is also about arriving at the Games in peak fitness and getting it absolutely right on the only day that matters – the final. The 100 metres final in Helsinki proved to be one of the closest in the Games' history and, just like the final 20 years earlier, it remains a talking point even today with

Helsinki 1952, arguably the closest finish of any Olympic 100 metres final. American Lindy Remigino (third from the right) lunges for the tape just as Jamaica's Herb McKenley drives past him

the silver medallist still insisting that he was not beaten. But it all could have been so different for Lindy had he not been accidentally chosen for his high school sprint team when their first-choice sprinter fell sick.

Born in New York in 1931, Lindy and his family moved to Hartford, Connecticut, when he was still quite young and he has lived in the pretty New England town ever since. His father was clearly a fan of the famous and christened his eldest son Rudolf, after Valentino, and the youngest Lindbergh, after the aviator, although both boys shortened their names – to Rudi and Lindy. Even before high school Lindy was a keen runner, chasing cars and running to school but he was not bitten by the competitive bug until he was about fourteen years old when he entered a race at his local YMCA.

Lindy said later, 'My brother and I went down to see what was going on and there were all kinds of events, so I entered a 40 yard dash. We had to run up and touch the far wall of the hall, turn around and come back. I won it and the guy handed me a little blue ribbon. I thought, "Hey, that's a lot of fun, I think I'll keep this up when I get to high school," and that was my introduction to track and field, and I still have that blue ribbon.'

However, when he eventually got to Hartford Public High School the coaches pigeon-holed him as a quarter miler, rather than a sprinter. In his first competition, he shot off his marks like a bullet and with the tape just in sight and the rest of the field some 30 metres behind, his legs turned to rubber, he fell flat on his face and vomited in front of the stands.

'That's when I found out I was a sprinter,' laughs Lindy, 'and not a quarter miler. I was humiliated. My brother was in the stands and at first he was ready to pass out cigars, but after that he was hiding. He was so disappointed and I decided not to run any more quarters.'

A little while later, he got the opportunity to run a shorter distance when the school's senior sprinter reported sick just before a meeting and Lindy was drafted in as a late replacement. Determined never to run any longer races again, he charged down the track in the 100 yards, winning

the race in 10.3, and never looked back. He went on to excel as a high school sprinter, winning the state championship in both the 100 and 220 yards in 1948 and 1949, and holding the New England 100 yards title and record in the same years. But despite a prediction in the 1949 Hartford High yearbook that Lindy would win in the 1952 Olympics, the Games in reality seemed an impossible goal, and Lindy was considering giving up the track when, during a New England meeting, he was approached by a man who said: 'I like the way you run, we'd like you to come to Manhattan.' That man was coach George Eastment and, thanks to him, Lindy was able to improve his sprinting and set his sights on reaching those Games.

Although he became a member of Manhattan College's successful track team he still did not reach the standard required for Olympic team selection, and during 1950 and the following year he did nothing on the track. It was not until the beginning of the 1952 indoor season that he started to train hard, but even then his form was inconsistent and there were times when he genuinely felt like quitting.

'I was certainly my own worst enemy,' admits Lindy, 'because whenever I got beat I took it real hard, but when I won I felt great.'

His first big win early in 1952 came at the Milrose Games, in New York's Madison Square Garden, where he won a 60 yard dash. During that indoor season he had to race with his two Manhattan team mates John O'Connell and Joe Schatzle almost every time and he only managed three victories, winding up with another 60 yard win at the K of C Games, also at Madison Square Garden. Despite Milrose Games tournament director Fred Schmertz publicly announcing to the press that he felt Remigino was going to win at the Olympics, few people felt that he was going to be a serious contender. The experts had already singled out the likely trio for Helsinki: the powerful Jim Golliday, from Northwestern University, who was the world number one in 1951; Andy Stanfield; and Art Bragg.

Lindy's coach George Eastment, however, felt that there was more to come from his protégé and tried to boost his ego with the help of a friend on the *New York Herald Tribune*, the great track and boxing writer Jesse Abramson.

'Do you think Remigino is a great sprinter?' asked Eastment.

Abramson agreed that he was.

'Then will you please write a piece saying so? I can't make him believe it.'

The article seemed to galvanize Remigino, and, with just three major meetings left before the boat sailed for Helsinki, Lindy began to hit form at just the right time. At the IC4As he was third in the 100 metres and won the 200 metres, but it was a race in which he finished fifth that proved to be the turning point of his track career. Soon afterwards, the great Jim Golliday pulled a muscle and was out of the Olympic running then Andy Stanfield announced that because of his own muscle trouble he was going to run only in the 200 metres in Finland. Lindy's luck turned when he entered the NCAAs, a race that was won by Golliday in 10.4, ahead of Art Bragg with Lindy fifth in 10.8, but suddenly he began to believe that he could run well in the Olympic Games.

A fifth spot in the NCAAs guaranteed him a place in the Olympic trials and it was then that Lindy chose his moment to start running really well, placing second behind Art Bragg, with Dean Smith third, to grab that coveted place on the American sprint team, even though the US press described their chances of retaining the prized fastest man on earth title as remote. One writer even criticised Lindy's running style, commenting that he looked like a dairy farmer when he ran, with shoulders hunched together as though he was carrying two milk churns across a barnyard!

'Of course, Jimmy Golliday was the favourite in the trials. I think he was the fastest of all of us,' recalls Lindy. 'But he got injured. When I ran against him I'd be hitting the ground like a machine gun but I wasn't going anywhere. He just held onto his lead.' Golliday, according to track experts, may well have won the Olympic final by a couple of yards, but he will always be remembered as the man who might have been. Sadly, the same catastrophe befell him just before the 1956 Games and he died from pneumonia after a long illness at the age of 39.

With his berth on the boat booked, Lindy realised that he had a winning chance. Golliday and Stanfield were out and Bragg was only just beating him. He was not even afraid of the international competition, namely Jamaica's classy Herb McKenley, the 400 metres silver medallist in 1948 and destined to repeat the feat at Helsinki, who was dropping down to the 100 metres for some speed-work, and Britain's McDonald Bailey, the Trinidadian-born star who finished last in the 1948 final after coming back from injury, but was now joint world record holder after running a 10.2 in Yugoslavia in 1951. But Lindy was improving all the time and his confidence rocketed during pre-Olympic training at Princeton, where the US coaches got him into excellent shape. 'I felt really

Jim Golliday who ran for Northwestern University missed two Olympics because of injury and died tragically young at the age of 39

Helsinki was a particularly friendly Games, even though the Russians had their own Olympic village away from the capitalist influences of the Western athletes. Lindy remembers: 'We had the western camp, and the Russians, the East Germans and the rest of the Eastern Bloc nations had the eastern camp. They were completely separated from us and I remember them coming into the stadium, all dressed in white, and nobody knew who they were, because we didn't know what CCCP meant, so there was a great mystique about them.

'But our shot putters Jim Fuchs and Parry O'Brien decided to pay them a visit and they went over to the eastern training camp. They weren't supposed to go, the place was covered with barbed wire and there were secret police walking around, but it didn't bother them. After all, who's going to argue with two guys who weigh 280lb and stand about six four. But they didn't show for a couple of hours and we started to get worried about them, when finally they came back carrying piles of souvenirs from the Soviet Union.'

Again, as happened in 1948, the American sprinters were not permitted to march in the opening parade, and Lindy and his team-mate Dean Smith watched from the stands as the rain poured down on the athletes who filed into the stadium, with tears pouring down their faces. When the parade finished, doves were released, a cannon boomed a 21-gun salute, and then out of the tunnel ran a small, balding man carrying the Olympic torch. It was the legendary Finnish runner Paavo Nurmi, a nine-time gold medallist in the 1920s and holder of no less than 29 world records, who, despite rumours that he was suffering from rheumatism, bounded into the stadium. He then passed the torch to fellow countryman Hannes Kolehmainen, the winner of three gold medals in the 1912 Olympics, and he jogged to the torch at the top of the opposite stand and lit it. The 70,000 crowd, undaunted by the appalling conditions, cheered wildly as the spectacle unfolded.

The first day of the Games was reserved for the first round and quarter-finals of the 100 metres, and with 72 entrants the competition took its time. 'It seemed like an endless number of heats were being run,' says Lindy. 'While waiting for your turn you're pacing up and down under the stadium because you're not allowed to go on the track. I must have run the 100 metres about 50 times up and down, up and down that stadium – and then you're on. So I got up on to the track and what a feeling that is, especially at your first Olympics, with all the people watching. We had

good. After all, the Americans had dominated the event for so long and we felt confident one of us was going to win,' he said.

Lindy's belief was strengthened still further when the training workouts began in Finland and he won every starting practice, thanks to his indoor running earlier in the year. He was still out in front at 60 metres, something that delighted the crowd at the practice sessions, especially a large Italian contingent which shouted continually, 'Bravo, Remigino'. The atmosphere in Helsinki was also helpful to his confidence, with 21 hours of sunshine every day, enabling the athletes to have two or even three workouts if they wished.

to learn the Finnish commands, then the gun goes off like a cannon and you're flying, running much faster than you have ever run in your whole life.'

Lindy cruised through the first heat, easing up in 10.4, then took his quarter-final in the same time, still looking relaxed and comfortable, just like his closest rivals Bragg, Smith, McKenley and Bailey, who all ran well. The next day saw the semis and the final, and Lindy was hoping that he would draw Bailey in his semi whom he had beaten in practice. But as luck would have it, he drew McKenley with his fast finish, and as if to preview what was to come in the final, they seemed to hit the tape together in a photo finish, with the Jamaican getting the vote over Lindy by the merest whisker. However, there was one final card to be played before the final got underway, and that was the American number one, Art Bragg, going out of the competition when he pulled a muscle and finished a miserable last in his semi. So there was only a quartet of athletes – Smith, Bailey, McKenley and Lindy – with a genuine crack at the gold.

'Now I knew that any of the four of us could win,' recalls Lindy, 'and it was all going to boil down to just 10 seconds in the final.' There were a few hours' break between the end of the semi-final and the start of the final and all the athletes were asked to leave the track and return to their dressing-rooms.

'The main dressing-room was under the stadium and there were tables there, but I didn't want to get a rub-down, I just wanted to have my legs relaxed, so I laid on one of the tables and covered myself with a large white towel. So I'm laying there and trying to get my thoughts together on how to tackle the race when in pops McKenley for heaven sakes and he's got a big smile on his face.

'He says to me, "Lindy, McDonald Bailey is ready to be had, he's so doggone nervous. I just left him and he's so nervous you can forget him." So that kind of perked me up.'

Today McKenley, an influential figure in Jamaican athletics, does not remember the incident, although he agrees that Bailey did have the jitters. 'I really didn't expect to get to the final,' he said. 'I just went into the competition for the speed and I just kept going all the way to the final.'

Finally the athletes were called, returned to the track and began to warm-up ready for the big race. Mac Bailey, the 31-year-old whom even the American press had voted the favourite, looked the most ill at ease of the whole bunch. 'When I was named favourite I became very tense and nervous,' recalls Bailey, now 67 and living and working in Trinidad. 'Remigino, by contrast, was probably the most relaxed person there, because no-one was looking for him, in the same way no-one was looking for Dillard in 1948. What unnerved me was the track. The conditions were awful, it was a very heavy, sodden surface and my lane was the worst of the lot. I looked down at my running shoes and I couldn't see the spikes because of the huge cake of mud and cinders on them. The track was so bad they even poured kerosene over it and set light to it to try and dry it off.'

As the six finalists lined up at the start – the Russian Vladimir Sukharyev, McKenley, Remigino, Smith, Bailey and the Australian John Treloar – only one thought flashed through Lindy's mind and that was to get out of the blocks like a bolt of lightning, while McKenley, the world 400-metres record holder, had been trying to convince himself throughout the competition to stay down at the start and not pop up too early.

As the gun fired, it was Lindy who sprang into the lead and just when it mattered McKenley got off to a bad start, standing straight up after just a few strides, so that by about 50 metres Lindy was way out in front. However, with about 20 metres to go, the rest of the field began to bear down on him, particularly the long-striding McKenley and Bailey. 'It was then I did something tactically wrong,' admits Lindy. 'When I saw the tape coming up real fast at me I thought, "I'm gonna win this damn thing" and I stuck my chest out, but I wasn't anywhere near the tape. I'm leaning and I didn't realise how far away I really was. So instead of hitting the tape and leaning, I started slowing up because my stride is getting shorter, then everyone is coming at me and as we hit the tape I thought McKenley had got me and I was angry because I thought I'd blown it.'

The last 10 metres of that final were among the most dramatic in Olympic sprint history, and even today there is disagreement over exactly what happened. It is true that Lindy had leaned far too early and as he reached the tape his right shoulder and arm flicked towards the line, just as McKenley came flying past him like an express train. The photo showed that Lindy had just beaten Herb on the line by getting his shoulder there first, but the judges had to study it closely and even a set square was brought in to ensure that they made the correct decision. Some journalists felt that McKenley had won it, some thought it had been a dead heat, whereas others agreed with the judges, but even with the aid of the old black-and-white moving pictures it is still

Above: the first four athletes in the Helsinki 100 metres final were all credited with the same time of 10.4 and Remigino won by an inch
Left: the winners (left to right): Herb McKenley, Lindy, the champion, and McDonald Bailey

difficult to tell. In the end, the final verdict was Lindy by one inch, in 10.4, with McKenley second in the same time, Bailey third in the same time and Smith fourth also in the same time. The distance between first and fourth was just 14 inches.

Lindy says, 'I thought Herb had won, as other people were congratulating him, so I shook his hand and said, "I think you won it". He said he thought it was close and then I saw the photo. My name went up and I just jumped for joy. That moment has stayed with me for the rest of my life.'

The Jamaican team manager, Herb McDonald, conferred with the Olympic jury, asked to see the

photo and then said that he felt it should have been a dead heat, but added that he had no intention of lodging a formal protest. The *New York Times* considered that McKenley had done no better than barely draw even with Lindy, whereas Peter Wilson, the doyen of British track writers, was never convinced that the gold medal had gone to the right man and always maintained that McKenley had won it by a whisker. One of the abiding memories of the Games, Wilson recalled, was of McKenley sitting in an empty stadium still studying the photograph and insisting that he had won, something he still feels even today. 'If the tables were turned, I'm sure I'd feel the same way,' says Lindy. 'But I think I won and Herb and I have remained friends for years.'

One of the first people to rush to congratulate Lindy was the giant shot putter Parry O'Brien, who had just won a gold himself, and he bounded across the in-field after the result of the 100 metres was announced and grabbed him in a bear hug, lifting him off his feet. 'He took all the wind out of me and said, "Lindy, you've just won a gold medal, you don't realise what you've done, it's going to change your whole life." Lo and behold he was right because once you're a gold medallist, you're a gold medallist for ever.'

After the medal ceremony, there was another moving experience which prompted more tears from Lindy. He was whisked into a giant press conference by the organisers and sat behind a large desk on which were placed dozens of microphones. Lindy was answering in Italian and English, while all sorts of questions were thrown at him, especially about the American sprinters who did not make the final. 'Are you kiddin'?' he told one interviewer, who asked about being the world's best. 'If those guys were in I wouldn't be here.' When the press conference began, Britain's Harold Abrahams stood up and began to ask a question, but he was interrupted by Red Smith of the *Herald Tribune*, who said: 'Wait a minute now, this guy's a New Yorker, I get first shot.'

Eventually he managed to escape the media madhouse and returned to his room in the village to think about what he had achieved. But there was little time for relaxation – he was in the relay team, alongside his own teenage hero Harrison Dillard, so there was still practising to be done, even though it nearly ended in disaster on the day.

Harrison, who had been wishing that he had entered the 100 metres, never practised the relay at full speed – in fact, the US team rarely got together at all, such was the strength of the sprinting. Lindy explains: 'During one practice we would all be tearing about but Harrison would just jog up and give me the stick and I would give it to Andy. So in the final we're in with the Soviets, who didn't have any outstanding individuals, but were a pretty good team. Smith starts off and he hands to Harrison who comes barrelling down the straight and almost whizzes straight past me. Because we haven't been practising at full speed I have no timing and he was going so fast I almost missed him. But I got the stick and got round the bend and handed to Andy Stanfield who drew away to win by two metres. Later he tells me I wouldn't let the stick go and he had to pull it out of my hand.'

But it was another victory and that meant Lindy could return home with two gold medals in his pocket. Before heading home for Hartford he ran a series of races and during that post-Olympic time he remained almost unbeaten, running all over Europe, against Smith, Bragg and Thane Baker, a silver medallist behind Stanfield in the 200 metres. He won every 100 metres, but McKenley got his revenge by beating him in the 200 metres. Lindy even managed to tie the world record of 10.2 in Oslo, although the mark was said to have been wind-aided and was never officially ratified by the IAAF.

He finally returned to Connecticut and a huge welcome party was held in his home town, with parades, banquets, speeches and awards. He was really looking forward to seeing his fiancée, June, after his long absence, and they were married in 1953. That same year, he graduated from Manhattan. He continued his coaching career, something he had set his sights on before going to Helsinki, and joined Hartford Public High School, where he still teaches physical education. But between 1952 and the next Olympic year, he continued to run competitively and set his sights on the 200 metres in Melbourne, feeling that he would be outgunned in the 100 metres by the newcomers to the sprint scene. Shortly before the Olympic trials, he beat the reigning champion, Andy Stanfield, only to be struck down with a throat infection, so while Stanfield went off to Los Angeles to train in the warm climate before the trials began, Lindy was languishing in bed. He stayed there

A celebration parade through the streets welcomes Lindy Remigino home. He is seen with his fiancée June and his mother

until just a few days before the trials, and although he felt very weak he flew to California, where he was promptly wiped out of the competition. It was the greatest disappointment of his track career and at the age of 24 he retired from athletics.

'So I went back to my coaching career. I knew I could coach, I knew I could help youngsters and I started going to clinics to become a better coach, then before long I was giving the clinics and writing papers. I really enjoyed it.' When he retired as a coach from the school in 1984, Lindy had stacked up no less than 29 state championships, coaching 10 all Americans and presiding over 11 undefeated seasons on the track. He won the National High School Coach of the Year Award no less than three times, and one of his closest coaching rivals was Irv Black, of the New Britain High School, who said: 'We had some great rivalries, but our athletes were always friends. He had the credentials to be an Olympic coach. He had good technique for training sprinters, but a lot of Olympic champions wore it on their sleeves. Of all the guys I knew, Lindy used it less than anybody.'

Lindy clearly misses the coaching, although he still has a few more years as a teacher at the school. He now has a new venture – a sports store he recently opened near his home. It is called, naturally enough, Remigino's 1st Place, and it is home to some of the photos from the 1952 Games and the shoes he wore in the final, with no spikes, just golf-style cleats on the toes. They have pride of place in the store, but they look a little strange hanging above the high-tech shoes that he sells today.

'I hope to work in the store after I retire. There are just so many times you can paint the garage door, you know, and I don't want to drive my wife nuts hanging around the house,' he says. Even though he has retired from professional coaching, he still has more than a passing interest in a young half-miler – his son Michael, who is just 18 years old. Michael is the youngest of five children (the only son) and Lindy still joins him for a training run, although he does get left behind most of the time. Michael has already run 1.49 for the 800 metres, good for his age, and Lindy has high hopes for him, maybe even a place in an Olympic Games in the future to carry on the Remigino tradition.

Winning the gold medal certainly opened a lot of doors for Lindy and he admits that getting his first teaching job might not have been so easy had it not been for his Olympic success. He took full advantage of the opportunity and paid the invest-

Lindy Remigino pictured in 1987 on a training run in Hartford Park in snowy Connecticut with his talented half-miler son, Michael

ment back in full. Many people dismiss Lindy as a lucky winner, but that is too much of a simplification. It takes more than luck to win an Olympic title, and although some of the big names were missing, that was not his fault. It is all part of the Olympics – getting there is the first part of the race while winning a gold medal comes later.

Frank Litsky, of the *New York Times*, probably put it best when he said: 'It's true that Lindy was the third best sprinter on the Manhattan College team. In his defence it was a very good team, but he wasn't a great sprinter. It was a time when many sprinters were eliminated for one reason or another and he survived. People say he wasn't a great sprinter, maybe not, but he's an Olympic champion and there's no asterisk in the record book that says, "Not as good as he should be". He was there when he had to be there and while he never really won anything huge again, he won the gold medal at the Olympics.'

1956 Bobby Morrow

Remigino's scepticism about successfully defending his title at the 1956 Olympics was well founded, with three new young stars exploding onto the American track scene all hoping to write their own names into the history books. They were the diminutive, but fast starting, Ira Murchison, Duke University's giant Dave Sime and smooth-running Bobby Morrow, one of four top sprinters gathered together at a tiny Christian college in Texas. In addition to this talented trio there was the promising Leamon King, who twice equalled the world 100 metres record a month before the Games, plus the Helsinki 200 metres champion Andy Stanfield, and runner-up Thane Baker returning to do battle again in Melbourne. Thus making the US team was going to be an uphill struggle for any top sprinter.

However, one man emerged from the pack to

Bobby Morrow (vest 55) hits the tape in the 1956 Melbourne Olympics 100 metres final in a time of 10.5. Thane Baker (dipping) received the silver and Hec Hogan (vest 2) the bronze medals

dominate the Games in Australia and that was the Texan Bobby Morrow, rated by many as the most relaxed sprinter of all time, even more so than his hero Jesse Owens. Bobby would eventually discover that winning a haul of Olympic gold medals had a down side as well as an up side, and even today he is still not certain whether they were a blessing or a curse. It is possible that his background was related to what happened after his Olympic success, closeted, as he was, in a strict and devoutly Christian family, growing up on a cotton farm in San Benito, way down in the lower Rio Grande Valley. For Bobby the atmosphere was one of discipline and regular trips to church, three times a week and twice on Sundays, and he never tasted a beer until after he left high school. Such a puritanical upbringing hardly equipped him to deal with the enormous pressures

that would be placed on him in the wake of his Olympic triumph, and Bobby, the man some writers liked to call America's 'Mr Clean', would have his name dragged through the mud by people who sought to exploit his success on the track. But, as he points out, were it not for his God-given speed he probably would never have attended college and would have remained in San Benito working quietly on the farm.

Bobby Joe, as he was christened, did not realise his natural ability for sprinting until junior high, when he was already 16. The coach at San Benito High School, Jake Watson, spotted his potential and set to work to fulfil it. Watson was an uncommon talent, a high school coach who actually knew something about track, and Bobby is keen to acknowledge the debt he owes him. Watson set him on the road toward the Olympic Games

(although they were never in his thoughts at the time) and began to teach him the rudiments of relaxation as a key to top-class sprinting – something that he would later perfect at college.

Bobby had not considered going to college – his plan was to marry his childhood sweetheart, Jo Ann, on leaving high school and return to the farm, but Watson convinced him that he could be a great sprinter and so he had to attend summer school to build up enough credits to get to college. By this stage, he had already excelled on the track as a high school athlete, with a schoolboy record of 9.6 in the 100 yards, so there was no shortage of offers when the time came to leave San Benito High. One came from Lamar Hunt, the owner of the Dallas Texans football club, who had seen Morrow excel as a tailback for his school team and wanted him to try out as a pro. However, in those days the money in football was nothing compared to the sums that players can earn today, and Bobby decided against it, preferring to travel around the country on the free trips he was being offered by some of the top colleges who were keen to sign him up. In the end, he opted for Abilene Christian College, a Church of Christ school, the conservative organisation to which he and his family belonged, and the school his older brother attended. But there were other reasons for choosing Abilene. Bobby liked the smallness of the school, around 2,000 students,

Right: down on the farm. Bobby Morrow lends a hand on the tractor on the family holding in San Benito, in the Rio Grande Valley. Below: Bobby (extreme left) poses for a San Benito High School football team photograph. His tailback skills earned him the chance to play professionally

compared to 40,000 at the big colleges, and he was a shy, farm boy who felt happier in the more modest surroundings at Abilene. Most important of all, he knew the pedigree the school had in track, where despite its size it had won a pile of national titles and boasted one of the best sprint relay teams in the country.

Now married, Bobby settled straight into the Abilene track team. In his first outings for the college, as a freshman in 1955, he began to run some impressive times, culminating in June with an astonishing run in Abilene, at a cold and rainy NAIA meet, where he tore down the track to

register a 9.1 for 100 yards, which was two-tenths of a second better than Mel Patton's world record. Unfortunately for Bobby, the wind was over the legal limit so the record never stood, but the run convinced him that he could make it to the very top – the Olympic Games.

The man responsible for his improvement was the Abilene coach Oliver Jackson, who honed Bobby's natural speed, polished his technique and taught him how to relax and run. Relaxation was the key to his form, and the fluidity that Jackson managed to build into his running was something to behold. One writer described Bobby's style quite succinctly: 'He doesn't appear especially to pull, push or drive as he runs. He's never struggling. He just runs. He's like a wheel rolling down the track.' A test Morrow used to ensure that he was running properly was to waggle his jaw muscles as he ran, especially coming off the curve in a 200 metre race, where lots of athletes tend to tighten. Films of his races show this technique, as if he is running in his sleep!

Early in 1956, Abilene had the best sprint quartet in the United States, with Morrow, Bill Woodhouse, James Segrest and Waymond Griggs, and in the two years that followed they would break or equal world records a staggering 11 times. Training was quite advanced for its time, with Jackson supervising weight-training, almost unheard of in those days, and insisting that Bobby ran throughout the year, although it was mostly cross-country during the off-season and then running bare-foot on grass before moving on to the track. Of course he was barred from playing football at college because Jackson feared that he might get injured. The coach also stopped him long jumping, an event in which Bobby had shown great promise at high school.

'Most of my work was done barefoot on the grass,' recalls Bobby. 'In fact, I hardly got on the track before the season began and then only to get conditioning for the 200 metres. We always concentrated on relaxation. We trained so your cheeks would bounce up and down when you ran, making sure your arms were relaxed and we worked on that every day of the week. I worked on starting a lot because I never tried to roll with the gun, like a lot of other sprinters, so consequently I was usually behind at the start and had to make up a lot of ground. I was never a great starter.'

One of Jackson's chief ploys to ensure that Bobby would never tighten up, even if he was a long way behind the rest of the field, was to use a colleague in training and to start him about 10 yards in front of Bobby in a 220 yards run, and tell him to catch up without tensing while keeping his jaw muscles bouncing. All this training paid off when the Olympic year finally arrived and after a short tour of Australia, which proved invaluable experience, he tore into the opposition around the United States.

At the same time, newcomer Dave Sime was hitting the headlines with a series of spectacular indoor wins and they finally met at the Drake Relays in Iowa, in April, where during a torrential downpour Sime leaped out of the blocks to beat Bobby by a yard. It was his first defeat over 100 yards for three years and it would be his last defeat of the season in major competition. There are those who maintain that Sime would have presented Bobby with a tougher challenge at the Olympics than the athletes who eventually competed in the final, but Dave Sime never made it to Melbourne. Shortly after his victory over Bobby, he was thrown by a horse and injured a groin muscle. The following week he ran in California and smashed the world 220 yards record in 20.0, but in doing so aggravated the injury leading to complications that dogged him throughout the season. When he and Bobby met again at the NCAA championships in Berkeley, California, in June, Sime could only manage a third place, blaming the injury, whereas Bobby cantered home by two yards. Despite these victories, many sports writers still did not rate his chances of making the team, especially with the line-up of sprinting talent in the US all vying for places, but Bobby shocked them all by winning the AAU 100 metres and following that with a double win in the final Olympic trials.

The Games were held late, in November, of 1956, and the Americans had led a wholesale assault on the sprint records, with Dave Sime twice equalling the 100 yard mark and Leamon King making it once. In the 100 metres, Bobby equalled the world record of 10.2, set by Jesse Owens, no less than three times, whereas his colleague Ira Murchison equalled it twice. The Olympic trials were held in late June, so all the athletes had to keep their form for another four months, with Morrow, Thane Baker and Murchison selected in the 100 metres, and Morrow, Stanfield and Baker in the 200 metres and Leamon King as the odd man out who travelled as part of the relay team.

The unluckiest man was Willie Williams, who broke the world record in 10.1 in early August, in Berlin, but had been edged out of the team during the trials. The following day Murchison equalled the new world mark, and during October Leamon King hit form and twice equalled the new record

Left: Dave Sime was forced out of the Melbourne Games due to injury
Above: Bakersfield, California, June 1956. Bobby Morrow equals
Owens' world 100 metres record in 10.2 seconds

in California – on both occasions beating Morrow and Murchison. Meanwhile, in the 200 metres, Bobby had equalled the 20.6 world record twice, so it was still anybody's guess which of the American stars would be right on the day and take the top prize. Bobby's surprising defeats had come during a specially selected series of pre-Olympic tests, but it was reported widely that he was suffering from a debilitating virus infection, which caused weight loss and a general loss of sparkle. By the time he left for Australia, he was well on the road to recovery.

The journey, undertaken a fortnight before the Games were due to start, was a tortuous one. 'Back in '56 we had no jets,' says Bobby, 'so we travelled by a prop-driven Pan-Am Clipper. The team was broken up and I was travelling with the lady swimmers, which was a great experience for me, but it was a long trip, about 48 hours' flying time and it was horrendous sitting there all that time with no sleep. We all tried to find somewhere to lie down and my feet swelled up and I couldn't get my shoes on. We made three stops, at Honolulu, Fiji and Canton, but we were glad to get off when we finally arrived.'

Despite the political turmoil around the world, Melbourne was a happy place for the Olympics. There was still fighting between Hungary and the Soviet Union and the Suez crisis continued to bubble, so it was no surprise that there were suggestions that the Games should be scrapped

and a number of countries chose to boycott them in the belief that turbulent world events prevented them being staged in the right spirit. But the charm and efficiency of the Australian organisers and the amazing enthusiasm of the fans meant that the Olympics not only went ahead but proved a tremendous success, with 120,000 enthusiasts packing the main stadium, the Melbourne Cricket Ground, during every day of competition.

Bobby realised immediately that Melbourne was a sports-minded city when he saw the kids heading for the tennis courts instead of church on a Sunday morning. 'I loved Australia,' he says. 'I loved the people there, they packed the stadium and there were thousands of people outside who couldn't get in. It was a warm experience, especially visiting the various athletes from all over the world and to be able to talk to them and learn their training methods. Of course we were particularly interested in talking to the Russian athletes and they were keen to talk to us, so we'd sit down and find out about each other's training, eating and preparation.'

For the first time at the Olympics, the Russians were part of the main village, at Heidelberg, where the Australian government had built houses, each of which accommodated four athletes during the Games. The US team had all their food flown in, even their water, and the village cafeteria was open 24 hours a day and became a popular meeting-place for the athletes. Bobby said: 'I was just in a fantasy land being one of the youngest members of the Olympic team – just 21 – and being able to meet and talk to all the athletes from around the world. Sport was the international language and everyone understood. If we could keep politics out of it, what a better place it would be.'

The 100 metres competition was, as always, the first major track event, and so Bobby missed the opening parade, remaining in the village. Apart from the American team there were few top-class sprinters to worry about, although the Australian Hec Hogan, the darling of the crowd, had equalled the world 100 yards record two years earlier on a grass track in Sydney, and therefore could not be completely discounted.

Abilene Christian had sent Oliver Jackson to Melbourne to help out and to ensure that Bobby was in the right frame of mind. Thus the team coaches had little to do with him. They worked together on the relaxation exercises and he went through his normal workouts, but in addition he and the three other American 100 metres contenders worked daily on baton passing for the relay, sometimes three times each day.

When the 100 metres competition finally opened, under blue skies and bright sunshine, Morrow and Murchison took complete control of the early rounds, both equalling the 10.3 Olympic record without looking unduly troubled. Disaster almost struck in the quarter-final when Bobby pulled a groin muscle, but the team managers worked tirelessly to ensure that he would be fit for the next heat, using heatlamps, whirlpool baths and finally strapping it tightly to prevent the pull worsening. He did not suffer any after-effects and although the press almost wrote him off because of the injury it did not worry him unduly. After the semi-finals, in which the 6ft 2in Morrow and 5ft 4½in Murchison took first place, again equalling the Olympic record, the two Americans were made pre-final favourites.

The Australian starter came over to the US camp to join in the training, as he did with the other countries' teams, so that the sprinters would be accustomed to his technique, but Bobby did not pay much attention because he knew that he would be the last one out of the blocks and would then have to make up lost ground.

The six finalists included the three US stars, Morrow, Murchison and Baker, augmented by Hogan, the German Manfred Germar and Michael Agostini from Trinidad. As they settled into their blocks the wind gauge told them that there would be no world records, with a nine-miles-an-hour wind blowing straight into their faces. At the gun it was Hogan who leaped into an early lead but Bobby had not got a bad start and caught him at about the halfway mark, switching into overdrive and pulling away to win easily by five feet, in 10.5 (thanks to the wind), with Thane Baker lunging past Hogan on the line to take the silver. The Australian took the bronze, while a

Left: the electronic photo shows the distance by which Bobby Morrow won the Olympic title
Above: big smiles from the winners: Bobby Morrow (left) won the gold, Baker (centre) the silver and Hogan the bronze

disappointed Murchison finished fourth. 'I just couldn't believe it,' recalls Morrow, 'and I wondered to myself after I hit the tape, "What am I doing here?" It was a very big surprise to me and all the sports writers said, "Well, he's won the 100, but he can't win the 200".'

Standing at the top of the medal rostrum remains one of the best moments of his life. 'It's the greatest experience an athlete will ever have. The American flag is raised on the centre pole and they play the anthem. There's dead silence in a crowd of 120,000 people and you could literally hear a pin drop. Chills ran up and down my spine as they gave me the medal and I'll never forget it as long as I live.'

The cynics among the American press corps predicted that Bobby would have tougher competition in the 200 metres, especially with reigning champion Stanfield, but they also thought that he would not last the pace of four rounds with his muscle problems. However, Bobby insisted: 'I felt confident, much happier than I did in the 100, because I liked to run the curve and I felt very comfortable.' Despite the bandaging wrapped around his left thigh he breezed through the heats and lined up with his old adversary Thane Baker as well as Stanfield. Baker was given the unfortunate draw of the outside lane, while Morrow was in the middle. It was particularly galling for Baker because he had been alloted the same lane in the 1952 final; in Melbourne it made him so nervous that he put down his starting blocks pointing in the wrong direction and thus the race had to be delayed, the error pointed out and the blocks changed. It was Bobby's race all the way, powering past everyone on the curve, jaw muscles waggling in familiar style, and he tore down the home straight to win by a yard and a half over Stanfield, with Baker overcoming his nerves to finish third. Bobby's victory made him the first double gold winner of the Games, and his time of 20.6 beat the old Olympic record set in Berlin by Jesse Owens, who was watching up in the stands and was among the first to congratulate the big Texan. But it was not the only record that Bobby would take from Owens and, as everyone expected, the relay team, comprising arguably the four best sprinters in the world, had little trouble in winning the gold medal, with a particularly fast start from Murchison and efficient handovers to King, Baker and finally Morrow who galloped down the track. He broke the tape in 39.5, three-tenths of a second better than the world record set by the Owens quartet in 1936. Bobby was the first man to win three track and field gold medals at a single Olympics since the 'Ebony Antelope' and he became one of the star attractions in Melbourne and one of the main targets for the photo and autograph hunters.

He always shunned publicity, because he was a quiet and shy young man who felt distinctly uncomfortable in the role of the conquering hero.

Bobby Morrow (vest 55) completes his Olympic sprint double with a gold in the 200 metres despite the strapping on an old thigh injury

To this day he insists that he has never read a newspaper or magazine article about himself, and although he has always been helpful and responsive to most requests for interviews over the years, Bobby still tries to avoid publicity whenever he can. In Melbourne this took an unusual form when he and his close friend Glenn Davis, the hurdler, devised a foolproof scheme to escape the hordes of autograph hunters who stood guard outside the only entrance and exit to the village. 'There were so many people outside it was impossible to get anywhere, so when Glenn and I decided to go to a movie or ride downtown we came up with this scheme. We went to the training room and had the trainers wrap our hands with tape, so when we walked out of the gate our hands were all bandaged up and nobody bothered us.'

Bobby's reception in Australia was nothing compared to the one awaiting him when he returned home to Texas. In Abilene the entire college turned out at the airport as he flew in on a private plane from California, with a huge crowd of local banner-waving fans eager to catch a glimpse of their new star. His success in Melbourne put his name on all the headlines around the United States and established Abilene Christian firmly on the map. As Bobby was paraded through the streets, given the key to the city and attended banquets in his honour, little did he know of the traumas that would follow.

On the day he returned home, a local sports reporter wrote: 'If Abilene loved Bobby Morrow in October when it sent him around the world to compete against the best the world had to offer, it threw itself in admiration at his feet in December when he returned triumphant over all.' Bobby began to travel on the lecture circuit where his abilities as a public speaker kept him in high demand, talking to many groups around the country. He was a good speaker, even an inspirational one, in the Jesse Owens tradition, but then he was a speech major at college and had preached to congregations in church and taught bible classes, so he had had many opportunities to improve his technique. His public speaking drew big crowds wherever he went, even a standing ovation at the state legislature, where he told the assembly: 'I sincerely believe that my greatest race, the Christian race, is the most important of them all and is yet to be won.'

In the months that followed his almost messianic return home he was in such demand that Abilene Christian assigned him a permanent public relations man, Bob Hunter, who toured with Bobby all over the United States, arranging his

The demands on Bobby Morrow to make public appearances after the 1956 Games were great. He was the epitome of the all American boy

flights, booking hotels, paying bills and even writing the speeches. 'He did everything in the world for me,' recalls Morrow. 'All I had to do was show up and be there. But it was real hard for an athlete that young to have all these things taken care of and even more difficult when you get out of that situation to then go out and do things on your own. It was very, very difficult for me.'

Bobby's epic tours were also placing a strain on his marriage to Jo Ann and his family life (he now had twins Ron Floyd and Vicki Jo). 'Because I was gone so long it put pressure on the family. I was away so much I couldn't keep up with my studies, so I laid out a semester because I was in South America, then in the Caribbean for the State Department and it was very hard to have a family life. It put a strain on everybody, not only on your wife, but the kids and yourself.'

Bobby Morrow had become the living embodiment of his country and all the things that made America great: God, clean living, family life and athletic success – he really was just too good to be true. His photo appeared on the covers of *Life*, *Sport* and *Sports Illustrated*, and politicians were eager to be photographed with him; he even appeared on the top-rated Ed Sullivan and Arthur Godfrey TV shows. A cascade of awards began to rain down on him, including the Sullivan Award, as the year's most outstanding amateur athlete. Similar awards came from *Sport* and *Sports Illustrated*, where he beat the top baseball and football players to be crowned America's number one sportsman. Early the following year, he was summoned to the White House for a conference with President Eisenhower, and the US Chamber of Commerce honoured him as one of the nine Great Living Americans. Bobby was not allowed to remain as just the fastest man on earth, he was promoted as an example to everyone in the country, and that put enormous pressure on him as he tried desperately to live up to his new reputation – a task that eventually proved as impossible as it sounded. Naturally his glory reflected on the college and the Church of Christ, the evangelistic faith dedicated to the New Testament, and their popularity grew with his.

Bobby continued to compete throughout 1957, tying the world 100 yards record at the NCAA championships in Austin in June, and putting together a series of impressive relay times, including four world records with the fast quartet from Abilene Christian. Between races he continued his speaking engagements and even made a movie. 'I took acting lessons and I had a coach,' recalls Bobby, who personified the athletic, handsome image that was admired in the mid 1950s. 'But I had to be up every morning at 6.30 for make-up, having already learned my lines the night before. It was an experience and I enjoyed it, but I didn't want to do it again.'

He played a high school coach trying to avoid the persistent attentions of a gorgeous student, but the movie was not a success at the box office and Bobby's movie career stopped right there although he was reluctant to continue acting anyway.

The following year, he graduated from Abilene and went to work as a vice-president at the Abilene Bank of Commerce, which allowed him time off to train and compete in major meets. His form was inconsistent and although he was beaten by his relay partner Bill Woodhouse and the improving Dave Sime, Bobby had already set his sights on defending his title in Rome in 1960. But he found training without the back-up of the college very difficult, even though the bank were always sympathetic and supportive. 'I had a hard time when I got out of college,' he recalls, 'because when I was in school I worked out with my teammates and I had a coach who would tell me what to do. He'd tell me I had to run repeat 200s or 300s and of course I'd do it, because if I didn't I wouldn't be on the team and my scholarship would be cut. But when you're on your own it's hard to go out there and work out on your own.'

To counter this problem Bobby got permission to continue training with the college and with Jackson, although he still missed the motivation of running for the team. The 1959 season was similarly inconsistent and it was then, before Olympic year itself, that the curtain was finally brought down on his career, when he travelled to Houston for the Meet of Champions, suffered a severe muscle spasm during the final of the 100 metres and crashed to the track. A large knot appeared on his thigh muscle and as the trainers worked feverishly to try and push the injured

The beginning of the end of Bobby Morrow's track career. Houston officials try to help as Bobby writhes in agony from a severe muscle pull

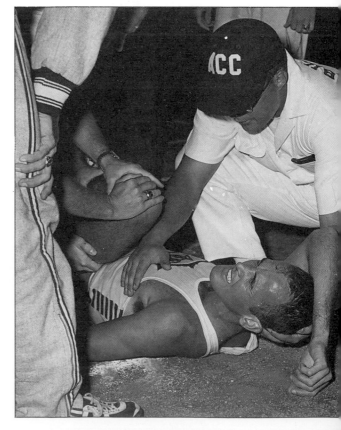

muscle back into shape, photographers gathered around to take shots of the Olympic champion lying in agony on the track, his face contorted in pain. But the efforts of the trainers were to no avail and his leg was never the same again. In fact, even today he still cannot stretch it out properly. But it was not just the injury that finished his running career at the highest level.

At that time, Bobby was on the verge of getting his pilot's licence, but he was still technically a learner and thus was accompanied by a qualified pilot when he flew down to Houston for the meeting. Naturally, he was not able to pilot the plane on the homeward bound flight, so his 'minder' had to do the job for him. 'It was a very cloudy and overcast day,' remembers Morrow, 'and my wife and her brother were in the back of the plane as we took off and climbed up. I was on the radio trying to give Houston our flight plan when I looked over at the instrument panel and saw that the artificial horizon, which tells you how the plane is flying, was vertical. I told him and when he saw it he just went crazy, he grabbed the wheel to his chest and started screaming and hollering. I finally managed to pull the wheel away from him and pushed it down so we'd pick up our air speed and as we broke out of the clouds there was just enough time to see the ground and straighten out. We had flipped and stalled and if the clouds had been any lower we would have crashed straight into the ground. I had to fly on to Abilene and when we landed he got out of the plane, tore up his licence and vowed never to set foot in a plane again. It turned out he wasn't an instrument rated pilot, we'd popped some rivets in the tail and he couldn't fly it. We were very close to being killed.'

The shock of escaping death so narrowly in the plane had a lasting effect on Bobby and after the incident he found it increasingly difficult to relax, which was the whole essence of his running. Willing to try anything, he accepted Jackson's offer of hypnosis in an effort to relax. 'I went to a doctor in Abilene and he did help me to relax and he told me that if he had enough time he could teach me to go into a hypnotic trance at the sound of the gun and come out of it when I hit the tape. We didn't have time to work on self-hypnosis, but he travelled with me to the big track meets, stayed in the same hotel and before each race he'd hypnotise me to relax.' Bobby is convinced that he only touched the surface of his problem with the technique, which he likens to a form of deep concentration, and thinks that today's athletes would do better trying to relax rather than dabbling in drugs.

In the AAU championships, a route to the final Olympic trials, he strained a muscle during the warm-up and failed to qualify for the 100 metres. He still managed to take fourth place in the 200 metres, thus qualifying for the Olympic trials. The injury healed before the trials and although the break in his training was to prove critical, there were those who still felt that he would be sufficiently good to make the team for the second time around. He came in fourth in the 200 metres, just missing the team, but the US coaches and officials were keen for him to continue training with the team and invited him out to the Olympic camp in California. So he gave up his job in Abilene to spend five weeks there in the hope that his performances would improve and he would be selected as a reserve. His form began to improve and in the pre-Olympic meets he started beating the athletes who had finished ahead of him in the trials. On the last day of the training programme, on the eve of the team's departure for Rome, Bobby asked the officials if he would be going. They told him that the decision would be made at a meeting that night. 'Finally they said I should meet them at the airport in the morning and they'd tell me then if I was going or not. I asked if that meant I had to pack for the Games or pack to go home, but they said they didn't know. So I packed for the Games and turned up at the airport all ready to get on the plane and they said, "No, you're not going." So I turned around and came home.'

The decision and the manner in which it was executed devastated Bobby, and even today he admits that it is still a thorn in his side. He feels that there could have been two factors behind such shabby treatment of a reigning champion.

The first was, perhaps, an understandable fear on the part of some of the eastern coaches who did not want Bobby to be vying for places with their own athletes, but the second was far more sinister. Shortly after the Melbourne Games, Bobby had spoken out about the misuse of money during the Games by the American officials and had met the Attorney-General in Washington to talk about the AOC and a possible investigation of the AAU. A committee of inquiry held hearings on the AAU and Bobby testified with several other athletes, but nothing was ever followed up and the investigation fizzled out.

Bobby had been upset by the freeloaders who had flown in with the athletes to Melbourne and clearly remembers that there was one official whose job it was to hand out the soap – and his wife went with him! 'The Olympic team is supported through public donations,' he says. 'It's not Government sponsored. But it's so political that all the AOC and AAU officials, their friends and relatives came along and jobs were found for them.' One of Bobby's biggest opponents during the investigation was a man whose name has appeared with unerring regularity throughout Olympic history, and that was AOC President and Olympic 'Godfather' Avery Brundage. Bobby and Brundage had crossed swords before over the issue of expenses for athletes, which the AOC chief vehemently opposed, and Bobby feels there may have been an element of revenge in the way he was left out of the 1960 team at the eleventh hour. As it turned out, the Americans put up a poor showing, by their standards, in the sprints and relay and could have benefited from Bobby's experience, but it was something the AOC would never have admitted.

After such a dramatic turn of events at the airport in 1960, Bobby decided to retire and never ran competitively again. Despite failing to make the Olympic team he was still a popular figure in Texas, especially in Abilene, and it was at this time that he began to experience the attentions of commercial vultures, who descended on a man they perceived as an easy marketing ride because of his clean image and good name.

Bobby and his family were still living in Abilene, but he decided to leave the bank for a short time and formed a company to market a pill called Stim-o-Stam, which he had used during his college days. It contained a mineral that helped relieve muscle soreness and fatigue and was widely used in athletics at the time and by hunters on long trips into the mountains. He employed a local man as sales manager and they set to work selling stock around the country to raise money to form the company. Many of the investors were friends from Abilene and the Texas area, some of whom were involved in the church and the college. It soon became clear that the business was not running properly and it transpired that Bobby's partner had been using his name to sell stock to his friends and pocketing the money. The partner was arrested but all the money had been spent and Bobby's friends were not repaid as the company folded.

'They were mad at me because everything had been done in my name,' says Bobby. 'But I really had no idea what he was doing. It hurt my image, especially in Abilene, and I had to have my phone disconnected because of all the strange phone calls I was getting. I was just one of many athletes who were being taken advantage of. People want to use your name and your notoriety for their own gain. Of course today athletes have agents and that's a good thing. That would have helped me a lot.'

The Stim-o-Stam affair was not the last occasion on which he got his fingers burned by a sharp operator. A few years later he suffered another image battering when he got involved with a man described by the locals as the Church of Christ's most famous criminal, a man called Billy Sol Estes. Bobby had made a few speeches for Sol Estes before he fell foul of the law and went on trial for selling fertilizer tanks that did not exist. He was out of prison on a bond, and in Abilene one night when he telephoned Bobby, asking him out for supper. Bobby tried to refuse but Sol Estes insisted on meeting him if only for a coffee. Bobby relented and arrived at the restaurant and, while they were drinking their coffee, Sol Estes excused himself saying that he had to make a phone call. He returned a few minutes later, and soon the place was crowded with reporters and cameras, wanting to know what was happening. It was an embarrassing scene, with Bobby trying to hide his face behind his hands and repeating, 'No comment' over and over again. The whole sorry episode appeared on the front page of the *Abilene Reporter-News* the following morning.

'I think he did it primarily to get publicity for himself,' says Bobby, 'and to get public sympathy on his side. Of course that really hurt me being seen with him at a restaurant and I had people calling me all hours of the night and eventually I had to have my phone disconnected again because of the animosity it caused. I definitely think Billy Sol did it on purpose to help himself.'

The Sol Estes fiasco put additional strain on Bobby's marriage and Jo-Ann went on record as saying: 'Nobody can stay on a pedestal and he fell pretty fast. It was really hard on him and our marriage, too. Neither one of us was very communicative. He came through the Stim-o-Stam deal pretty well, but he was disappointed in people because they were disappointed in him. But the blow he couldn't take was when he tried to go to the '60 Olympics. They strung him along and used him to help other sprinters train. When they didn't take him after that, it was a hard blow. That was a kind of turning point. He felt used and got down on himself and then he got down on everyone else. He got more cynical and chose some friends that he would never have chosen before.' The strain finally proved too much and Bobby and Jo-Ann were divorced in the 1960s, which estranged him from his twins, a situation that has been resolved quite recently with his son Ron.

Bobby worked for a couple of banks and, while in Houston, became involved in some promotion and coaching work with the Houston Striders athletic club, where he helped future Olympic champion and world record holder Jim Hines, especially on his starting, which seemed ironic as that was the weakest part of Bobby's racing make-up. He was delighted when Jimmy won in Mexico in 1968 but never felt like taking up coaching on a permanent basis. On leaving Texas he got involved in a children's education programme in Ohio, where he met his second wife of more than 15 years, Judy, who had two children of her own. They also have a 13-year-old daughter. In the early 1970s, Bobby returned to his roots to run the family farm when his father underwent back surgery. The family still own the farm (his mother lives there) although it is rented out. When the economic realities of the farming business caught up with him, he switched from farmer to store owner, opening a clothes store in the city of Harlingen, followed by a pool and leisure centre, but he did not persevere with either and decided to move to Austin, the state capital, where he still lives today. He runs an insurance business from home with a partner, and appears to be prospering.

'We're looking forward to the future very much,' he says. 'I'm enjoying the insurance business, working with and helping people. It's what I've been doing all my life. I don't keep that keen an interest in track, because there aren't many big meets in Texas, but I watch the ones on TV.'

One noticeable change is the influence of the church on his life. He no longer attends church regularly and explains: 'I think because I was brought up in a strict, religious family, it's probably a rebellion on my part. I'm still a religious person, I just don't go to church and participate in church activities.' He has always been interested in speed – running fast, cars, planes and boats. He has a pilot's licence and a ski boat and admits that speed is a lifelong passion. He last ran, just for fun, in a 1956 Olympians relay race in 1976, alongside Thane Baker, Ira Murchison and Earl Young, but the next morning he could not even get out of bed. He does not aspire to the ranks of the morning joggers and promised himself that he would never run again.

Winning three gold medals affected Bobby's life in many ways, enabling him to travel around the world and meet people but he also admits that his Olympic success prompted a lot of people to try and take advantage of him, and some of them succeeded. Oliver Jackson recently compared Bobby to Carl Lewis, saying: 'He had great

Bobby Morrow today is a more contented man than in the post-Olympic years of turmoil, and he lives comfortably with his family in Austin, Texas

strength and he was unbelievably disciplined. He never jumped a gun in the four years I had him and that was when you could jump and not be disqualified. We said he had ice water in his veins. I'm biased but I've never seen anyone I thought could beat Morrow. He ran on cinders in Melbourne and the track had been laid the week before the Olympics and it was so mushy you could stick your fingers down into it. If he ran on the tracks we have today there's no telling what he could do.' Many people in athletics mistake Bobby's laconic style and dismissive words about his career as a sign that he wishes he had never competed in the Olympics, but that is far from the truth. A Texas magazine recently quoted him as saying that he regretted winning the gold medals, but they only got half of the story, because he still feels that those days were the greatest of his life. It is only the bad things that subsequently happened to him as a direct result of that success that he now regrets.

But he is not haunted by the past and it is history as far as he is concerned. He won the medals, enjoyed the experience immensely and now that period of his life is finished and forgotten. Forgotten by many perhaps, but Bobby Morrow remains as probably the greatest white sprinter of all time, by virtue of his competition success and world records, and certainly one of the most beautiful runners ever to grace a track.

1960 Armin Hary

By the time of the 1960 Rome Olympics, the United States had dominated the sprints for nearly 30 years. Although the rise of the fast-starting young blonde European champion Armin Hary from West Germany had caused a few ripples of interest in the world track scene, there was still little thought given to the possibility of an American defeat in the forthcoming Games. As the Olympic year began, the world 100 metres record of 10.1 was held jointly by no less than four US athletes – Willie Williams, Ira Murchison, Leamon King and, most recently, Ray Norton.

Norton was widely regarded as the world's premier sprinter and had taken his share in the world record at a San Jose meeting in 1959, a year in which he also swept the board in both sprints at the big USA–USSR meeting and the Pan American Games. Apart from Norton, the Americans also had the improving Frank Budd and big Dave Sime, now back to full fitness and ready to prove a

A wide-angle view of the finish of the 1960 Olympic 100 metres final in Rome. West Germany's controversial world record holder Armin Hary (extreme left) wins the gold ahead of American Dave Sime (vest 397) and Britain's Peter Radford

point after the disappointment of missing out on Melbourne through injury.

Of the nine athletes who jointly held the 9.3 world mark for 100 yards, an astonishing eight were American, including Norton and Sime, while at 200 metres only Britain's Peter Radford could claim a share in the world record alongside the USA's Stone Johnson and the inevitable Norton. So it was hardly surprising that the American coaches were sceptical about the seriousness of the challenge from Germany and were supremely confident that one of their 'boys' would successfully retain the 'fastest man on earth' title for the United States. Their nationalistic arrogance would prove to be their undoing because the Germans had at last unearthed a real world beater in the young Hary, after years of turning out world-class sprinters, such as Houben, Kornig, Jonath, Fütterer and Germar, only to see them beaten in the major inter-national championships. Hary enjoyed a short but controversial career and was regarded by the German athletic establishment as an oddball character who seemed to delight in causing friction in the sport. His arrogant style and off-beat behaviour often upset other athletes and his incredible 'speed' out of the blocks earned him the title of 'The Thief of Starts' because of his persistent gun jumping. Off the track his antics continued to provide copy for the newspapers, though mostly for the wrong reasons, with stories about an abortive film career, a ban from the track for bringing the sport into disrepute, a fairy tale romance and marriage to a wealthy society heiress and finally the shame of arrest and prison.

Today, Armin Hary is not regarded as a national hero, as one might expect from the sports loving German public, and he prefers to stay out of the limelight. His name is seldom mentioned and he has been described by some of the

country's top sports journalists as something of a forgotten man. But back in the fifties all that was ahead of him as he practised hard to fulfil his childhood dream and become a football player in a small village near the industrial town of Saarbrucken, where he was born in March 1937, the son of a miner. His father was also a versatile sportsman and had a reputation as a wrestler, so it was no surprise when Hary Junior began to excel in sports, particularly soccer and gymnastics, before he switched his attentions to athletics.

He first became a keen decathlete and sprang to prominence during 1956 when he established a new Saarland record of 5376 points and ranked among Germany's top 15 decathletes by the end of the year. However, while competing in the 10-event discipline it became clear that by far his best event was the 100 metres, and he proved the point the following year by running a 10.4 in Dusseldorf, followed by a 10.5 second place in the German championships behind the favourite, Manfred Germar. The year proved to be a crucial one for Hary, because he left his athletic club in Saarbrucken to join the big Bayer club in Leverkusen, which was backed by the giant Bayer chemical works, where he worked as a precision toolmaker. Once there he came under the influence of coach Bertl Sumser, who quickly realised Armin's potential as a top-class sprinter. 'Hary has the temperament, unprecedented ability and enormous start speed,' he told pressmen. 'He is powerful and muscular, has a good supply of ambition and in addition a real charge of nervous energy – vital in a sprinter.'

During a series of tests conducted on German athletes at the Freiberg University Clinic, eminent professor Herbert Reindell also

Armin Hary, seen here in a 100 metres heat in Rome, is two strides ahead of the rest of the field and showing the advantage of his 'Blitz Start'

discovered that Armin's body had the capacity to endure a tough campaign of athletic training because his heart was that of an undeveloped, non-athlete.

Sumser recalls the day he first saw the young Hary: 'I knew straight away he was going to be a world-class sprinter. He had everything, marvellous reactions and he was so well motivated. Although he had tremendous natural talent, he allied that to hard work in training – he was just a genius.' So during the winter of 1957–58, Sumser worked tirelessly with him to improve his sprint times and hone his technique, with cross-country runs and hours of gruelling gym work, including weight-lifting, wall bar exercises and medicine ball training. The result was a new look Armin Hary – stronger, quicker, more confident and with additional stamina allied to his natural speed and ability. When the 1958 season opened and he was able to beat Germar over 60 yards, people were ready to start taking him seriously. His electrify-

ing start, referred to by the German press as the 'Blitz Start,' was clearly his main weapon, and in most races, when he was not called back for jumping the gun, he would be two or three strides in front of the rest of the field within the first five metres. Naturally there were cynics who suggested that Hary was simply a master at anticipating the gun, so a series of tests were conducted using a high-speed camera which showed that his reaction time was superior to other athletes. The researchers suggested that the average human reaction time to a starting gun was 15 one-hundredths, whereas the reaction time of top German sprinter Heinz Fütterer was eight one-hundredths. But when they studied the films of Armin's starts, his reaction time was an astonishing three one-hundreths of a second. Some scientists doubted that anyone could react to a gun at that speed, and it was rumoured that the new boy must have a sixth sense to anticipate the gun.

His reaction time was only a part of Armin's phenomenal starting ability because he himself admitted that a more important part was getting into full stride quicker than the other athletes. 'In the time it takes other runners to take their first step,' said coach Sumser, 'Hary has taken two or three.' Armin had learned, through hard training and relaxation, how to achieve full power soon after the gun and, together with his explosive reactions, this created the 'Blitz Start'. Hary himself believes: 'It was my speed of reaction to the gun. There was no real technique – just pure reaction speed.'

His ability was appreciated more widely during the European Championships, in Stockholm during the same year, where he won gold medals in both the 100 metres and the sprint relay although his start in the 100 seemed a little too good. His excellent form continued right through the year and in September he actually recorded the first 10 second flat time for 100 metres in Friedrichshafen, but when officials investigated the time they discovered that the track had an 11cm downhill gradient – just one centimetre more than permitted – and the time was invalidated. His 1959 form was a disappointment compared to that of the previous year, but he did get an invitation to California by San Jose State College, where Ray Norton was based, to talk over terms of a sports scholarship. An agreement

Armin Hary dips to victory in the 1960 Rome Olympic final, just ahead of Dave Sime in lane one while Peter Radford powers past Figuerola

was not reached, however, and early in 1960 Armin returned home.

One of the problems he had encountered was his inability to speak English. He earned some money by washing dishes and when an offer came to return to Germany he jumped at the chance. He joined the athletics section of the FSV Frankfurt Football Club, where he trained under the auspices of Coach Haefele, who had aided the 1954 European Champion Fütterer in the early 1950's. The club also helped find him a job as a salesman in the TV and radio department of the giant Kaufhof stores. His form, which had dipped during 1959 because of the lack of proper training and his trips to America, began to return early in 1960 and on 21 June, in Zurich, he wrote his name indelibly in the record books, reaching an athletic barrier that many felt would not be achieved for another 10 years.

By this time Armin was already showing signs of non-conformity. He appeared to enjoy bucking the system and was unconcerned about upsetting anyone who got in his way. It was reported in the German press that before he left Frankfurt to fly to Switzerland he called the organiser of the meeting and told him that he needed to be motivated 'additionally' before he would set foot on the plane. It had been customary for some years to pay a small amount of expenses to athletes but under-the-counter payments were more rare. Hary was well aware of his value to the meeting in terms of pulling people through the gates and thus the organisers agreed to his demand for 1,000 Swiss Francs. He did not disappoint them nor the large crowds in the Stadion Letzigrund hoping to see some fireworks from the new German sprint star. On a warm and sunny evening, Armin tore off his customized starting blocks, clearly before the gun, and won easily from the rest of an international field to record another 10 seconds flat. There was no re-call from the starter, it was later discovered, because the second shot would not go off, but the officials agreed that it had been a false start, and again his 10 seconds flat time was struck off.

Armin protested vehemently, claiming that it was not his fault that the re-call had not gone off. The organisers eventually conceded to his demands for a re-run to take place some 50 minutes later. Two of the original line-up were persuaded to race again with him, so the three of them took their places at the start and this time there was no question of Armin jumping the gun and he sprang out of the blocks incredibly fast and strode away from to two other athletes, hitting the tape in yet another 10 seconds flat.

This time it was legal and his run became a sprinting landmark.

Three weeks later, the Canadian Harry Jerome became the second man to run a legal 10-flat during the national trials in Saskatoon, but despite these two world record shattering performances both Hary and Jerome were still expected to play second fiddle to the Americans Norton and Sime when the Olympics began in Rome. The Italian capital was bathed in summer sunshine for the opening of the seventeenth modern Olympics, a setting that contrasted the beauty of the ancient world with modern facilities, in the city that ironically gave the order to end the original Olympic movement all those years ago.

As usual, the 100 metres competition was among the first to get underway, and 61 competitors from around the world were in the Olympic stadium to contest the first round, with the most notable absentees being the defending champion Morrow, the injured US sprint star Charlie Tidwell and the Italian find Livio Berrutti who wanted to save himself for the 200 metres, which he considered his best event. While Hary and the other favourites cruised easily through round one, the only real big name casualty was fellow German Germar. One man who did impress was the young Cuban Enrique Figuerola, who had set a national record of 10.2 before leaving for the Games. The packed stadium had not seen much of the real Armin Hary, but in the second round he unleashed one of his famous 'Blitz Starts' and sped to a new Olympic record of 10.2, beating his close rival Dave Sime in the process.

The following day, all the favourites had made it through to the last twelve for the two semi-finals, but tragedy befell the Canadian joint world-record holder, Harry Jerome, when he pulled a muscle at 50 metres and crashed to the track. Bitterly disappointed, he threw himself in the in-field turf and wept. At the finish of the race it was Britain's Peter Radford, a Walsall school teacher, who demonstrated his famous blazing finish to pip Figuerola on the line, with Budd just making third place to qualify for the final. In the second semi, Armin led from the gun to the tape, with Sime and Norton trailing in behind, so with the exception of Jerome, all the big guns had qualified. With the Canadian now out and Norton looking as though he had peaked a year too early, the final seemed to be a question of whether Sime could catch Hary, with Radford, Budd and Figuerola as outsiders.

The draw for the final, in blazing sunshine, put the two favourites, Hary and Sime, as far apart as

ARMIN HARY

they could be, with Sime in lane one and Hary on the outside. The field was under starter's orders for fully 20 minutes before the starter got them away. The heat would take its toll on some of the athletes, but Hary was among those who remained relaxed. At the first attempt to start, both he and Sime bolted before the gun fired, but it was declared a faulty start and neither was penalized. Then Figuerola decided to adjust his blocks, so there was further delay, and when the starter tried a second time to get the race underway it was Armin who jumped, and he was warned by the official. One more false start and he would be out of the final. However the warning did not appear to worry the cool German – it had happened to him before on many occasions and it was what his racing was all about.

Finally, at the third attempt, the field got away cleanly and, as predicted, it was Hary who catapulted into an extraordinary early lead, taking a metre out of the field in the first five, a lead that seemed impossible to close. On the inside, after a terrible start, big Dave Sime was accelerating fast and as the tape loomed it looked as if he might get there first, but the German just managed to hang on and as he hit the line the big American lunged desperately forward and crashed in spectacular fashion on to the red track. The two of them were clear of the rest of the field, in which Radford had suffered another poor start, but his amazing finishing speed brought him past the field to pip Figuerola for the bronze, with Budd fifth and the pre-Games favourite Norton a disappointing last. When the judges examined the photograph it was clear that Hary had won the gold by a foot from Sime, although it was felt that the result might have been different had the two men been drawn together instead of in opposite lanes.

Sime, who had beaten Armin earlier in his career, remembers: 'The German had a tremendous start, but I didn't see him at any time during the race. I might have beaten him had I been in the lane next to him because then I would have known when to dip.'

The big American, now a respected eye surgeon in Miami, also remembers Hary as an arrogant champion and said that he did not want anything to do with him. Sime had only just made the US team because his medical studies had not enabled him to train properly, but once he made the Olympic line-up he then spent some time getting back into shape, beating the seemingly invincible Ray Norton in three of their four pre-Olympic meetings, defeats that may have damaged Norton's confidence and been responsible for his poor performances during the Games. As for that famous Hary start, he was never close enough to see exactly what the German was doing, but he says: 'Our initial reaction to the gun was about the same, but after the first step Hary would be two feet ahead. He had a second and third step that were out of this world.'

The bronze medallist Radford was clearly in the best place to understand how the Hary 'Blitz Start' had worked and he has his own views on how the German won his gold medal. Now a respected lecturer at the University of Glasgow and an authority on physical education and sport, he recalls: 'There was a lot of debate about Armin Hary and his start. The German press had been carrying stories about how he had the fastest reaction time ever recorded and there were stories going around about how he'd been in a laboratory and demonstrated that he reacted faster than anyone who ever lived. The stories were put around quite deliberately by his coach, so there was a lot of tension at the Olympics and the Americans were quite hostile to him.'

The final itself gave Radford the opportunity to experience the Hary starting phenomenon at close quarters and he agrees with those who feel that the German could easily have been disqualified for false starting twice, holding him to blame for the first faulty start as well as the 'jump' for which he was officially warned. As for Radford, his concentration was wrecked by the long delay in getting the race underway, a well-meaning group of cheering British fans in the stands who were chanting his name and the realisation of how Hary had been getting off the blocks ahead of

All friends together. However, silver and bronze medallists Dave Sime and Peter Radford say they had little respect for the champion Armin Hary

everyone else. 'When we'd had our first run out of the blocks Hary was in lane six and I was in lane five, we were shoulder to shoulder, and I knew instantly how he'd set his world record and how he had a reputation for being a stride and a half faster than anyone else out of the blocks. I knew how he did it and I then had to make a decision whether to do the same, because it was a technique rather than an ability.'

Radford explains that under the international rules that applied at the time, the athletes moved into the 'set' position on the command 'set'. Once they were all in the 'set' position, the starter then fired the gun and the race was underway. The starter alone decided when all the athletes were motionless in the 'set' position before he fired his pistol. 'In unison all the athletes moved into the "set" position,' says Radford, 'but Hary didn't move. He came into the position later than everyone else. The starter couldn't start the race until everyone was still and Hary knew that, so the starter waited for Hary to get into position before he fired the gun. Hary knew as soon as he was still the gun would fire, so after waiting a moment he moved into the "set" position, paused momentarily and then charged off. Most of the time his move would coincide with the gun.'

Shortly after the Games the rules were changed making it illegal for an athlete to stay down after the 'set' command, but in 1960 Hary had the flying start down to a fine art. 'My opinion of Hary is tainted by the knowledge that he tricked us all in the final,' admits Radford, and he has little feeling for the 1960 champion, something unusual in the sprinting world, so often a close fraternity. 'He wasn't an easy person to like. I think a lot of athletes have to be arrogant in a way, they have to believe in themselves and their own ability. There can't be any half measures or fraternizing with the 'enemy' too much, so you don't expect a warmth with your main rivals as you go around the world, but you do expect a certain sort of respect, almost like fellow professionals in the same trade. You never got that feeling with Hary. He was quite aloof and he had an uncomfortable arrogance about him that wasn't just based on his ability as a sprinter, but his feeling that somehow nobody else counted but himself. That was unusual with sprinters and he was very different in that respect.'

But respected or not, it was Armin Hary who climbed on to the medal rostrum to accept his gold, the first German to win a 100 metre medal since Arthur Jonath's bronze in 1932 and the first German to win an Olympic gold in a track event. Even in victory, standing in the gold medal posi-

tion as his national anthem played and his flag was raised, he was causing a furore. As the cameras beamed pictures around the world, millions could see that to ensure he made some money from his Olympic enterprise he was wearing an Adidas shoe on one foot and a Puma shoe on the other. In the eyes of the sporting world, particularly in Germany, his fame turned to silver on that medal rostrum. On his return, the German press exacted revenge, with stories about his fiancée Christine, and even scandalous suggestions of causing a road accident in which he irreparably damaged his knee – an injury that would ultimately end his sprinting career just two months after the Games. Germany wanted a winner but Armin did not project the desirable clean-cut, gracious image. His old coach Sumser said: 'I found Armin a nice, honest boy, not the bad boy the newspapers liked to paint him. He got a lot of success very quickly and he simply couldn't handle it.'

He had returned home with two gold medals in his pocket, one for the 100 metres and the other alongside Bernd Cullman, Martin Lauer and Walter Mahlendorf in the sprint relay, where they finished second behind the USA quarter of Budd, Norton, Johnson and Sime, but took the gold when the Americans were disqualified after the luckless Norton ran out of the passing zone trying desperately to compensate for the acute disappointment of coming last in both the 100 and 200 metres finals.

The 200 metres, which Armin did not enter, was won by the home crowd's favourite Berruti, dark glasses and all, in a world record equalling 20.5, with the USA's Lester Carney second and Frenchman Abdoulaye Seye in third place. It had been a torrid time for the American sprint team and an Olympics they would want to forget in a hurry. Meanwhile, in the Olympic village Armin had committed the ultimate sin, especially for a German sprinter, bearing in mind what had happened in 1936. He had snubbed Jesse Owens. The great man had asked him for an interview but the new champion had refused point blank. Three days later it seemed clear that efforts had been made to ensure the insult was rescinded, and Armin Hary was part of a large German retinue that descended on the US sector of the village and the traditional 'champions together' photos were taken. 'He is a strange boy sometimes,' admitted Gerhard Stöck, the chief of the German party. 'He can be difficult. When Owens asked to meet him Hary was busy and he said so. I don't think he intended to be so rude.'

But Hary's individualism was taking monstrous proportions and on his return from the Olympics

Armin Hary relaxes on the shores of Lake Tegern near Rottach-Egern after his medal-winning success in the 1960 Rome Olympic Games

he decided to cash in on his new-found international fame and voiced his intentions of becoming a major movie star. It was not to be a smooth passage and in a highly publicized row with a big German film distributor it became clear that he had demanded the lead roles in a western and a detective film for a fee of 100,000 marks each. The film company maintained that for a totally unproven, inexperienced 23-year-old, this was sheer arrogance, and Hary's claim that his name was as valuable as that of the major German film star Curt Jurgens was, they said, plainly ridiculous. The affair earned him another nickname – the 'Callas of the Race Track', after the temperamental opera star Maria Callas, and he eventually rejected an offer from the company of 7,500 marks to appear in one of their films in a character part.

As one row finished, another began. After his car crash in November he fell foul of the German athletic establishment in another highly public row, this time over the alleged fiddling of his expenses and damaging the image of German sport. In January 1961, he was banned from competition for a year after being found guilty on both counts, namely that he had brought the sport into disrepute by painting a poor picture of athletics in a magazine article the previous summer, and had injured team spirit prior to the Olympics.

He admitted that he had claimed travel expenses to and from two sports festival meetings even though he had shared a car with a team member from Frankfurt. The 'trial' at Frankfurt Sports College lasted eight hours and the normally cheerful and bouncy Hary could not hide his disappointment when he heard the result. 'I was so sure of myself and did not expect a single day's ban,' he told one newspaper. 'I had plans for the near future. I had been invited to Tokyo and the USA. The Japanese I could have beaten on one leg, but the American competition was a challenge and I would have loved to run. Now everything is over. What I did and admitted, others would also have done. With me they set an example of German thoroughness, but I shall fight this hard sentence. If I don't succeed I shall stop running. I will not be slapped in the face.'

Hary recalled later. 'I don't think I was the one who started demanding money for racing. There were sums of money floating around and all I did was the same as the others at the time – I took my share'.

Whether it was his threat to retire or mounting public pressure at the severity of the sentence that changed the mind of the athletic establishment is unclear, but a fortnight later the punishment was rescinded by the German Athletics Union, which reprimanded Armin for his actions and substituted a ban which would effectively stop him competing for just the first week of the track season in May. The GAU Committee stated that 'too much attention was paid to Hary from sport and other circles and he obviously lost the right sense of measure. Anyone who was pushed to the forefront in public life would require an enormous amount of maturity. This maturity is not possessed by someone young and still growing, such as this egotistic Olympic winner.'

However, there was no happy return to the track for Hary because the injury to his left knee, sustained in his car crash, had not improved. In fact, doctors warned that the chronic inflamation would not clear up unless he took a year's break from sport. It was discovered that Armin could not stand or run for any length of time without considerable pain, and he decided that rather

Above: March 1966, Armin Hary and 21 year-old heiress Christina Bagusat leave the chapel of the Castle Possenhofen after their wedding

than wait a year in the hope of reviving his career he would bow out now at the top and try and make some money from his success while he was still a big name.

'If I am forced to take such a long break,' he told newsmen, 'I will lose contact. It makes sense for me not to begin. My career as a sprinter is over.' He quit the track and went into business, including selling shirts, telephones, gambling machines, his own brand of sports shoes, insurance and finally property, becoming an estate agent.

In 1966 he married his fiancée Christine, the beautiful daughter of the wealthy Bagusat family, whose fortune was founded on the production of the 'Rex' motorcycles and a brickworks, her family home was the magnificent Bavarian Castle Possenhofen. It seemed to be a fairy tale ending to a troubled story and although Armin and his family did not live in the castle itself, but a smaller house in the grounds, he seemed content as a finance and property broker in what appeared to be an idyllic existence. But in 1980 the world caved in on the former Olympic champion, just as he was setting off on a skiing holiday in the Austrian Tyrol.

He and his friend, Karl-Heinz Bald, a tennis partner, were arrested by the police and charged with defrauding the German Catholic Church of more than a million marks and causing financial damage to the Archdiocese of Munich estimated at several million more. Although the older Bald, another property dealer, was clearly the prime mover in the sad affair, 43-year-old Hary worked as his right-hand man and together they had milked large sums of money from buying and selling property for the church. The original trial lasted several months and at the end he was sentenced to two years in prison. The once proud track star spent a nightmare five months in a tiny cell at the Stadelheim Prison before he was released on bail pending an appeal, at which his punishment was commuted to an 18 months suspended sentence.

The sorry affair, which understandably made banner headlines in the German newspapers, ruined him, both as a businessman and in the eyes of the German public. After the trial, his licence to work as a property agent in West Germany was withdrawn and he made a living selling mobile steam baths. He did not win back his licence until 1986, and today he still practises in Possenhofen, where he lives in the castle grounds with his loyal wife who stuck by him throughout the court drama. Armin, always looking for money-making opportunities, was in many ways a man ahead of his time during his track career, where he maintained a professional attitude to both running and winning at a time when such professionalism was simply frowned upon. Today he would probably enjoy a reputation as a showman and would certainly be wealthy from his track earnings, but in his day such enthusiasm to make money only succeeded in alienating the German press and public, and consequently he did not enjoy the popularity a man of his stature might have expected. However, that was certainly of his own choosing and it is difficult to understand his motives in many of the affairs in which he was involved. It would be easier to understand if he would talk openly about the past, but he is keen to avoid publicity and does not enjoy talking about old times, making it difficult to tell his side of the story. Perhaps one day he will give his version and we might understand a little better.

THE GOLDEN YEARS

1964 Bob Hayes

'The man just exploded, he was absolutely fantastic just like a clenched fist travelling along the track'

1968 Jim Hines

'As soon as I hit the tape I knew it to be the greatest race of my life, good acceleration and strong finish . . . it had to be a world record'

1964 Bob Hayes

From an American point of view, the Rome Olympics were a complete disaster as far as the sprints were concerned. It was one of their worst showings in the history of the Games, an embarrassing failure that they did not want to repeat. A new sprinting hero was needed, someone who could dominate like an Owens or a Morrow, and the United States found one. 'Bullet' Bob Hayes was tailor-made for the role of the avenging American sprinter, a muscular, all-American boy who hauled himself out of the Florida ghettos to beat the world. His sporting talent spanned two of the world's most demanding sports – track and American football – and he dominated both camps. But while his career was a series of breathtaking highs, his life since has been one of tragedy, humiliation and near death. Only now has Bob Hayes got his life back on the right track.

Back in the early 1940s, when Bob was born, track and field did not figure prominently on the list of sporting favourites in the east-side ghettos of Jacksonville. He grew up in a tough neighbourhood, the youngest of three children in a struggling black family, and much of his early life was spent playing truant from school and hustling on the street. His family were poor and things were made worse after World War II when Bob's father returned home in a wheelchair. Their only steady

'Bullet Bob' Hayes, running in the inside lane, powers through the finishing tape to win the 1964 Tokyo Olympics 100 metres title in ten seconds flat, seven feet ahead of Enrique Figuerola (vest 80) while Jerome comes in third

source of income was his disability pension plus anything else the family could make. As the youngest, Bob was able to dodge the strict, almost military family atmosphere. 'I was always the best athlete in my age group and being the youngest in the family I kinda' got everything I wanted,' he remembers. 'I wasn't the best student because I didn't have to hustle to get the best grades.'

From an early age, it was quite clear that Bob was a natural sportsman, but his real love was football, so he hardly gave track a passing thought, and it was not until high school that he began to attract attention as a possible sprint star of the future. 'I was in junior high and the coach had a physical education class,' recalls Bob, 'and he saw me running in the class with the other guys. He noticed that they were in tennis shoes or running barefoot, while I had on my every-day shoes, but I was out-running them, so he convinced me to take up running.'

His first real meeting for the high school saw him entered in no less than seven events – the 100, 220, 440 and 880 yards, the sprint relay, the long jump and high jump, and he won them all. His speed not only earned rave reviews from the school's coaches, but it also proved to be something of a moneyspinner. Bob explains: 'My friends used to organise races for me against the

senior guys in the school and then bet on me. Naturally the older guys always thought they could win, but they never did.'

However, despite his athletic success, he was still convinced that his future lay on the football field and it was his ability as a speedy running back that earned him a scholarship to Florida A&M University, in the state capital of Tallahassee. In his first year at college, he hardly set foot on a track, preferring to use his speed to run rings around opposing defence men in the college football league. But it was not long before the track department persuaded him to audition for the track team and he came under the caring eye of coach Jake Gaither, who not only helped Bob become the world's greatest sprinter and vastly improved his football technique, but also became something of a second father to him.

Bob certainly needed guidance in those early days – he had been on campus only a short time when he fell foul of the law and received 10 years' probation for armed robbery and assault, although in reality the offence was hanging around with a young man who held up another youngster with a toy gun and took his chewing gum and 11 cents. It was a ridiculously harsh sentence for such a petty crime, but Bob promised himself and Coach Gaither that he would not get

into trouble again. He began to pay back Gaither's faith in him on his very first college track meet, in March 1961, when he went out and equalled Jesse Owens' long-standing freshman record for the 100 yards in 9.4. Two months later, he narrowly missed a record in the 220 yards, and people were beginning to take an interest in the new boy from Florida.

His improvement on the track continued and in June of the same year he became the thirteenth man to tie Mel Patton's 100 yards world record of 9.3, although it was never officially ratified because just over a fortnight later Villanova's Frank Budd became the first man to duck under the record with a run of 9.2 at the AAU championships in New York. But Bob was not downhearted – after all, youth was on his side – and he disappeared into a football season with his college team and did not return to competition for more than six months. When he eventually exchanged his football strip for running spikes, things began to happen almost immediately. In his first race at the college, he tied Budd's world record, only for it to be ruled out because the starter had used a non-regulation, small-calibre starting pistol. However, his form earned him a trip to Europe, where he ran a 10.1 for 100 metres and the season also saw his first ever defeat, by the Canadian Harry Jerome, in Modesto, although some people still maintain that the judges awarded the race to the wrong man. Bob started the following year off in similar fashion, putting together a remarkable series of races, including two runs of 20.5 in the 200 metres, and 220 yards, which was then the world record, but again neither were officially ratified.

Bob was now being hailed as the rising star of the sprint world and all the press stories indicated that it would not be long before he took a record of his own. That day finally arrived in June 1963, at the AAU championships, on the fast rubber-asphalt track in St Louis, where he hurtled to victory in the semi-finals in a new 100 yards world record of 9.1, repeating the feat, albeit wind-assisted, in the final. Now he was out on his own as the premier sprinter in the United States, and there were few men elsewhere in the world who could give him a serious race. If confirmation was needed that Hayes would be the man whom everyone would fear at the Olympics in Tokyo, then it was provided in chilling fashion during a series of indoor meets early in the Olympic year itself. He had already given warning of the kind of form he was in when he ran a 9.1 in the 100 yards and a 20.1 in the 220 yards in Miami on New Year's Day, but when he came indoors he equalled the world

record for the 60 yards dash on no less than five occasions, clocking six seconds flat.

One man who remembers the indoor series clearly was the up-and-coming American sprinter Charlie Greene, who would become one of the great stars of the sixties, but was then just starting out as a freshman at the University of Nebraska. 'Bob was simply the best sprinter I ever saw,' he says. 'At that time I was a brash, young college boy. I knew I was good but I had a lot of trouble convincing other people. I was running indoors at Madison Square Garden and I'd won my heat and semi-final and felt pretty good. There were some newspaper people around so I went up to Bob and said, "You're gonna' have to run a new world record to win this race, because I'm gonna' tie this one." Sure enough I tied the record, but Bob ran 5.9 and broke it!'

Charlie's amazing confidence and fast-talking showmanship would make him a hit with the public in the years to come, but for now he had to take a back seat while Bob moved to centre stage. Tokyo was fast approaching and he had endeared himself to the American track fans but not the coaching purists, because his running style, or rather the lack of it, had them holding their heads in disbelief. 'He doesn't so much run a race as beat it to death,' suggested one American sportswriter, an off-the-cuff description that actually summed up the essence of Bob's running. He was a heavily built athlete and very muscular – in fact, he looked more like a boxer than a sprinter and when he ran he seemed to roll from side to side as he pawed his way down the track.

New York Times athletics writer Frank Litsky remembers vividly the first time he saw Hayes in action. 'I looked across the starting line at all these sleek model sprinters and there's this guy with these huge shoulders, he looked like a weight lifter in the wrong race. The gun goes and the others go gliding off and he's rolling all over the place. I figure he must be 20 yards behind in the middle of the race, but then he's in front and he wins going away. I was astounded and after the race I saw his coach and said, "I've never seen Bob before, but it seems to me that he's wasting an awful lot of motion sideways and if he went straight he could go much faster." The coach agreed and I asked him if he had plans to do anything about it. He just looked at me and said, "No, I've got the best sprinter in the world here. He's going to win an Olympic gold medal".'

Hayes was one of the heaviest sprinters around, scaling over 190lbs, and he is the first to admit that he was not the most beautiful runner in the world, with his unorthodox style, broad shoulders

Bob Hayes, with a build more akin to a boxer than a sprinter, powers forward to another indoor victory in New York in early 1964

and pigeon toes, but he points out: 'I might not have had the correct arm pump, the right body lean or the proper stance, but I won my races. I'm built funny, different from other athletes, so what I did got the job done. As I told some of the critics at the time, they don't take pictures at the start, only at the finish.'

There was certainly no intention to change his running as the Olympics loomed and as expected Bob muscled his way to first place in the 100 metres trials in 10.1, with the rest of the field trailing some way behind, but he was beaten in the 200 metres, finishing third behind Paul Drayton and Dick Stebbins, so he dropped out of the event allowing fourth placed Henry Carr, the world record holder, to make the trip. So with his closest rival, Frank Budd, dropping out of track in 1962 to try his luck in football with the Philadelphia Eagles, the American hopes of getting back their prized 100 metres gold rested squarely on Bob's big shoulders. The team set off for the Games in October, flying from California via Alaska to Tokyo, where they arrived completely exhausted in the early hours. However, the Japanese organisers, who had no intention of allowing them to sleep, rolled out the red carpet for the team. 'All we wanted to do was sleep,' Bob remembers, 'but when we got off the plane they had laid out chairs with our names on the back, just like you were a movie star, and everyone wanted interviews. I'll never forget it, here I was, a kid from Jacksonville, and everyone wanted to talk to me.'

The atmosphere and the setting in Tokyo suited Bob perfectly and he immediately felt at home in the village, where the athletes rented bicycles to get around and all the competitors were allowed to mix freely. The Games were a triumph of organisation from start to finish and are now regarded as probably the greatest advertisement for the Olympics in their long history. The Japanese seemed to create a spirit of enjoyment and goodwill that had never been witnessed before or matched since. All the Games that followed Tokyo would be tarnished by political problems and controversy. The cost was massive, estimated at £30 million, but the stadium was always full, even for the most obscure qualifying heats.

A record 94 countries took part and for the first time the Olympics reached an international television audience with the aid of satellite technology, so Bob knew that all American eyes would be on him when he stepped onto the track for the first major final. 'I didn't know if I was going to win or not, because there was Harry Jerome, who I knew, and the Cuban Enrique Figuerola, who I had never met before. But I knew I was in the best condition of my life and I was going to give 100 per cent to win that gold medal back. We had lost that tradition to Germany in 1960 and we wanted it back, we felt it was ours to own, so there was a little pressure on me to win.'

No less than 75 sprinters entered the competition and in round one, on the first day of Olympic competition, Bob battled through appalling wind and rain to ease home in 10.4, while the best time was recorded, perhaps fittingly, by Japan's Hideo Iijima, in 10.3. In the afternoon, when the wind and rain cleared, Bob romped through the quarter-finals in 10.3 and was through to the semis, which were held the following day. Here the draw favoured Bob by keeping him clear of his two main rivals, Jerome and Figuerola, and while the weather had been improving slowly, the track was still a little wet. Bob set the packed stadium alight by running 9.9, although the wind gauge reading indicated there was a strong wind blowing in his favour so it would never be a record.

The final itself was held just an hour and a half later, and after the semi Bob felt confident of success, despite a practical joke that almost cost him the race. During his stay in the village he had been going around with long-jumper Ralph Boston and boxer Joe Frazier, and on the eve of the final they had been playing around in their room when, unbeknown to Hayes, one of his running spikes had been kicked under the bed. 'I was so nervous I had everything packed hours ahead of time,' he said, 'so you can imagine how I felt when I got to the stadium and found I only had one shoe. Fortunately I only wear size eights, small for a guy of my build and I managed to find another athlete with the same size shoes and he let me borrow them for the final.'

Bob had been assigned the inside lane for the biggest race of his life, where the cinders had been chewed up so badly by the recent finish of the 20 kilometre walk that the officials had to rake it. The Americans tried to protest, after all their man had run the best time in the heats and deserved a better lane, but their appeals fell on deaf ears. Bob and Mel Pender were the only Americans in the field, with injured third man Trenton Jackson failing to make it, but the real competition for Hayes would come from Jerome and Figuerola, while the other finalists, Poland's Maniak, the German Schumann, Tom Robinson of the Bahamas and the Ivory Coast's Gaousso Kone, were really unknown quantities.

From the gun, Bob was quickly into his running and from about the 20 metres mark he unleashed a sustained burst of power that carried him hurtling down the inside lane and crashing through the tape an incredible seven feet in front of the next man, Figuerola, with Jerome third. His 10 seconds flat, which equalled Armin Hary's world record and established a new Olympic record, was amazing when the track surface is taken into account, and remains one of the greatest sprints in track history. Jesse Owens, watching from the

Bob Hayes (vest 702) wins the 100 metres final in Tokyo and destroys a world-class sprinting field in the process

stands, said: 'When he comes out of the starting blocks he looks like a guy catching a ball behind the line of scrimmage and dodging people.' Owens described the victory as the greatest since 1928! He estimated Hayes' margin of superiority as three metres. Bob remembers the race vividly and one thought was flying through his mind as he took off out of his blocks. 'I was thinking, "Well, I got a bad lane, I've just got to run faster and harder, I've got to be more determined." As I hit about 40 yards, my acceleration started coming on and I stayed calm and relaxed, made sure I didn't run out of lane and there was the tape. It was an unexplainable feeling.'

Hayes had become one of the heroes of the Games and the Japanese fans loved him, especially when he wore his distinctive cowboy hat around the stadium, nor did he disappoint them at the medal ceremony, standing at the top of the rostrum looking as if he had stepped out of a John Wayne movie. As he walked back across the track studying his medal, he looked up into the stands and spotted his mother, who had been able to come and watch the Games thanks to the generosity of the Mayor at Jacksonville, and he went straight up and gave it to her. Understandably, the moment was one of Bob's greatest, but another one was just around the corner in the sprint relay, a run that some experts maintain was the fastest ever run by a human being. But first he had a little score to settle with a certain boxer over that missing shoe. 'I got a bit cocky then,' says Bob, 'and I went back to the village, found Joe and told him, "I know you're a world class boxer but if you ever kick one of my shoes again I'm going to knock you out." Then I smiled real quick and said, "Hi, Mr Frazier, how are you? I love you".'

BOB HAYES

A close-up view of the finish of Hayes' Olympic victory: he crashes through the tape and the rest of the field fight for the minor places

Later that night he and his mother celebrated the gold medal with a special dinner for two in Tokyo – it was a day that neither of them would ever forget. A few days later it was time to get back on the track as part of the American relay team, but there was concern about the lack of proper preparation and poor baton changing, and fears were growing that the USA could see a repeat performance of their 1960 disaster. Just before the race the French anchorman, Jocelyn Delecour, went up to Paul Drayton, the American lead-off man, and dismissed the US team, saying, 'You can't win, all you have is Bob Hayes'. His prediction looked like coming true when poor changeovers between Drayton, Gerald Ashworth and Dick Stebbins put Bob in a terrible position in fifth place and about three yards behind the leaders. What followed was astonishing. Bob's pick-up was electric and he roared after the field, catching and then passing them in just 30 yards, as if they were all standing still, and running on to hit the tape a clear three yards ahead in a new world record of 39.0. Various times were given for his anchor leg, but the slowest was an amazing 8.9, though the fastest clocked him in 8.5. It is enough to say that his performance has never really been equalled, and the run also went down in history – just as his 100 metres final did – as one of the landmarks in sprinting. Hayes also felt that it was the fastest he had ever run and fittingly it was to be his last race.

The British journalist Neil Allen, reporting for *The Times*, still remembers the gasps of amazement in the stand as Hayes got the baton. 'I'd never seen any sprinting that impressed me as much as Bob Hayes' final leg. The man just exploded, he was absolutely fantastic, just like a clenched fist travelling along the track and as he crossed the line up went the baton into the air and his team-mates were rejoicing. Until Johnson broke the world record last year it was the greatest explosion of speed I'd ever seen.'

Paul Drayton enjoyed meeting the Frenchman Delecour after the race, in which the French took the bronze medal, and the American just smiled as he saw him and said: 'All anyone ever needs, pal!' Dick Stebbins, who handed off to Hayes, recalled: 'On my last steps I was really moving and Hayes was only in his twelfth or thirteenth stride, but I could feel the force of him about to explode and in one more step he'd have been out of my reach. In 10 yards he was going faster than I was at 110 and I think he ran the last leg in 8.5. It was unbelievable to make up all that ground and win going away. Just to have won in the circumstances would have been superb, but to annihilate them was out of the question.'

So Bob returned home with two gold medals to a hero's welcome, and American President Lyndon Johnson invited all the golden athletes to a special dinner in Washington, where Bob, at just 21, and the quadruple gold medal winning swimmer Don Schollander, who was only 18, were the stars of the show. With the Olympics over, Bob returned to college and the football season, but his track career was finished. He had decided to give up running and was drafted by both the Dallas Cowboys and the Denver Broncos, at a time when there were two different football leagues, and opted to play for Dallas in the National Football League in 1965.

It is likely that had he continued to run he would have broken more records, especially with more specialized training and synthetic tracks, because at just 21 he had many more years' running in front of him. Lindy Remigino, the 1952 sprint champion and a lifelong coach, thinks that Hayes was simply the greatest. 'If he'd have run on the plastic tracks he'd have just taken off. I really feel he would have been running then the sort of times Ben Johnson is running now.'

Bob only lost two 100 races, the first being the doubtful verdict against Harry Jerome and the second at the NAIA meeting in 1962, when he was beaten by Roger Sayers after missing training for three weeks with a virus infection. No other sprinter can claim a record anything like his. 'A lot of folks asked me to stay in track because they felt I hadn't reached my potential, but there was no money in the sport and I didn't know all these all-weather tracks, better equipment and training methods were coming, so I decided to join Dallas and play football. I suppose I could have brought my 100 time down a couple of tenths.'

Even though Bob had been an outstanding college football player, there were many people in the sport who poured scorn on the idea of transforming track stars into ball players, simply because history had told them it had never worked. Glenn Davis, the 1956 and 1960 Olympic champion in the 400 metres hurdles, had one disappointing season with Detroit; sprinter Ray Norton fared a year better with the San Francisco 49ers; and Frank Budd was disappointing, too. Worse still was the tragedy of Stone Johnson, who finished fifth in the Rome 200 metres and joined Kansas City, where he died after breaking his neck during a pre-season game in 1963. But, undeterred, Bob joined the Cowboys, while the 200 metres champion from Tokyo, Henry Carr, teamed up with the New York Giants. Dallas signed Bob to a three year contract worth around $100,000, but there were some anxious faces during his first practice games as a wide receiver when he kept dropping the ball. These problems were soon ironed out and he introduced himself to the Dallas fans by pulling in a wobbly pass from quarterback Don Meredith and sprinting 45 yards for his first touchdown.

Long serving head coach Tom Landry recalls: 'It wasn't too difficult for Bobby to make the transition because he had played college football. He wasn't just a sprinter, he was a football player who could sprint.' The President and General Manager Tex Schramm, who signed Bob, remembered: 'He had such speed and such unusual skill that instead of him learning the game, it was more a case of the game having to learn him, because he revolutionized our game in the early years.'

Schramm was right, because no-one in the NFL had ever had to cope with world-class speed allied to a football brain, and Bob was creating havoc in some of the best defences in the league. Finally the coaches around the country decided to abandon the tried and trusted man-to-man marking system and introduced a zonal defence scheme, which is still used today, and all because they could not cope with Bob Hayes. Bob played for nine years at Dallas, an unusually long career in a game with an enormous casualty rate, and he was one of the greats, his high point coming in 1971 when the Cowboys beat their arch rivals, the Miami Dolphins, in the Superbowl. From his very first season, when he married his college sweetheart Altemese and adopted baby girl Adrienne, the Cowboys fans took him to their hearts.

The legendary Cowboys quarterback Roger Staubach, who joined Dallas midway through Hayes' career and remained a close friend, rates Bob as one of the all-time great football players and the fastest wide receiver he has ever seen. 'He made me look a hero,' he said. 'We played in a lot of key games, including the Superbowl, and not only did he have incredible speed, but he was also a great football player. It's very rare to have both attributes.'

Landry adds: 'I regard him greatly. A coach can't say anything but good things about a player as great as Bobby Hayes. He came to us when we became a championship team and in 1966 we won a division for the first time and went into the world championship game that year. It was mainly because of Bobby.'

The record books show that Bob still holds a fistful of records at the club, including a career record 76 touchdowns and the best record in punt returns. In 1966, he chalked up 1,232 receiving yards, which is still a record, and during one game he managed 236 yards and that will also take some beating. 'I knew I was faster than anyone in the league,' says Bob, 'and they had to prevent me from getting behind them. But I was in good condition and I could run around the big, aggressive linemen instead of getting hit head-on and I think that's the reason I stayed in the game so long.'

The Cowboys were one of the most successful sides during Bob's career, and from 1966 through the seventies they won more games than any other team. There were plenty of good moments, such as Bob's record 95 yards touchdown in 1966, but there were also some unhappy ones, especially the infamous 'Ice Bowl' game in Green Bay, when the Packers beat the Cowboys for the NFL championship, with the temperature at 13 degrees below zero. 'I never could get a drink of water on the sidelines,' said Bob. 'Every time I'd squirt the stuff near my mouth it would freeze before it got there.' At the peak of his career, it was estimated that Bob was earning around $75,000 a year, but he certainly was not among the highest paid players in the league, and when persistent injuries and complacency dogged him in 1974, he was traded to the 49ers. However, things did not improve there, and after just six months with the San Francisco club he quit the game. This sudden departure from the sport marked the beginning of Bob's decline. He had made few plans for financial security and had entered too many business deals that failed. The worst period of his life was about to start.

'It was a kind of empty feeling,' he remembers. 'We all say we can adjust, but it's very difficult. All of a sudden you're down and no-one recognises you. Anyone who says they don't miss

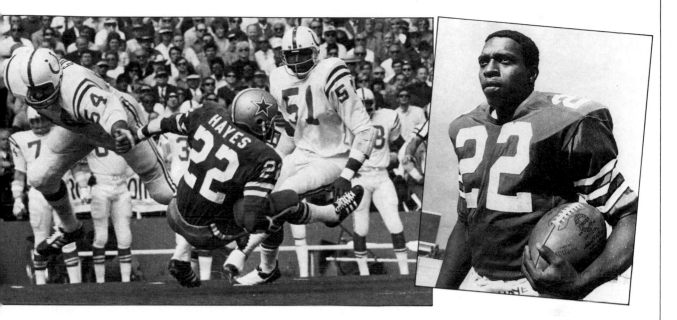

*Left: Superbowl 1971. The Dallas Cowboys beat
the Miami Dolphins with the help of Bob Hayes
Above: Bob revolutionized American football with
his incredible speed and won many club records*

that is lying. I certainly did and everyone I've
spoken to did as well.' The problem was that Bob
achieved his greatest sporting highs at a very
young age, so the downward journey was a tough
one. Many people tried to use him as a front, and
in those days he found it difficult to differentiate
between the good ones and the others. Bob later
admitted that he was just an immature boy in a
grown-up body who tried to please everyone and
that landed him in trouble.

Roger Staubach explained: 'Bob could have
gone on playing longer, though he had a good
career, but he certainly wasn't as dedicated as he
could have been. Athletes in his position are put
on a pedestal. You are earning good money, but
many don't have the vision to look ahead to when
they stop playing. They are more interested in
having a good time and living for today rather
than tomorrow. So when they do stop playing
they are just not prepared.'

However it was not only the money problems
that hurt him, because he still had money in the
bank and even when his football career finished
he earned a little on the professional running
circuit for a while. He became an alcoholic and
got involved in the drug scene, both of which
combined to pull the Cowboys' famous No. 22 all
the way down. Bob stresses his problems with
alcohol were rooted in his family, because his
grandfather and father were both alcoholics and
died from the disease. 'I suffered just like they did
because when I drank I just wanted more. I wasn't
a social drinker, I was greedy and after a while
my tolerance for alcohol increased and it started
to destroy me.' At the same time, he got involved

in drugs, mostly cocaine, and fell prey to the NFL
hangers on who could brag to their friends that
they knew the big names and sold their mer-
chandise to the starry eyed. It might have been
that playing football for so long could have made
Bob susceptible to the drug scene, because drugs
were, and still are, widely used in the NFL to
ensure that players are back in action as soon as
possible after injury. 'During that time your body
gets accustomed to it,' says Bob, 'and all of a
sudden it's cut off, but you still want it. While
you're playing it's legal, but when you're not it's
illegal, so you get caught.'

The *Washington Post* sportswriter Ken Denl-
inger felt that Bob's problems stemmed directly
from his sudden departure from the NFL, because
he was using the drugs and alcohol as a substitute
high for the thrills of sport, but it is more complex
than that. 'We have a wonderful flair for shooting
our youth with large doses of fantasy, for getting
them passionate about sports,' he wrote, 'but
shockingly few bother to consider the trip back
down, or that some sort of sporting phaseout, or
at least an academic cushion, is necessary for
someone whose career ends before middle age.'
Bob's former Cowboys team-mate Pat Toomay
told the Dallas newspapers that it was 'like telling a carpenter at age 32 that he couldn't hammer
a nail again – ever'.

Bob, however, is convinced that while the

drugs may have been partly a by-product of the NFL, it was his alcoholism that drew him further into the web, and that was caused by his childhood. 'It doesn't affect just big sports stars, it's an across the board illness,' says Bob. 'It's not black or white, it has no religious boundaries, it's not people that have money and it's not just a problem – it's a disease. If there's someone who's an alcoholic or a drug addict in your family then it can carry on to you. It started when I was young because my Dad was an alcoholic, he gave me whisky when I was 12 and I had been drinking ever since.' Looking back, he remembers those days as the worst of his life, physically and emotionally. In 1974 he was divorced from his wife Altemese and shortly afterwards married Janice and had a son Bob Junior.

Finally events caught up with him and in 1978, while he was working for a computer firm in Dallas, he acted as a middle man for a drug deal and one of the would-be purchasers turned out to be an undercover narcotics agent. There were questions about entrapment and whether the authorities had pursued Hayes because he was a big name, but it did not really matter, because for Bob everything was now out in the open. He had to sink right to the bottom before he could start to climb back up again. Within a year he was in court to face the charges, and as he sat quietly in the dock his world crumbled dramatically around him. He pleaded guilty to the drug trafficking charges before State Judge Richard Mays, and his defence counsel tried desperately to keep him out of prison – an array of character witnesses were paraded before the judge in an attempt to get probation.

Among them were Tex Schramm, Tom Landry and Roger Staubach, while Bob told pressmen: 'I could see my wife out there with tears in her eyes. I could see Jake Gaither with tears in his eyes. On every row I could see someone I could say I was personally close to. It was a rock bottom feeling, the emptiest I ever felt in my life.' He took the stand admitting: 'I'm not the smartest guy in the world. If I was, I wouldn't be up here. I'm guilty, I was wrong, but I've paid the price in my image and my respect. People see me as Bob Hayes dope dealer, not Bob Hayes the citizen, and that hurts.'

Judge Mays listened carefully as he was told how Bob had a tendency to say 'yes' to the wrong sort of people and how he had lost untold commercial opportunities as a result of the offence. Staubach stated that Bob was a good person who had fallen in with the wrong crowd, while a psychiatrist explained that Bob had found it difficult to sustain himself as a person of value since quitting

football and would not gain anything from prison. But the prosecution lawyers argued just as persuasively that a special case should not be made for Hayes – after all, a similar incident had recently ended with a disgraced track star going to jail for 15 years on similar charges. Apart from that, they said, there was concern about the influence Hayes had on young people. The judge decided, after listening to both sides, that Bob would go to prison for five years for selling cocaine and receive a seven-year probation on another charge of selling methaqualone.

He was taken to the Texas State Penitentiary in Hartsville, to start his sentence a completely broken man. 'You're standing on the rostrum winning a gold medal and all of a sudden you're in jail,' said Bob. 'It's like going from the penthouse to the outhouse. It's very difficult to explain, but it's the lowest and worst I have ever felt.' He certainly did not receive any star treatment inside, but he kept his head down, refused all but

On the way down: Bob Hayes is freed on bond from Dallas County jail after his arrest for drug trafficking. He later served a ten-month sentence

one interview, which was for the Cowboys newspaper, and did everything he was told. 'I didn't learn anything,' he says. 'There was no rehabilitation. You were just locked up and developed anger and resentment. All I did was play some basketball and softball and lift some weights.' But his good behaviour earned him a parole and in February 1980 he was back home in Dallas after serving just ten months of his sentence.

However, he soon returned to his old way of life, drink and drugs, as he tried to rehabilitate himself into society and build a better future. Fortunately, Bob is the sort of person who attracts a lot of friends as well as hangers-on and it was his real friends who came to his rescue when he needed them most. 'I tried living my way, but it didn't work,' said Bob, 'so I decided to try it another way and that meant going to a rehabilitation centre. It was there I found out who Bob Hayes really is. Not the track star, not the football star, but the real person. Today I'm fortunate because now I do know who he is.'

The people responsible for pushing him into the centre were old friends like Staubach, Drew Pearson, Ron Horowitz and Jethro Pugh and they paid for him to stay there for six months. 'It was there that I got my life back in order,' says Bob, 'and there that I found a greater power in my life that I choose to call God. I had been taking drugs for about three years – they were stimulating, they improved my reflexes, but they also made me miserable. Cocaine is very powerful, it's very fatal. It takes away your ability to think, it takes away your ability to love, it takes away your ability to remember, it takes away all of your goals and I know that if I ever did it again I would end up in a mental institution or I would die. So I made a willing decision to hand my life over to the care of God and He's still in my life.'

The centre made Bob acutely aware of his problems and how to cope with them, and he believes that he is now a much more balanced person for the experience, a bit older and a lot wiser. He owes his real friends a huge debt and says of Roger Staubach: 'He's the kindest man who has ever been in my life. He did more than just help, because if I had continued to drink and take drugs I would probably have died. He was probably the most important guy in my life; without him I wouldn't be here today.' But Bob is also a realist and the centre taught him that there is no cure for his problem. 'I just take one day at a time and I can't promise that I won't do it again, but I'm not doing it today.'

Tex Schramm says: 'He did some things that were wrong, but he's paid the debt and now he's doing a very fine job and we're all extremely proud of him.' Bob worked in the real estate business for Roger Staubach's company, shortly after coming out of rehabilitation, but today he spends his time working for Athletic Associates, a company that looks after professional athletes in all sports, handling their finances, their marketing and their problems. There is no man in the world better qualified to counsel on all these things than Bob Hayes. He still keeps a keen interest in track and football and makes regular trips to the big meetings and to the Cowboys, where he is instantly recognised as 'Speedo', the nickname he had throughout his career, and fans besiege him for autographs. It seems that Dallas fans have forgiven him for what happened, but the club have yet to install his name on their famous 'Ring of Honour', which runs around the giant Texas Stadium celebrating their greatest stars (although Mr Schramm says it may well be in the pipeline). It would be fitting for a man who gave such glorious service to the club for nine years, especially now that he is suffering the consequences of his long career. He walks very slowly, pronounces himself a middle-aged cripple and on some mornings he cannot even move around. His knees are damaged beyond repair and his shoulder needs another operation, all legacies of his football career.

On the plus side, he has his family back, although his second marriage also ended in divorce, caused by his drink and drug problems. Son Bob Junior is an important part of his life, although he seems more interested in soccer than American football, and daughter Adrienne is doing well in college. Bob spends a lot of time helping out on charity events and drug abuse programmes, including a major 'Say No To Drugs' campaign last year run by the Florida National Bank, and he tells every youngster who will listen that there is no short-cut to success. He is enjoying life again, and it is amazing to think that in spite of everything he has been through, he has still managed to stay the fun-loving and ebullient character he is today. He is great company with a powerful personality, and he is glad to be back and respected for what he is now and not necessarily what he was in the past.

He may have excelled as an Olympic athlete on the track, he may have been a spectacular wide receiver for the Dallas Cowboys on the football field, but Bob Hayes' greatest achievement has been to pull himself out of the gutter and fight to regain his self-respect. There are no gold medals nor Superbowl rings for achieving this, but it is simply his most impressive success.

1968 Jim Hines

When Bob retired from the track after Tokyo it opened the door to a new wave of sprinters who were all keen to establish themselves as America's number one. The mantle fell on Charlie Greene, who was still kicking himself for messing up the 1964 trials and coming in sixth when he had been the only man to push Hayes all season. 'Sometimes when I'm by myself at night I still think about it,' says Charlie, now a Major in the US Army, 'and I really believe I'm two medals short, because I feel I could have got second or third to Bob in Tokyo and a place on the relay team.'

Missing the trip galvanized Charlie into action and he dedicated himself to ensuring that he did not miss out when the Games opened in Mexico the next time around, quickly establishing himself as the world's top performer for the next two years. Charlie even created an image for himself on the track – a fast-talking, super-cool unsmiling facade aimed at frightening his rivals and entertaining the fans.

'I was so disappointed after the trials in '64

A big smile breaks across Jimmy Hines' face (vest 279) as he prepares to break the tape and win the 1968 Olympic 100 metres title in Mexico City. Jamaica's Lennox Miller (vest 536) is second while Charlie Greene (vest 275) comes in third

because I knew I had to wait four years, so I devised a kind of poison for myself, so that everytime I raced I made it a deadly serious business. I developed this really tough exterior and I ran for one purpose only and that was to be the best sprinter in the world.'

Charlie's most famous prop was his dark sunglasses, and he delighted in telling reporters who questioned him about them,'Hey, these aren't sunglasses, they're re-entry shades!' He picked up the idea from Henry Carr, and the reasoning behind them was that nobody could see him, which, when coupled with the rest of his image, presented a larger than life figure on the track, especially for the other competitors.

It was not until midway through the 1967 season that his dominance was seriously challenged by a new hope, a 20-year-old from Oakland, California, called Jimmy Hines. They had met during the previous season when Greene had shown the younger man the way home on each occasion, but in 1967 Charlie began to recognise

that Hines was a genuine threat to his supremacy, and when he won the Drake Relays, in April 1967, beating both John Carlos and Hines, Charlie realised that he had to be very careful indeed. The next time they met was about a month later at the Modesto Relays, and Charlie went into the 100 metre race knowing that he was unbeaten at the distance since September 1964, so when Jimmy not only beat him, but also equalled the world record in 10 seconds flat, it was a shocking experience for Charlie, but one to which he would grow accustomed. Jim Hines had arrived and he was not going to go away.

Jimmy was actually born in Dumas, Arkansas, in 1946, but his parents moved with him and his nine brothers and sisters, to California when he was only a five-year-old. It was only at junior high that he discovered his ability to run fast, when a track coach spotted him darting around in a baseball match and asked him to try out for his team. He remembers running the 100 yards in 10.6 at the start of the ninth grade, and by the end of the

same year he had reduced the time to 10.2, so when he started at McClymonds High School he already had something of a pedigree as a sprinter.

In his second year at high school he cut his 100 yards time to a very respectable 9.6 and then managed to drop it by a tenth of a second in the next two years until he matched Jesse Owens' high school record of 9.4. His talent ignited the usual mass interest from big colleges, but he chose Texas Southern in Houston, not because it was a black college, but because it had the best track and field team in the country and a top coach in Stan Wright at the helm. As an 18-year-old freshman, he won his first international vest in early 1965 on a team touring Europe, but back home he was still finding Charlie Greene a difficult hurdle to overcome. It was not until early in 1967 that he started to set the sprinting world alight, when indoors he reeled off three world-record-equalling 5.9s for 60 yards, made some impressive runs for Texas Southern and in May tied Bob Hayes' world 100 yards record in 9.1. The next big race was the confrontation at Modesto between Jimmy and Charlie, where for the first time Hines managed to beat his old adversary and match the world 100 metres record.

The victory started a riveting rivalry between the two men, which had not been seen in the sprinting world since the days of Owens and Metcalfe, and created an immense amount of interest in the sport wherever they ran, just as Carl Lewis and Ben Johnson's battles have increased the appeal of the sprints today. Even now Charlie and Jimmy argue about who won more races and who was the better man, although it is more good humoured than it used to be on the track in the sixties. 'When I lost that race in Modesto to Jimmy it was shocking for me,' says Charlie, 'and it wasn't just because I lost or that I made a mistake, it was because on that day he was better than I was. But I found that hard to understand after being unbeaten for so long. How could he be better than me?'

Charlie's confusion was further complicated when less than a month later Jimmy beat him again in the AAU championships with the aid of a dubious start, with the evening temperature still in the nineties. Both men ran 9.4 for the 100 yards into a five-mile-an-hour wind and appeared to hit the tape together, but the judges gave the verdict to Hines. It was at about this time that Jimmy got some extra coaching from the 1956 sprint champion, Bobby Morrow, who was working in Houston. He helped Jimmy to improve his starting, which had been causing him problems and even disqualification from races. The coaching obviously helped

as the run-up to the Games in Mexico City got underway, and may have proved a decisive factor in the races that led him to the Olympic title.

Jimmy and Charlie were still running neck and neck, prompting one *Sports Illustrated* journalist to describe them as 'the fastest four-legged sprinter ever sent to the Olympics'. Charlie had tied Hayes' 9.1 for 100 yards in the summer of 1967 and, despite losing a couple of races to Hines, he went into Olympic year still confident of becoming the Olympic champion, but nevertheless aware that Jimmy was the man he would have to beat.

As the 1968 season began, it was Charlie who still held the upper hand, with wins in the Drake Relays, Modesto and San Diego, but the biggest sprinting occasion would be the AAU championships in the heat of Sacramento, California, in June. The AAUs of 1968 are recorded quite correctly as the greatest evening of sprinting in track history, with a wholesale assault on the world record that had never been seen before and probably never will be again. The stars of the show? – who else but Jimmy Hines and Charlie Greene. But they were ably supported by one of the finest line-ups of sprinting talent in the world, most of whom would return to do battle in the Olympics in October. The scene was set for a memorable evening in the heats, when Jimmy ran 9.8 in the 100 metres, which would have smashed the existing 10.0 seconds flat world record to pieces had it not been for a tail-wind of about six miles an hour, but it sent a rush of excitement through the crowd. In the next heat it was Charlie's turn to get the fans on their feet, running a legal 10.0 seconds flat to equal the world record, but slowing down from about 15 metres out.

A couple of hours later, in the first semi-final , Jim Hines made history by becoming the first man to claim a legal run under 10 seconds, with a 9.9, beating, by a metre, Ronnie Ray Smith, who was given the same time. Not to be outgunned in his semi-final, Charlie Greene then went out and ran exactly the same time, becoming the next man to run a legal 9.9 and setting the scene for an epic confrontation in the final to decide who was America's number one. On this occasion it was Greene, nipping Jimmy at the tape, but despite a strong tailwind the time was 10 seconds flat for both men, with Lennox Miller third, Smith fourth, the Frenchman Roger Bambuck fifth and Mel Pender sixth. It was one of the classiest sprint fields ever assembled and probably the greatest outside an Olympic Games. Five of the athletes there that night would be among the eight finalists in the 100 metres in Mexico.

'I felt confident after that race that I had a hold on Jimmy,' says Greene, 'because I'd beaten him the first five times we'd raced in '68, but I knew if I made the tiniest error, he'd beat me.'

Jimmy remembers: 'In the final, Charlie jumped out on me, but I made a close race of it. But I had run an official 9.9 and become the first man in history to break the 10-second barrier, so for me that night was the greatest series of sprinting of all time.'

The next hurdle to overcome was the start of the US trials for the Games, and it was then that Jimmy began to ease into top gear and beat Charlie in the semi-trials and then again in the finals. So just before the Games, their 'score' in terms of finals won and lost was Charlie Greene seven, Jimmy Hines four. They still argue about the other races and who won more, with Jimmy saying: 'We were battling for three years and I still say the record stands about 80/20 in my favour, but I know Charlie will say differently.' Not surprisingly, Charlie does: 'Jimmy was a great sprinter, not a mathematician, so if he read the record books he would see. But it's not important, because it's all there in black and white; in our head-to-head matches I won by far the greatest number of races.'

The greatest night of sprinting in track history! In the 1968 AAU Championships in Sacramento the ten seconds barrier is broken three times

The US trials meant the 1-2-3 line-up for the 100 metres team was Jimmy, Charlie and Mel Pender, who had just returned from Vietnam to run and would return there after the Games. The fourth spot, for the relay, went to Ronnie Ray Smith, and so the Americans had by far the strongest sprint team. Jimmy says that he would have liked to run in the 200 metres, despite the presence of Tommie Smith, John Carlos and Larry Questad, because he could have run a world record, but it was impossible to double-up when the events were run back to back in the trials. Hines and Greene may not have been the closest of friends, but when they found themselves together in the American team, the Olympic cause became something of a common bond between them. As Charlie says: 'Overnight we were transformed from a group of competitors into a close-knit outfit. Stan Wright told us it was absolutely vital that one of us win the 100 metres to be the world's fastest human – a title that traditionally the American sprinter holds. So for the good of the country individual ambitions and ideas were suppressed, so we developed a common appreciation for our talent. Going to Mexico we had one objective – that one of us should win.'

The political temperature in Mexico was red-hot, for a lot of different reasons, and for weeks before the opening ceremony was scheduled, it looked as though the Games might not take place at all because of student demonstrations at the university opposite the Olympic stadium. The students were objecting to the huge amount of money that the Government had spent on staging the Games, a luxury that contrasted sharply with the abject poverty experienced by the majority of the people in the country. They threatened to disrupt the Games and as the opening day drew nearer so the demonstrations grew bigger. The Government reacted by sending in the army, and tanks were a common sight outside the university, but few people expected the kind of solution to the problem that the Mexican military finally adopted. On 2 October, in the Square of Three Cultures, in the middle of Mexico City, the army surrounded the demonstrating students and opened fire on them, killing 260 and injuring 1200 more, an atrocity that assured there would be no more trouble throughout the Games.

When the Games finally opened, there was a lot of discussion about the effects of the heat and the altitude, with the city 7,000 feet above sea-level and the thin air making life easy for some events and much more difficult for others. Tests showed that the altitude meant 27 per cent less atmospheric pressure and 23 per cent less air density, both of which made life easier for the explosive events, particularly the sprints.

These would be the Games where millions of people around the world saw the Fosbury flop for the first time, but they will be remembered most for the prodigious long jump of Bob Beamon, who almost jumped out of the pit with his 29ft 2½in (8.90m), and the other surviving world track and field record from the Games, Lee Evans' 43.8 400 metres. But they could have been the Games that had to go ahead without the talents of Jimmy Hines, who had been seriously considering giving up track before Mexico because of his precarious financial position. He was married and had a one-year-old son, but sprinting was not paying the bills, so when the Miami Dolphins football team stepped in and offered Jim a lucrative contract to sign and become the new Bob Hayes, he saw an immediate solution to his money problems. 'I almost signed that contract, I really did,' says Jimmy. 'But after talking it over with my wife and my parents I finally decided to go for the goal I had set myself in college. I wanted to be like Bob Hayes, who was my idol, so I decided to do it his way.'

Arriving in Mexico City, Jimmy could not believe the scenes that greeted him: 'There were soldiers everywhere, down all the streets, all around the Olympic village. We had to be guarded when our bus took us to the stadium and my mind wasn't actually on training for the race, but more on would I be safe? Was I going to make it to the stadium to be able to compete?'

The 100 metres competition, the first to be held on a synthetic track, was a tough one, with 64 sprinters lining up for a first round that saw all the favourites come through unscathed, with Charlie Greene looking particularly good in a slightly windy 10-flat and repeating the feat in the quarter-finals held about six hours later. Meanwhile, Jimmy was unhappy because his races had been against the world's top men and he was having to run hard just to qualify, especially in the quarters when Jamaican Lennox Miller pipped him on the line. It was a very strong competition, so much so that in the very next heat East Germany's Heinz Erbstösser had the distinction of being the first man ever to run a 10.2 and not even make the semi-finals.

After the first day of racing in the 100 metres, fate was still pointing her finger in Greene's direction and Jimmy knew that he had to come up with something special for the semi and the final on the following day. He decided that the best thing he could do was to go and see his wife Joyce, who was staying some miles from the village on the other side of the city, so he went to the coaches and told them where he was going. 'They looked at me like I was crazy,' said Jimmy. 'The coach said, "You wanna do what, you wanna stay with your wife the night before the biggest race of your life." They thought I was joking, so I went back to my room, packed my things and left. Meanwhile, the coaches had been on the phone to my wife and told her to stay away from me. So when I got to the hotel, with a couple of bottles of champagne, she would not let me in. Finally I persuaded her to open the door but she's acting like she doesn't know me, because I'm drinking the champagne and she won't have any. After a while I said, "It's time to go to bed," but she's still not sure, so I said, "We're married, aren't we, let's go." So I had sex with my wife and the next day I got up and went down to the stadium and the rest is history.'

The night's entertainment had relaxed him so much that he felt almost unbeatable when he stood on the track for the semi, running an easy 10-flat to beat Bambuck, Jerome and Pender. In

Above: Jimmy Hines reaches the tape ahead of dipping Lennox Miller and Charlie Greene
Left: Jimmy can hardly believe it – a gold medal and a world record
Right: Jimmy waves to the cheering crowd

the other semi it was Greene who now looked a little ragged, even though he managed to win in 10.1, holding off Miller, Cuba's Pablo Montes and the little man from Madagascar, Jean-Louis Ravelomanatsoa. As the final would prove, the first all black field in Olympic history, Charlie Greene had been 'up' on the first day of competition, but he was just under 100 per cent on day two, just enough to make him beatable as far as Hines was concerned.

After a false start by Ravelomanatsoa, the gun sounded and the 60,000 crowd burst into life as the veteran Pender, the captain of the US track and field team, burst out of his blocks and into an early lead, holding on until the 30 metres mark. Then Hines drew level and in a few strides had passed him smoothly, with Charlie Greene on the inside lane struggling to go with him. But Hines was not going to be caught and kept on accelerating to run through the tape unopposed in a new world record of 9.95, with Miller edging out the lunging Charlie Greene for the silver.

'I just hoped and prayed I could come out near Mel,' said Jimmy, 'because he was the fastest starter. I think I got the best start of my life and there was Mel out in front and Charlie and I were together. But I felt good because I knew I had another gear and when I switched it on I just went away. As soon as I hit the tape I knew it had to be the greatest race of my life, with a good start, good acceleration and a strong finish, so I felt it had to be a world-record time.'

Both Miller and Greene recorded 10 seconds flat, but for Charlie it was a disappointing end to his four years of hard work and dedication. 'From about 30 metres Jimmy and I started to make our move,' he said, 'but at 60 I felt a little pull on the outside of my left knee, just like somebody tapped me. So for a split second I had to decide whether to stop or keep going, but in that short space of time I decided I'd come this far and I was going to get one of those medals. But I couldn't increase my speed and I couldn't go with Jimmy the way I normally did and I ended up with third.'

Charlie was sporting in defeat and one of the great pictures of the Games was of he and Jimmy hugging each other in the middle of the track. Even on the rostrum they were clowning around as Jimmy stepped up to receive his gold medal. 'It was – and still is – the greatest feeling of my life,' says Jimmy, 'because you are number one and nobody can take that away from you. There will never be anything to surpass it.'

Jimmy's time, which was an electronic timing, is still the Olympic 100 metre record and remained the world record for nearly 15 years, so it ranks as one of the great track runs at any distance. But there are plenty of people who have poured cold water on it because it was set at altitude, where the thin air meant less resistance and helped the sprinters achieve better times. Jimmy disagrees: 'Since that day people have been saying I ran so fast because of the thin air, but it was the hardest race I ever ran in my life. It was the only time in my life that I finished a race and felt absolutely dead. That thin air didn't help me one bit, in fact it hindered me, because at 80 metres my chest was burning and if that hadn't happened I probably would have broken 9.9. I know I could have run faster if I'd been in any other part of the world.'

So Jim Hines was now the fastest man on earth and there seemed to be time to sit back and enjoy the feeling, because the relay was not scheduled to start until the end of track competition. But a few days later a new political storm erupted right in the middle of the American team and every athlete in Mexico was touched by it. It happened when the 200 metres medallists from the United States, Tommie Smith and John Carlos, conducted their infamous Black Power demonstration on the medal dais as the Star Spangled Banner echoed around the stadium. Both Smith and Carlos were members of the Olympic Project for Human Rights, a group of athletes organised to campaign for better treatment of blacks in the USA, and they caused an enormous storm by standing barefoot on the rostrum with their heads bowed and black gloved hands in the air. It was a gesture to express the view that freedom applied only to whites in America.

Hines and Greene were present at the meetings that followed and both saw the demonstration first-hand. Jimmy says: 'I was a member of the US Olympic track team and although there had been talk of a possible black boycott we all stepped on that plane to Mexico as Americans. What happened was something that was done by those two individuals, while the 40 or so other black athletes, including myself, were just as surprised as everyone else when the gloves went up.' The storm had not really died down when the sprint relay team went out. Although the coaches knew that Greene was still not completely fit, they decided to persevere with him, and in the final it was poor baton passing and not Charlie's injury that held them back as it came to the last leg, with Jimmy five feet behind Cuba in third place. But in a storming run, reminiscent of Hayes' performance in Tokyo, Jimmy tore past the field and hit the tape about a yard clear of the Cuban Figuerola, jogging to the side of the track and hurling his baton into the crowd with delight.

He now had two gold medals and Charlie had finally got his, but as they stood on the rostrum they knew their careers would now take completely different paths. Charlie would continue running until 1972, although he never surpassed his 1968 performances, and carry on as an officer in the army, where he still works, on Fort Mead in Maryland. Meanwhile, Jimmy was now confident of becoming the next Bob Hayes and even as he stood on the rostrum the men from the Miami Dolphins were waiting in the wings with a contract and a pen, eager for him to sign. Looking back, Jimmy genuinely believes that at just 22 he could have carried on running for a good many years and been a top contender for medal honours in the 1972 and 1976 Olympics; he was even quoted recently as saying that he should have stayed in track and earned a few thousand dollars

Jimmy Hines, wearing his two gold medals, poses for the press, as he signs a $150,000 contract with Miami Dolphins President Joe Robbie

under the table. But at the time, the attraction of big money in the NFL was impossible to resist and he signed for the Dolphins almost as soon as he returned home, with both parties hoping to see a re-run of the success Bob Hayes was having at the Dallas Cowboys. Sadly it was a false hope and although his arrival and four-year $150,000 contract were fanfared in real American fashion, with Miami President Joe Robbie claiming it was 'the safest bet we ever made', Jimmy could not produce the goods on the field.

There was a major difference between Hayes and Hines in terms of their footballing careers, at college, Hayes was a star, but Hines actually did not touch a ball. Jimmy had gone to Texas Southern on a track scholarship and while he had been a good football player in high school, the coaches at college were not keen to see their sprinting investment knocked around on the football field. 'I think I suffered a little bit because the Dolphins drafted me with the expectation of being another Bob Hayes. But they didn't realise, or perhaps they didn't particularly care, that I had missed four very important years of college football. They were expecting me to come in and do what Bob had done with the Cowboys and that put me under pressure.'

Meanwhile, some of the other players in Miami resented a newcomer arriving from nowhere with no college pedigree and picking up a big pay

cheque. The Dolphins wanted to use his speed as a wide receiver but Jimmy was having trouble catching the ball and the Miami fans uncharitably christened him 'Oops', while others suggested he had 9.9 feet and 12.9 hands. So Jimmy spent most of his time on the bench and in three years at Miami he caught 11 of the 14 passes that were thrown his way in game competition, but the press only seemed interested in the ones he dropped or fumbled. He feels that given more opportunity, he could have done better at Miami, but after he was cut from their side he tried his luck briefly with the Kansas City Chiefs and finally joined the Oakland Raiders, but he never got on the field for the Californian club and in early 1973 he was laid off and decided to give up his dream of emulating his hero Hayes for good.

Throughout his football career he had been running occasional professional races, sometimes against other former Olympic stars and other times against horses, but the one good thing about hardly setting foot on a football field was that he came out of the game without a scratch. So when a professional track circuit was set up in 1973, Jimmy was able to take advantage of it and for three years he plied his trade around the world, even setting a world record of 11.7 in Australia for the 130 yards on grass. It was nearly 10 years after his triumph in Mexico when the pro circuit folded and he had to start looking around for work, but 10 years is a long time and he had little to show for his efforts during that time; the money had gone and so had his fame. Even though he was still the fastest man in the world there were no commercial opportunities and he was not even recognised on the streets of his home town. He had to face the unpleasant fact that he was an ex-Olympic champion who was looking for a job, and those years since Mexico had effectively been nothing more than a waste of his time and talent. First he worked in recreation in Houston, then moved to Austin, where he became director of the city's Human Services Department, an important and responsible position, organising welfare programmes, helping the underprivileged and doing counselling work. However, he gave that up and came home to Oakland where he got involved in more local government work, before he ran into an old friend, Dr Thomas Jones.

Dr Jones had known Jimmy for 25 years and was saddened by seeing him unable to fulfil his potential, especially when he watched him still racing horses in 1984 and losing. He put Jimmy to work in his own company, P.A.S.S. (Professional and Amateur Sports Services), a business that looks

Jimmy Hines today. Despite the suit and tie he is still very involved in sport: he scouts for new talent and represents sportsmen all over the USA

after men and women at all levels of sport, from high school through to top professional competition, and gave him a job as an agent and scout. Jimmy still feels that he is due some of the commercial and other opportunities he missed in 1968, so the selling of Jim Hines, Olympic Champion, is now well underway, masterminded by Dr Jones and including the publication of an autobiography, called *Diary of an Olympic Champion*, the chance of TV work, speaking engagements and a variety of other marketing schemes.

'I don't want to paint a halo over him,' says Dr Jones, 'but I think he must be given his due. With respect to the kind of things he's done for his country and the athletic community I think it has been long overdue.' Running alongside Dr Jones' organisation is a laudable scheme to aid and house abandoned, abused and neglected children in the area, administered by an orthodox priest called Father Gregory. There are eight such homes housing at present 48 under-privileged kids and Jimmy is heavily involved in the project. 'He's a great morale-booster,' says the Father. 'He uplifts their spirit and gives them a sense of expectation, a sense of the future. The message Jim gets across to them is that they can succeed as long as they try and that there is hope for them in life. There are good role models, people who have succeeded and maintained a high level of success and that's what I see in Jim Hines.' So 20 years after winning the Olympic title and creating

the oldest Olympic record on the books, Jim is now in the best position of his life to take on the world.

'You know life is hills and valleys, ups and downs, and I've experienced that. But I've always been a positive person and now the future looks very good for me. Of course, people always expect you to be rich, with a gigantic car, a million dollar house and fine clothes, but when I meet people I just let them know I'm not like that. I've had ordinary eight-till-five jobs and I'm just an everyday person.' This attitude is easy to understand because even at his present offices, in San Mateo, on the outskirts of San Francisco, few people know who he is, other than the quietly spoken, easy-going guy who works upstairs. Sadly, he is separated from his wife now, but his two children are doing well and Jimmy predicts that his daughter Kimberley could well be following the 'old man' into the Olympics. She ran a 13.5 for 100 metres at just 10-years-old and her father is keen to get involved in coaching her as a sprinter; while son Jim Junior is excelling both as a student and as a football player at Rice University in Texas. Jimmy is proud of their achievements and looking forward to seeing what they can achieve in the future.

His story has a lot of parallels with the life of Jesse Owens, in that Jesse spent a lot of years in limbo before he found his way, so perhaps the same thing is happening to Jimmy. 'I can relate to Jesse Owens' story step by step,' he says, 'and I consider him to be the greatest sprinter who ever lived. But my life has taken some similar turns and Jesse got things late in life and my success is coming later, so there is a parallel.'

It is strange to think that even though Jimmy was the first man to break the 10-second barrier, his name is rarely mentioned when track people start talking about the greatest, but perhaps that is because he was so quickly off the scene and forgotten. He admits that he will not be mentioned in the same breath as Owens or even Hayes, but he hopes that when knowledgeable people talk about sprinting his name will come out.

As the Seoul Olympics begin, Jimmy will be 42, but despite his balding, middle-aged appearance he still thinks that he can give today's sprinters a run for their money. Perhaps, as some people say, his mind is still back in 1968 and his body in 1988, but he meant every word when he threw down a challenge to Ben Johnson and Carl Lewis to race him over 50 yards before the Olympics get underway. But for a man who still looks in good shape, seems to have his life in order and was still running good times only a couple of years ago, maybe it is not as ridiculous as it sounds.

OUT IN THE COLD

1972 Valeri Borzov

*'I was absolutely elated.
. . . But it's impossible
to express in words the
state one is in when you
get an Olympic medal'*

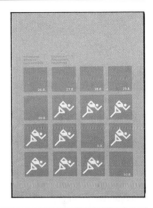

1976 Hasely Crawford

*'I knew I was on a
winner . . . I had
corrected all my
mistakes and I was
running well'*

1980 Allan Wells

*'The feeling of running
fast is unforgettable; the
exhilaration you feel
running around a bend,
it's like you're in
charge, you're a Ferrari'*

1972 Valeri Borzov

'The Fastest Human is a Commie,' screamed the eye-catching headline in the *New York Times* after both sprint events at the 1972 Munich Olympics. They were totally dominated by the powerful and fluent running of 22-year-old Russian Valeri Borzov, the poker-faced hero of Soviet athletics whom the newspapers had christened 'The Ukraine Express'. He destroyed two top-class fields in successive sprint finals, tearing from the grasp of the Americans the two gold medals that they considered their's by divine right.

What was even harder for the United States to bear was the fact that their two best men had missed their heats in the 100 metres, following a bizarre error by the US coaches, leaving the Russian star with a reasonably clear run at the gold. After the controversy had died down, the

With an uncharacteristic victory salute, Soviet star Valeri Borzov is shown to be the clear winner by the judges' photograph of the 100 metres final at the 1972 Munich Olympic Games

press turned their attention to the inoffensive Borzov, describing him as an automaton and hinting that the reason for his emergence was the existence of a high-tech Soviet sprinting 'factory' somewhere in the Russian hinterland which was busily churning out athletes in production-line fashion. Of course, it was all complete nonsense but it demonstrated the strength of feeling in the United States about losing their prized 'Fastest Man on Earth' title.

Today, Valeri Borzov, a little heavier than in his prime running days, just smiles when he's reminded of those newspaper stories, 'R-O-B-O-T,' he says with a big grin, giving an admirable impression of how R2D2 might have tackled an Olympic sprint final. He can afford to laugh about it now but even today there are still people who write him off as a man-made sprinter, who was pushed into a pair of spikes just because he was the right height and weight and could pass a few biological laboratory tests. The reality is different and the obvious reply to those who doubt Borzov's right to a place alongside history's great sprinters is to ask them to name all the other top Soviet sprinters. Borzov is the only top-class sprinter to emerge from the Soviet Union, in fact the only one to come out of the Eastern Bloc. Even their advanced training methods cannot create the ability to sprint – it is an inborn quality and few have it. The Soviets quickly recognised Borzov's potential, coached it well, allowed it to develop and flourish naturally and then applied science to hone his technique to world-class standards. However, without the

original talent all the work that followed would have been to no avail.

Valeri's speed first materialized as a child in the town of Sambor, in the Lvov region of the Ukraine, where he was born in 1949. Nearby was a long stretch of sand dunes, and young Valeri spent many hours playing in them, unconscious of the fact that the soft ground was strengthening his legs. The sand gave way underfoot and anyone trying to walk over it would sink in ankle-deep, so each footstep needed two or three times more effort, which in turn strengthened the muscles and tendons and encouraged Valeri to move fast so as not to sink.

'Only now I understand that spending a great deal of time playing energetic games on sand contributed to the development of my leg muscles,' says Valeri, 'and as I got older I often used sand in my training, either on the beaches of Novaya Kachovka, where I used to live, or in Kiev. It was very effective.'

He was always running as a child, whether it was an errand for his parents or racing his friends at school, but he did not realise how fast he really was until the day he overtook a moving car. 'I used to try and catch the cars in the town as they went past,' he says, 'and on one particular day I succeeded in catching and passing one. It happened on several other occasions and it was then I realised I had an aptitude for sprinting.'

Before his twelfth birthday, he was spotted by coach Boris Voitas, who kindled in him a genuine love of athletics, and although he put him through a rigorous basic coaching regime to prepare him for what was to come, Voitas always stressed that sport should be enjoyed. His methods ensured that Valeri would not tire of athletics before he fulfilled his true potential. To that end he invented games for Valeri to play, which stood him in good stead for the years ahead and included one essential lesson for a great sprinter – relaxation. 'We made paper tubes and Voitas would order us to run 100 metres holding them in our teeth,' recalls Valeri. 'The one who did not bite or squeeze the tube was considered a sprinter, while the rest were considered to be simply runners.'

After Voitas laid the foundations he handed over his protégé to the scientific approach of Valentin Petrovsky, a senior lecturer at Kiev's Institute of Physical Culture, where Valeri was studying biomechanics. At the time he came under Petrovsky's guidance, he possessed natural speed and all the correct basic habits and the right mental approach to the sport; so all that was needed was to tap his vast potential. Petrovsky's

method of achieving this goal was to take a scientific view, breaking down the 100 metres race into small component parts and analysing the requirements for each section and how Valeri should reach them, even to the extent of studying in minute detail his running patterns, from the push-off at the start, the pick-up, the middle of the race, right through to the finish.

His movements were calculated to within hundredths of a second and Petrovsky demanded that each individual movement was speeded up in order to get a faster overall race. The calculations were made with slide rule accuracy and resembled the designing of an aircraft rather than the training of a sprinter, although Petrovsky liked to compare it to the detailed training of a top ballet dancer. In his quest to find the perfect sprinting model, he even made use of slow-motion films of some of the past sprint champions so that Valeri could watch and learn from them both the things he should emulate and the bad habits he should avoid.

'After the basic preparation I had gone through there would not have been a better coach than Petrovsky,' says Borzov. 'We suited each other and I was good material for him. Voitas handed me over to him for a very specific purpose and it produced very positive results. I believe it is better to have a first coach, then a second to train you to the highest level of performance. I don't think that one coach can prepare an athlete from the beginning right up to Olympic standard, though there have been such cases.'

At the age of seventeen, Valeri ran 10.5 seconds for 100 metres in the Ukraine schools championships, and Petrovsky knew that he was ready to make the breakthrough from average sprinter to world class, although it was not to be a painless transition. For two years, Valeri pushed himself to the limit only to be frustrated by repeated injuries and breakdowns, spending weeks hospitalized in plaster after a succession of tendon, ligament and muscle injuries' – a depressing run that threatened to put an end to his track career before it even got off the ground. There were times when both athlete and coach feared that the breakthrough would never happen, but after two years their hard work and Valeri's suffering finally paid off.

In 1968, after winning the European junior sprints, he equalled the world indoor 60 metres best of 6.4 (hand-timed), and in 1969, he went into his first full season, clear of injury and with his body hardened to the stress he would now place upon it. He entered the Soviet championships in Kiev, where, on a rain-soaked, floodlit cinder

Valeri Borzov, the Olympic champion, is pictured while he was studying biomechanics at the Kiev Institute of Physical Culture

track, he set the crowd alight by taking the 100 metres title in an electrifying 10 seconds flat, equalling the Soviet and European records – a star was born.

The Soviet sprint title was the first in a series of targets that Petrovsky had mapped out for his rising young star, but he never made the mistake of pushing him too far, too soon. 'We planned the targets according to the state of my preparations,' Valeri says. 'That is to say, we never planned any goal which I would not be able to achieve. This gave me great confidence in my potential and kept me mentally in balance. There were indeed stages. Winning the Soviet championships was the first, then trying to "look good," as Petrovsky would say, in the European Championships, then trying to compete with the Americans and only when I had beaten the Americans several times, to try to get through to the final of the Olympic Games.'

In 1969, Valeri now Soviet champion, had his athletic 'coming out' at the European Championships in Athens, where he ran for the first time on the new Tartan track, a surface which he liked immediately. He responded by surprising even his Soviet supporters and winning the 100 metres title. He followed this success with more victories around Europe, and then horrified the Americans by beating their best sprinters in a USA-USSR meeting in Leningrad, a result that the US experts put down to a temporary aberration on the part of their athletes. However, there could be no excuses when Valeri defeated them again, this time on American soil, and continued to beat the best the world had to offer, including the top US stars Ivory Crockett, Delano Meriwether and Herb Washington, maintaining his unbeaten record over the 100 metre distance right through and, as it turned out, well beyond the Munich Olympics. The workman-like and unemotional way in which he went about his running led to his reputation as an automatic runner, almost programmed, which was something the Americans loved to claim, especially when their athletes were on the receiving end of another beating.

'There was a lengthy period when I lost to no-one, but I never considered competitions in such a superficial way,' says Valeri. 'Not a single victory was automatic. It was always achieved in a sharp, competitive struggle, though it's true that at this stage I was much stronger. I simply had greater speed. For an outsider it looked as if I took part and won a competition automatically, but for me at that time it was not always important to win. In every competition I developed some kind of tactical variation that I would be able to use in a race of higher standard where there was greater competition.'

The more he won, the more attention and publicity he received, especially in the Western press, where he was berated as merely the latest in a long line of products from the Soviet sports system, a man-made sprinter, cold as ice, with all the personality of a robot. 'I'm used to certain titles given to sportsmen who achieved some outstanding or just good results,' says Borzov, 'and I was no exception. I was called the human rocket, a robot and many other names. My attitude towards it was a positive one. I thought journalists had the right to give sportsmen various titles, but I was never a machine, I've always been an active participant, not just a robot. The fact that I expressed no emotions was true, it was a tactic. I never jumped around after a race and this contributed to the journalists' opinion that I was a robot. I was a normal human being just like now.'

Eddie Hart (above) in the heats of the 100 metres at Munich. Unfortunately, neither Hart nor Robinson competed in the final

A typical study of the power and concentration of the Eastern Bloc's greatest sprinter, Borzov, as he cruises around the turn of a 200 metres race

The acid test of just how good he really was would be in the ultimate athletic competition, the Olympic Games, where his unbeaten record and consistency made him one of the favourites. His real competition, suggested the pressmen, would come from the two Americans Eddie Hart and Rey Robinson, who had both clocked 9.9 seconds in the US Olympic trials, as well as Jamaica's 1968 silver medallist Lennox Miller and the improving Trinidad sprinter Hasely Crawford.

The first heat of the competition began just after 11am on Thursday, 31 August, with Borzov, Hart and Robinson all cruising easily from the first round into the quarter-finals, which were due to start at 4.15pm, with the semis and the final on the following day. What subsequently happened is now part of athletics folklore and robbed the two American sprinters of the chance of continuing in the Games, because as their heats were called neither athlete was in the stadium, unaware that they were required on the track for several more hours. The sad tale has never been explained properly and at the time US sprint coach Stan Wright took the blame for their non-appearance but it was more likely that his out-of-date schedule, rather than suggestions that he could not read a 24-hour clock, caused Hart and Robinson to be disqualified for turning up late.

The story goes that the three American 100 metres men, Hart, Robinson and Robert Taylor, were told that their races were at 7pm, so they were wandering around the Olympic Village when, by chance, Robinson began watching one of the monitors in the ABC-TV offices. As he saw some athletes lining up for a 100 metre race, he asked the technicians if it was a re-run of the first round. When told that it was a live transmission, he realised that he was watching the start of the very heat in which he was supposed to be running. The three athletes were driven at high speed, in an ABC-TV car, to the stadium, but both Robinson and Hart were too late, while Taylor had just enough time to get changed before running out onto the track for his heat.

The Americans tried vainly to get their sprinters back into the competition, but the Germans, sticklers for the rules, refused. Many people remember the resulting controversy over the debacle, especially in the United States, but few are aware that Valeri Borzov also came close

to missing the same quarter-final. He says that he and Petrovsky were told by the German officials that their heat was to be put back by half an hour, which also suggests there may have been a little 'home' blame attached to the Americans' exit. Valeri wanted to go to the practice field but his coach told him to stay at the stadium, so Valeri found himself a comfortable spot to sit and promptly dozed off. 'When I woke up I saw my race had come up on the board,' he said, 'and I could see the competitors going onto the track. I tried to get on to the track but I was not allowed to, a German official would not let me through. I told him who I was and that my race was about to start, but he still refused, so I lifted him out of the way and ran out onto the track. I had just about enough time to install the starting blocks and take off my tracksuit when the official commanded "ready".'

To this day, he does not know what caused the confusion, but he thinks it was tragic that Hart and Robinson were deprived of the chance to take part in the event. 'These things just should not happen at the Olympic Games,' he says tersely.

A most un-machine-like reaction as Valeri Borzov takes the gold medal. He could not believe that a 100 metres Olympic title could be won so easily

As for America's number one sprinter, Eddie Hart, the pain of missing out on the biggest moment of his sporting life is something he has never forgotten. He now teaches physical education at a junior college in California, but the memories of that fateful day in Munich are still clear in his mind.

'I remember us driving to the stadium, speeding the wrong way down one-way streets, swerving around police cordons. I had got half way down the tunnel which connected the practice track and the stadium when my race went off – I was just seconds from making it.'

Hart is an intelligent and articulate man, but it is not easy answering the obvious question about what might have been had he made it through to the final. 'I was in the best shape of my life, with a 9.9 in the trials, and I felt very good. I really felt invincible and I was still on that plateau coming into the Olympics. At the very least I feel I would have given Borzov a real test, but I don't think I would have lost.'

One interesting facet of the sorry affair was that Valeri drew strength from the fact that his two main rivals were out of the competition, while Robert Taylor, the sole survivor of the US team in the event, was exposed to additional pressure. Hart was able to take a gold medal home in the relay, while Robinson left empty-handed, but for both men the feeling of disappointment and anti-climax was immense. 'I have managed to put it into perspective over the years,' says Hart, 'because I really had to come to grips with it. But it's still a big empty spot in my life. I could have accepted losing, but the idea of not even getting the opportunity to compete was really confusing for me.'

Despite the shock of almost missing the race himself, Valeri Borzov again proved his metal by winning the quarter-final in 10.07, easily the best time of the competition, telling Soviet sports reporters after the race, 'You could say I produced my best time out of sheer fright!'

After winning his semi-final, he lined up in the final, the ultimate goal on the list of coach Petrovsky's targets. Although Hart and Robinson were out, Robert Taylor was still a threat, along with Miller, Crawford and Valeri's fast-starting Soviet team-mate, Aleksandr Kornelyuk, so there was still plenty of excitement for the capacity 80,000 crowd. At the gun, the field seemed to get away together, but at the 30-metre mark Valeri, drawn in lane two and just coming upright after a copybook start, began to ease away and was never headed, crossing the line in 10.14, with his arms thrust high above his head in an uncharac-teristic display of emotion, with Taylor a metre behind and Miller third.

'Straight after crossing the line I thought, "I can't believe the Olympic gold medal can be won so easily". I was absolutely elated,' he remembers, 'I even wanted to talk to journalists! But it's impossible to express in words the state one is in when you get an Olympic medal.'

Despite the convincing nature of his win, the post-race press conference was very uncharitable, especially the American journalists. The mood was reflected in the *New York Times* article written by Red Smith, under the headline 'The Fastest Human is a Commie', which unkindly and inaccurately suggested that his race was 'mechanically perfect and in no respect remarkable'. Much of the questioning he faced at the conference centred on the absence of Hart and Robinson rather than the manner of his own victory, or the fact that he had become the first Soviet athlete to win a gold medal under 5,000 metres on the track. Some journalists even suggested that Valeri would not be wearing the gold medal around his neck had the two Americans been in the final. It's a question that he has heard many times since and he always answers firmly. 'Both at the time and now I think that a victory in the Olympic Games gives one the right to be justifiably considered the best at the time. In this particular case I do not think that Hart and Robinson would have changed the situation, though I always considered them to be strong sprinters. I think at the time I was better than them and I achieved victory in an objective situation. After the 100 metres race I took part in the 200 metres race with American sprinters and I won.'

His 200 metres success was actually more convincing than his win in the shorter sprint, even though he had not intended to run in both events and had to be persuaded to take part by the Soviet team coaches. He was already committed to anchoring the sprint relay team and was worried about how running in the 200 metres would affect his relay performance. But after the 100 metres, he felt in excellent shape and ready to take on the world, especially the Americans who had devalued his success. He almost ambled through the 200 metres competition to the final, and in one heat actually turned and spoke to US athlete Larry Burton as he cantered down the home straight, a sign of his relaxed mood and one of the factors that finally convinced him that he could win the final.

This time there could be no excuses from the Americans as the three US athletes – Burton, Larry Black and Charles Smith – had all qualified for the final and were beaten out of sight by a scintillating run from Valeri, who paced himself beautifully out of the turn, catching Larry Black down the home straight, shifting gear and roaring home with two metres to spare. He had enough time to turn and give the rest of the field a derisory glance over each shoulder before flinging his arms into the air, with the clock stopping at 20 seconds flat, a new European record, with Black second and Italian Pietro Mennea third. Victory made Borzov the first man to take the sprint double since Bobby Morrow in 1956, and the first non-American ever to achieve it.

After the race he refused, with some justification, to attend the usual press conference, saying that he had been treated unfairly by the US journalists after the 100 metres final. One of the more interesting things he told Soviet sports reporters was that he believed he had run only at 90 per cent power, although today he feels even that was probably an over-estimate. 'I now think I used much less than 90 per cent, maybe 70 per cent,' he says, 'but if I'd used 100 per cent I would have just fallen apart.' His suggestion that he beat all the USA could offer without even turning on full power antagonised the American press still further and from then on he always got a raw deal from them. He did get the last laugh, however, when a reporter from the respected *Track & Field News* asked him about the remark and he replied, with tongue firmly in cheek, that it was true and it had really taken it out of him throwing his arms in the air at the end of the race!

In the sprint relay, the Soviet team were handicapped by injury and in the final late replacement Juris Silovs got cramp on the third leg and only just managed to pass the baton to anchorman Valeri before he ran out of the end zone, which would have resulted in instant disqualification. Valeri was now way down the field in fifth place, with American Eddie Hart streets ahead, but another gutsy run brought him past everyone bar Hart and he crossed the line in silver medal position. He always insisted that had it been a 200 metres race he would have caught Hart. 'In Munich anything was possible for me,' he says. As the Soviet star of the Games, he was given the honour of carrying the country's flag at the closing ceremony, despite a threat that a bomb would be thrown at the team flag bearer, although it came amid the international recriminations over the Arab terrorist atrocities which cast a dark shadow over the Games and claimed the lives of eight Israeli athletes who were shot in the Olympic Village. The threat remained just that, and there were no further tragedies.

Valeri Borzov completes his Olympic sprint double with victory in the 200 metres final in a new European record time of 20 seconds

When Valeri eventually returned home he was treated like a superstar and had to deal with the hitherto Western problem of hero-worship, especially from the young fans. 'I had a great number of problems because people recognised me on the streets,' says Valeri, 'and I was forced into spending a lot of time telling them how I became Olympic champion, which was very exhausting. But I felt that people respected me because I was representing the city of Kiev, our Ukrainian republic and the Soviet Union at the Olympics and was worthy of representing them.'

During the Games, the newspapers in the Soviet Union had devoted huge amounts of space to reports of his progress and medal-winning runs. In fact, in one edition of *Pravda* he got practically an entire page to himself, while on the same day one-time hero Boris Spassky was relegated to just three lines when he lost the world chess championship to American Bobby Fischer.

What Valeri could not have known was the effect that competing and winning in Munich would have on him, and for more than a year the world seemed to cave in on him. Almost a lifetime's work had been fulfilled by victory, during a few fleeting seconds, at the Olympics. Now that all his goals had been achieved, there was nothing left except a terrible feeling of emptiness. He could not sleep and even his work failed to interest him. His condition was diagnosed as nervous shock and he was told that only time would find a cure.

There was nothing that he could do to cure himself so he surrendered to the depression and waited for it to pass. Gradually, as the months went by, it did diminish and his interest in both his work and the track slowly returned. However, to the outside world, especially the West, it appeared that he had gone into a sudden and premature retirement. Finally he forced himself back on to the track and began to train again, only then realising just how important the feeling of running had become to him. He told a Soviet writer-friend at the time: 'I very often have the following urge. I suddenly feel on the street that I have to run. I absolutely have to run, dressed in a suit, wearing my hat and tie, not paying attention to the passers-by. I have to because I feel a certain rhythm inside me that completely dominates my body. It's like a melody that won't leave you alone. Then convention gets the upper hand and I restrain myself. It's painful but I feel happy inside.' The remarks show the real drive inside Valeri Borzov – hardly the programmed thoughts of an automaton!

He finally made it back on to the track in the 1974 season and went on to reclaim his European 100 metre title in Rome, although he did not feel sufficiently strong to test himself over 200 metres. He returned home to begin preparations for the Montreal Olympics, with the Soviets convinced that he could hold on to the two gold medals he had won in Munich. His rivals always respected his talent and knew that he would still represent a threat in Canada. In the Soviet Union, the younger athletes hero-worshipped him. Just prior to Montreal, Aleksandr Aksinin, then an up-and-coming young sprinter from Leningrad, described how he felt about Borzov to a sports reporter. 'He is unique in terms of talent, inner reserve and also will-power. Probably will-power is his strongest point. It's uncanny, when you line up alongside him for a competition you just know, you feel it in your bones, that he'll win. You have no chance. Magnetism is just oozing out of him.'

Valeri clearly had a considerable psychological edge over his fellow Russian sprinters, but the rest of the world's top fast men, although holding him in high regard, genuinely felt that this time around he could be beaten. As it turned out, the improving Hasely Crawford took the gold, with Jamaica's smooth-running Don Quarrie second and Valeri in bronze medal position, just keeping the American Harvey Glance out of the honours. Valeri was disappointed but the Soviets regarded his run as a success – no 100 metre Olympic champion had returned to an Olympics and won a medal in the same event.

After the 100 metres he pulled out of the 200 metres, blaming a niggling injury, but he still turned out in the relay, anchoring a well-drilled Soviet team to another silver. During the Games, Valeri began making serious plans of a more personal nature. He and the four-times gold medal winning gymnast Lyudmila Turishcheva decided to marry, news that made major headlines, especially in the Soviet Union, where they were probably the two biggest sporting stars in the country. However, they were not brought together by their sporting success but by their political fervour.

'We first met at work,' says Lyudmila, who still looks as stunning as her days in the gym. 'Both of us were young Communists, active young Communists! We met at a Young Communist Central Committee Conference, then at various meetings, though at that time we didn't know we were going to be husband and wife. But when we were in Montreal we were already good friends and started making plans.'

They were married in 1977 and just over a year later daughter Tania arrived on the scene, an event greeted with great enthusiasm in the Soviet Union, especially by the newspapers, which immediately christened her 'supergirl'. At this time, Valeri was still hoping to make the Soviet team for the 1980 Olympics, held on home soil in Moscow, but a series of injuries, culminating in complicated operations on both achilles tendons, put an end to that dream and to his running career. However, he did take an active role in the Games behind the scenes and helped run the torch into the Olympic stadium. Retiring from the sport was not the enormous wrench it might have been for Valeri, as he was frustrated by the constant stream of injuries he had suffered, and he was relieved to hang up his running shoes.

Today, Valeri Borzov is a man of some influence and still lives and works in Kiev, in the Ukraine, where he is Deputy Director of the State Committee for Physical Culture and Sport,

Valeri Borzov and Lyudmila Turishcheva at their wedding and (inset) with their daughter Tania, on holiday by the Black Sea

responsible for organising and developing sport in the republic, encouraging youngsters to get involved and fighting for better facilities. While President Gorbachov is busy restructuring the country, Borzov says his main task is to restructure sport. He has also just been appointed as the Soviet delegate to the European Athletics Federation. He still enjoys athletics and attends as many meetings as time allows, but the only running he does these days is a little cross-country. He keeps fit by playing regular volleyball and is keen to take up tennis. He has lost none of the keen sense of humour or the razor-sharp intellect he displayed during his days on the track and there are those who predict a very bright future for him in sport and possibly even politics in the years to come. Valeri has few other ambitions, apart from one serious long-term desire to find an athlete with vast potential, take him under his wing and coach him all the way to the Olympic Games. The Olympics served as a platform on which Valeri based his career in sport, but it is likely that even without that triumph he would have still carved out a successful career elsewhere.

'Of course, both winning the Olympic gold medal and the popularity that followed changed my life in every possible way,' he says. 'For example, if I study at the university I am ashamed if I do not do well, because everyone knows me. If I work I'm ashamed if I do my work badly. If I'm amongst people I'm ashamed to say no to someone, not to tell them something, not to answer a question that someone asks me.

'That is to say, the Olympic medal put me in such a position that I have to behave as an Olympic champion, both at home and abroad, or wherever I am. I think it's a good saying that an Olympic medal has two sides – thorns and roses.'

Of the 20 Olympic 100 metres champions and the other great sprinters, there are probably five or six who stand out even among this elevated company, so there is no higher tribute than to place Valeri Borzov on the shortlist. Those who criticised him for being unspectacular, forgot that his power, fluency and almost effortlessly efficient running style were really a spectacle in themselves. His consistency at the very highest levels of world sprinting, his record in major championships and the high regard in which he is held by other top sprinters are clear testimony to his undoubted superiority.

1976 Hasely Crawford

At the precise moment that Valeri Borzov hit the tape to win the 100 metres final in Munich, more than 60 yards back down the track stood the fuming figure of Hasely Crawford. The big Trinidadian had pulled a hamstring in the semi-final and had only made the start of the final thanks to some intensive ice treatment and heavy strapping around his damaged thigh. But it took just four strides to undo all the team doctors' careful work, and Crawford, cursing his bad fortune, was out of the race. As he stood on the track watching the backs of the rest of the field disappearing towards the finish, he made himself a solemn promise to return next time and win.

From his earliest days, Hasely, one of 11 children, had shown an intense, almost unnerving dedication to any task he set himself, whether it was on or off the track. It is possible that this characteristic stemmed from his humble background, growing up in the industrial capital of San Fernando, Trinidad's second city, within sight, sound and smell of the giant oil refineries

'The Trinidad Flyer': Hasely Crawford (extreme right) gets it right on the day of the 1976 Montreal Olympic 100 metres final. Don Quarrie (in yellow) is second and Valeri Borzov (dipping) is third

that dominated the skyline. Life was tough for the Crawford family and made even worse when Crawford Senior, a rabies inspector with the Ministry of Agriculture, died of a heart attack when Hasely was just 14. By then Hasely had already been singled out by his school as a possible athlete after they saw him out-running boys several years older than himself in the playground.

Just over a year after his father's death Hasely took part in his first major race, finishing third in the Texaco Southern Games 100 metres for the under-16s, but it was not until 1968 that he began to have serious designs on the Olympic Games. He was injured and his close friend Carl Archer, whom he had already beaten, was selected for the Trinidad team for Mexico. 'Since he'd made the team I thought, well why not me?' says Hasely, 'but when I told my friends that I'd be on the team at the next Olympics in Munich, they all laughed at me.'

The Olympic year of 1968 was also his last at San Fernando Technical Institute. When he left, he took a job as an apprentice iron worker, spending much of his time in the docks working on the oil tankers. He might well have spent his life there had it not been for his running ability. He had only received a basic education, and paying to go to an American college was out of the question. But his luck began to turn after a promising season in 1969, so much so that he was picked for the Trinidad team for the Central American and Caribbean (CAC) Games, which were to be held in Panama City in February of 1970. Although Hasely had been running for the Texaco Sports Club, most of his training had been done on the tracks left by the sugar cane lorries at the giant Madeleine Sugar Factory, in the Philippines district of the island, so he was looking forward to his first ever trip abroad. It was one of his proudest moments walking out for the parade in the opening ceremony of the Games, wearing his maroon blazer and his welding goggles to shield his eyes from the sun. But the competition itself

was strong, particularly from the Cubans, so he did well to make the final and finish a respectable fifth in the 100 metres, won by Pablo Montes, who had been fourth in the Olympic final of 1968.

Having enjoyed the competition so much, Hasely now set his sights on the Commonwealth Games, to be held later in the year in Edinburgh, Scotland, where he would come face to face with a man who would become his greatest rival throughout his career, Jamaica's Don Quarrie. The Games were a key point in Hasely's life, even though he only managed a bronze medal in the 100 metres behind Jamaica's Lennox Miller and the winner Quarrie, because his performances in Scotland and also in Panama had been noticed by some of the major US colleges, who were always on the lookout for athletic talent around the world. The University of Texas, in El Paso, offered him a scholarship after the CAC Games, but after his bronze medal in the Commonwealth Games more offers began to arrive.

To move forward, both on the track and in education, meant leaving his home as there were few educational opportunities or financial help or sponsorship of sport from his government, so there were few events in which Hasely could compete. The college he selected, which was something of a tradition for Caribbean athletes, was Eastern Michigan University, where Trinidad's half-miler Eric Nesbitt was studying along with a handful of other West Indian track and field stars. So after completing his Texaco apprenticeship in December 1970, Hasely left for a better life and new opportunities in the United States.

Just before leaving, however, he was involved in a serious car accident and seriously damaged his back, a condition that doctors diagnosed as a pinched sciatic nerve and which still causes him pain even today. Thus the college's new acquisition could not even put so much as a foot on the track for nearly 18 months, until April of Olympic year itself, when he began to show the sporting powers at East Michigan what he could do. Hasely had beaten nearly every top sprinter in the world in the run-up to the Games, except for Borzov, Miller and the new American number one, Eddie Hart, so he felt that he had a chance of running well in Munich. The Russian star was a special motivation for him, particularly the way in which he was being upheld by the press as the great white hope of international sprinting. 'I must admit that when I was at college I was influenced by the Black Power movement,' says Hasely, 'and going into the Games I felt he was eluding me, I couldn't run against him and when he was being billed as the great white hope, I

didn't like it. So I built a kind of grudge against him, almost a rage inside me, and I was looking for him in Munich.'

This grudge was to prove Hasely's undoing at the Games, but before the team arrived in West Germany he embarked on a successful European tour, including a morale boosting victory over the US star Hart, in Italy, so he was in good shape when the Olympic competition began. Hasely finally got his wish to race against the Russian in the quarter-finals of the 100 metres, and he ran a national record of 10.18 in third place behind the American Robert Taylor and Borzov in what was to be the fastest race in the competition. It was enough to win him a place in the semis and again he was drawn against Borzov and felt that he had something to prove. 'I got a very bad start but I caught him after about 20 metres,' recalls Hasely, 'and I looked across at him as if to say let's go, let's see what you can do. I tried to crush him and to show everyone that he wasn't so great after all, but I pushed so hard that I damaged my right thigh muscle.'

The injury meant he had to line-up for the final heavily strapped and with virtually no chance of completing the race, but he decided to have a go and ignored offers of a pain-killing injection. Of course, it was a futile effort and the injury collapsed after only a few metres and Borzov ran away with the final. But the defeat was an important factor in how Hasely fought his way back to compete in the next Olympics in Montreal, where he would become an even greater force. He became a much hungrier athlete, having to live with his defeat in Munich for four years before he could return to the Olympic arena and correct the mistakes he had made. In 1972 he did not warrant a place in the world's top 10 sprinters, but in 1973 things had changed and he earned the number two spot, after an impressive victory in the AAU indoor championships in New York, where he beat Herb Washington, Borzov, Ivory Crockett and Steve Williams in the 60 yard dash final. His season continued in a similar vein, with a high-point coming in the last race of the year, in Kingston, when he beat the local hero Quarrie and great rival Steve Williams in 10.1.

Now well established on the international scene, Hasely had earned himself a title in his native Trinidad, the nickname of Raj Paul, a local 'badjohn', a big, mean person whom no-one crossed. The language on the island reversed 'good' and 'bad', so Hasely's running had been so good it became 'bad'. He is still known as Raj Paul even today. He had also been earning himself a reputation as the world's track tough guy, a

The great rivals: Trinidad's Hasely Crawford and Jamaica's Don Quarrie vied for supremacy from their early days in the Caribbean

Steve Williams was injured for the 1976 Olympics, but Crawford and Quarrie insist there would have been a world record had he been in Montreal

man who would stop at nothing to win a race. At nearly 6ft 3ins and over 190lbs, Hasely was a big, powerful man and he loved to frighten the life out of other athletes if he possibly could. 'I always believed that sprinting was relaxation, running and 25 per cent psychology,' he says, 'and I would do anything to win a race. I'd try to show you up, scare you, because I was always a bigger person than most other sprinters and I knew I could scare most people. I'd tease them, intimidate them and it often worked.'

After a dazzling season in 1973, he went off the boil the following year, but returned in May 1975 with a bang, clocking a wind-aided 9.8 in a 100 metre race with Steve Williams, at the Hampton

International Games, at Arima. That followed a successful indoor season, his best ever, where he won the Millrose Games, the NCAA title and the AAUs, where Williams again trailed Hasely in Madison Square Garden. One problem that Hasely faced at this time was the end of his scholarship, so while he worked towards his masters degree in materials engineering he had to take a job and cut down on his training. Nevertheless, he won the outdoor NCAA 100 in June, before starting work in the summer at Nash Engineering, near Detroit, where he designed gears for drag-racing cars, a job that lasted from six in the morning until four in the afternoon, so the only training he could do was in the evenings.

Despite these problems he still made Trinidad's team for the Pan American Games in Mexico City, just missing out on a gold medal to Cuba's Silvio Leonard in the 100 metres. When the 1976 season began, which would culminate in the Montreal Olympics, Hasely was still slogging towards his masters and working 10 hours a day, but he had the additional problems of a recurring eye inflammation which flared up occasionally following a stick-fighting accident as a boy; and an unhappy marriage. He had met and married New Yorker Linda Jones in the previous year, but by April 1976 they had separated.

Despite all these problems hanging over him, Hasely's hunger for Olympic success stayed as strong as ever and he kept his sights firmly on that 100 metres title. He qualified easily to run in the 100 metres, 200 metres and the relay in Montreal, and in the weeks leading up to the Games he chose his races carefully, ensuring that he did not overstretch himself and risk damaging any muscles. He chose well, because in a short pre-Olympic tour in Scandanavia he ran 20.2 for a national 200 metres record, and in Canada, a few days before the Games began, he set a new national 100 metres record running 10.0. 'It may sound cocky but I knew I was on a winner,' said Hasely. 'Because I had corrected all my mistakes and I was running well, though I did have some respect for Quarrie and Borzov.'

The Montreal Games had been marred by an eleventh hour boycott by 22 African nations and by the enormous cost of staging the Olympics which had plunged the city and the state of Quebec into massive debt. The boycott was announced just 48 hours before the opening of the Games, and the nations involved justified their actions as part of the campaign against apartheid in South Africa and as a protest against the recent tour of the country by the New Zealand rugby team. The Games themselves will be remembered for the boycott and the race to finish the stadium for the official opening by Queen Elizabeth but they were also the Games at which Finland's Lasse Viren retained both his 5,000 and 10,000 metres titles, and the giant Cuban Alberto Juantorena strode his way to double gold in the 400 and 800 metres.

Hasely was looking confidently towards his own sprint double when the Games opened on 17 July and he was awarded the honour of carrying the Trinidadian flag. The 100 metre competition began a few days later and he breezed through the first and second rounds, beating Borzov comfortably in the latter, and then beating his other closest rival Quarrie in the semi.

The final would take place with three notable absentees: the American star Steve Williams missed the Games through injury; his team-mate Steve Riddick had been surprisingly edged out in the second semi-final; and Cuba's Leonard had gone out in the quarters. Leonard had been injured in winning the 1975 Pan American title after falling into the 10-foot moat that surrounded the Panama City track, but he had regained his form and made the team. Just 10 days before the Games were due to start he stepped on a bottle, which broke and badly cut his foot, so unable to train or run as he would like, he crashed out early in the competition.

The US men left in the final were the teenagers Johnny Jones and Harvey Glance, but Hasely knew how to deal with them, in his own inimitable style, in the room where the finalists gathered before they went onto the track. 'It was a room about 20 by 20 and I think I came in last,' recalls Hasely. 'There were two attendants there. I came in singing a calypso to get the attention. Then I started swearing, cursing and shouting, pointing fingers at people, and I can remember Jones and Glance watching television like zombies. I shouted at them, "You two lose, you're in trouble, you're scared", and they stared at me like I was a ghost and I knew I had them beaten.

'Quarrie just kept saying, "Crawford's crazy", but I turned on him and shouted, "I'm crazy? You'll see how crazy I am when you go out there." The only person I couldn't move was Borzov. He just kept looking at me, making a kind of hissing noise, but he never once kept his eyes off me. So I went into the race knowing that he was the man to beat.'

Hasely had psyched himself up to an incredible pitch; he had hardly slept for nine days leading up to the final and the strain was beginning to show as he pumped himself up for the biggest race of his life. The night before the final he had been so restless that even his team-mates could not sleep. He had tried to read the Bible, he had got up and changed his outfit six or seven times and was making such a noise that his colleagues tried to quieten him by tying him to his bed and even cutting chunks of his hair.

'I remember saying over and over again, something old, something new, something borrowed, something blue. A lot of things go through your mind and you want to make sure you have the right clothes on, so I decided to get something old, new, borrowed and blue. I think it was my jersey, a jockstrap, my pants and my socks. Then I got out of bed early, had lunch, warmed up and went into the room with the rest of the athletes.'

Both Hasely and Don Quarrie are convinced that had their great rival Steve Williams been in the field then a world record could have been broken. 'I wish Steve had been there,' says Quarrie, now coaching at the University of Southern California and running his own business. 'We were the best of friends but we had a great rivalry. Hasely and Steve also had a rivalry, because Steve hated Hasely to beat him and vice versa and I think the tension would have been greater and the times a lot faster, maybe we would all have gone under 10 seconds.'

The eight finalists were Crawford, on the inside lane, the Bulgarian Peter Petrov, Borzov, Quarrie, Glance, Jones, East Germany's Klaus-Dieter Kurrat and Panama's Guy Abrahams. The gun went off but it was a false start, and Hasely jogged all the way to the finish line and then slowly back to the start, ever keen to pull some psychological advantage from any situation that arose. Back in the blocks the 70,000 crowd hushed again and this time the gun got the field away. Glance and Borzov were straight into the lead, but at halfway Quarrie was level with Borzov, while Glance was fading, but with 25 metres left the smooth-running Jamaican had eased clear of the Russian and was looking for the tape. Suddenly out of the corner of his eye he could see for the first time what everyone else in the stadium had been watching. In lane one, running in his own race, Hasely had been hurtling along in the lead and hit the line well ahead of the dipping Quarrie, who could not accelerate again. Hasely's right arm was raised in triumph, the big man rolled right around the bend and kept going for nearly another 100 metres until the realisation of what he had done must have suddenly hit him.

He hit the line in 10.06, with Quarrie second in 10.08 and Borzov snatching the bronze in 10.14, which was coincidentally exactly the same time in which he had won the gold in Munich. 'I went into the race figuring it was going to be between Hasely, Borzov and myself,' says Quarrie, 'and I didn't think the Americans would be a factor. I didn't get off that well and when I looked up I saw Borzov in front. Right away I said to myself, "Oh no, he's not going to win again." I took off after him, caught him and in going by him I thought I'd got it won. Then I saw Hasely. I made another effort but Hasely held on. But I wasn't too disappointed, I was hoping I would win, but that's what

Success at last. After disappointment in Munich in 1972, Hasely celebrated his golden moment in Montreal and said, 'I must admit I shed a tear'

the Olympics are all about. I should have been concentrating more on just running rather than paying attention to any one particular athlete. But I had the 200 to come.'

Hasely's reaction straight after the gun was similar to that of Quarrie. 'I saw Glance and Borzov out there and Borzov made a kind of high pitched hissing sound when he got off and I said to myself, "Jesus Christ, not again" because of '72. But in three strides I was past him and I opened a gap and I couldn't see anyone else. Then I saw Quarrie's yellow jersey and I picked it up again and went through the tape.'

Hasely's reaction as he cantered around the bend was understandable, cursing to himself – although he had finally achieved his long-time goal, he was probably still feeling angry that the Trinidadian Government had not given him the kind of assistance he had needed in the build-up to the Games. But he had become a national hero overnight, Trinidad's first Olympic gold medallist, so it was a sweet moment when he stood on the victory rostrum to receive his medal and he admits that there were tears in his eyes.

For the first time since 1928, there were no

Americans on the rostrum, and it was the second time in succession that an American had not claimed the Olympic gold and the title of the fastest man on earth. Hasely's next task was to take a second gold medal in the 200 metres, an event in which he had also run well in the build-up to the Games, but there was tough opposition in the field. After the traumas he had gone through before the 100 metres, he actually tried to get the Trinidad officials to pull him out of the competition, feeling that he could not face another four rounds of tension. But he was persuaded to join a field that included his great rival Quarrie, who was the clear favourite, plus the Italian Pietro Mennea, who had almost pulled out of the competition because of his poor performances in his national championships, and the Americans Millard Hampton and high school student Dwayne Evans.

One key man missing was the 1975 Pan American 200 metres champion, James Gilkes, but Guyana had decided to join the boycott of the African nations and, despite an appeal to the IOC by Gilkes to run under the Olympic flag, he was unable to take part. In the 200 metres heats, Crawford and Quarrie looked in good form, but in the final Hasely's injury jinx struck again and after about 50 metres he leaped high into the air and crashed onto the track with another muscle problem, this time a spasm in his left thigh. Again he had to watch as the rest of the field tore around the bend and Quarrie managed to hold off a late run by Hampton to take the gold, with 17-year-old Evans third. Hasely is listed in the official report as not finishing the race, but an eagle-eyed track fan in the stadium noticed that he never actually left his lane as he pulled himself to his feet and jogged to the finish line to retrieve his belongings. His time is the slowest ever recorded in an Olympic 200 metres race and went down as one minute and 19.6 seconds.

For Quarrie it was the culmination of a long struggle to take his prized gold medal. He had been injured in training after selection for Mexico in 1968, then went to Munich as the Pan American champion, with the second fastest electronically timed 200 metres ever (19.86) only to pull a hamstring in the semi-final and be carried off on a stretcher. Few would begrudge him his moment of glory, and Quarrie, one of the nicest and most respected men in the track world, now has a statue honouring his achievements in Kingston, Jamaica.

In Trinidad, a statue was just one of the ideas the authorities had to pay tribute to their new hero, who finally arrived home amid amazing scenes on 1 August – the same day that Trinidad & Tobago was officially proclaimed a republic. There had been rumours that Hasely had received offers to play football in Canada for the Toronto Argonauts and that the New York Jets were keen to use his size, speed and power as a wide receiver in the NFL, but if the offers existed then Hasely was not really interested. The welcoming party at Piarco Airport was led by his proud mother, Phyllis, and the Prime Minister, Dr Eric Williams, who joined thousands of people to congratulate Hasely as he stepped off the plane. After an overnight stay at the airport hotel, a motorcade took Hasely and the rest of the team to civic receptions past noisy, banner-waving fans in both the capital, Port of Spain, and Hasely's home town, San Fernando. The celebrations went on for weeks and the newspapers could print little else but eulogies to the island's new star.

One of the first honours to be bestowed on him was to have a British West Indian Airlines DC9-50 jet named after him, a plane that still runs regular services around the Caribbean, and Hasely was appointed as a public relations officer for the company. At the end of August he received the nation's highest civic decoration, the Trinity Cross, for distinguished and outstanding service, following in the footsteps of the great Barbadian cricketer Gary Sobers. There were reports in October of 1976 that he was seriously considering giving up athletics because of persistent trouble with bursitis, a painful inflammation of the joints, but he was treated for the condition in the United States and resumed light training the following year.

However, there were still more honours to come, including a postage stamp minted by the Trinidad Post Office to commemorate his win, and in 1977 he was handed the island's sportsman of the year award and appointed as a special adviser for sport and industrial education at the Ministry of Education and Culture. He was not even forgotten in the Carnival 1977, when no less than six calypsos were written about him, including one from Lord Kitchener called *de people's man* and another from the Mighty Sparrow which started –
'Crawford like a bullet
Take off like a jet
Flash o' lightning
He keep moving
People bawling
Everybody glad
Is Craw-ford, Trinidad.'
His achievement pushed him firmly into the public eye which, for a quiet and private person off the track, was something he did not always

enjoy. 'Winning the gold medal gave me world recognition,' says Hasely, 'and it gave me the opportunity to travel the world. I must say I was a hasty person before I started competing and it made me a disciplined person. I think I have a broader view of things now, though I must admit there are times that I do say to myself what was the purpose of winning this gold medal, because basically I'm a private person and there are times when people say nasty things to me and I feel resentful. I feel it's unnecessary, so sometimes I wonder what the purpose of it all was.'

Hasely did manage to squeeze in a few races in 1977, including another CAC Games medal, this time a bronze one in the 100 metres in Jalapa, Mexico, behind Cuba's Leonard, who won in the fastest time of the year, a 9.98, with Osvaldo Lara second. At around the same time he poured cold water on suggestions that he was going to abandon the sport and sign up with a major international promoter in the Middle East to run professionally. Instead, he set himself a target of gold in the Commonwealth Games in Edmonton, in August 1978. It was to be his last genuine chance of medal success in a major international competition, and again his rival Quarrie was still on the scene, but a newcomer was now challenging, Scotland's Allan Wells, for whom Hasely had enormous respect.

In the final in Edmonton, the first time that he had competed in Canada since the Olympics, with a seven metre per second wind behind the finalists, Quarrie edged the gold as the three favourites hit the line together, with Wells second and Crawford taking the bronze. He won another bronze in the relay and went on to take some important scalps on a European tour, including Riddick, Gilkes and England's Mike McFarlane. In 1979, he ran alongside Wells and Quarrie in Australia in the hope of getting into shape for the Olympics in Moscow in 1980 – he wanted to be fit enough to defend his 100 metres title. However, he could not regain the form of 1976 and he went out in the quarter-finals. That defeat looked like the end for Hasely and he disappeared from the track scene until March of 1982, when he started running in local meets to stay in shape. But he began to run some good times, including a 10.3 in Trinidad, so he went back into serious training in 1983 with one eye on the Los Angeles Olympics the following year. At the age of 33, Hasely again carried the Trinidad flag into the famous LA Coliseum and won his way through to the quarter-finals, placing fourth in the first round behind winner Carl Lewis and finally going out at the next stage in a race won by Canada's Ben Johnson.

Hasely Crawford today, demonstrating the best way of enjoying sugar cane, one of the gourmet delights of the Caribbean

It was his last major race and on returning from Los Angeles he decided to retire, after becoming the only Olympic 100 metres champion to race in four Olympics.

Since coming home from Montreal, Hasely has worked for the Government in the fields of youth, sport and recreation and is currently the country's acting Director of Sport, a position in which he hopes to improve sport in Trinidad. 'I hope I'll be able to pass on a lot that I've learned,' he says, 'and right now my whole future is my job. I would like to see Trinidad & Tobago sport in the place it's supposed to be, and that's high on the charts.'

Although he is recognised everywhere he goes in Trinidad, Hasely lives a quiet life, still suffering from his perennial back trouble and actually considering competing at a local level in 1988 just to keep his joints moving, but he also helps out on the coaching side at a club on the island and hopes to be one of the leading lights in getting more Trinidadian athletes to the Olympics and athletic success in the future.

He has come a long way since his struggling days by the oil refineries, but has not been spoilt by his achievements, even though he has competed internationally for 14 years, racing and beating the best in the world. Perhaps his tendency to pull muscles and suffer other injuries has conspired to rob him of a place higher in the rankings of the all-time great sprinters, but there are many top fast men who have suffered and never made it to the Olympics, let alone a gold medal.

1980 Allan Wells

While Hasely Crawford was rocketing to success in Montreal, few would have believed that 3,000 miles away, sitting quietly at home in rainy Edinburgh, his successor was watching the race unfold on television in complete anonymity. Allan Wells, the man who would ultimately inherit Eric Liddell's famous title of 'The Flying Scotsman', had only just taken up serious sprinting at the grand old age of 24, a time when many past champions had been retiring. He was not considered good enough for the British team in Montreal; in fact, the standard of sprinting in the country was so poor that the selectors decided to spare themselves the embarrassment of watching them lose and refused to send anyone to run in the 100 metres at the Games.

Allan had not long given up his dream of emulating his childhood hero Lynn Davies and becoming a great long jumper, but his lifetime best of 24ft $\frac{1}{4}$in (7.32m), which he set back in 1972, had been surpassed as a world record in 1898 and he eventually came to terms with the fact that he

Allan Wells' moment of victory, but the whole stadium waits for the scoreboard to confirm the placings. Allan dips to beat Cuban Leonard (extreme right) in the 1980 100 metres in Moscow

was never going to be an international threat at that event. He had always been a fast runner and during the long, tedious gaps at his club's long jump meetings he enjoyed watching the sprint races, particularly the 200 metres and the way in which the athletes ran the curve. The idea of running the curve himself appealed increasingly, so after yet another mediocre performance in the long jump he decided to abandon the event and have a go at sprinting. Four years later he was the Olympic champion.

It may be Scotland's capital and its most beautiful city, but most people agree that cold, wet windy Edinburgh is hardly the ideal place to find a world-class sprinter, but that is where Allan grew up and developed as an athlete. Born in May 1952, the son of a blacksmith and one of five children, his home was in Fernieside Crescent, a street that overlooked the famous Edinburgh Southern Harriers track, and which could later boast two Olympic athletes living within 50 yards of each other, Allan and hammer thrower Chris

Black. Allan first raced at the tender age of six, finishing second in a primary school 60 yard competition, but his interest in sport did not really take off until be joined Liberton High School, where he played football, basketball, badminton and ran cross-country. But even before then he enjoyed winning races against the other children in the neighbourhood, and he remembers: 'There was a friend of mine who used to leave his house in the morning and I could see him and he could see me. He would go around the bottom road and I would go around the top road and we would race each other to school. This would go on day in, day out and most of the time I'd win. I had further to go as well!'

Allan's greatest sporting success at school was winning the Scottish U-15 long jump title and it was at about the same time that he began to win trophies for his local Boys Brigade, the 9th Edinburgh Company, although his success came not in the sprints but in cross-country races, the type of character building event into which the Brigade

liked to push its youngsters. Allan joined the Brigade at a time when its code of strict moral and physical conduct and emphasis on clean living and manliness contrasted dramatically with the creed of the swinging sixties, but he had always been something of a loner, so he fitted in well. Of course, the Brigade boys were often the target of street jibes, particularly at their uniforms, but after Allan benefited from enrolling in a Charles Atlas bodybuilding course, few of the jokes were aimed at him. His hero in those days also fitted the clean-shaven, athletic figure endorsed by the Brigade, long jumper Lynn Davies, who had won the 1964 Olympic title and become one of Britain's top sportsmen. There is a famous and long running story about how Allan was spurred on to athletic success after raking the long jump pit for Davies during the 1970 Commonwealth Games in Edinburgh. This is false but Wells did work as a steward at the Meadowbank Stadium and on one occasion did manage to meet his hero. 'He was training out at the back of the stadium,' recalls Allan, 'and I just went up and interrupted his session and started talking to him. It gave me a real feel for the guy, because he didn't swear at me or kick me out, but took the time to talk.' Fittingly, it was Davies who would be the British track and field team manager at the Moscow Olympics when Allan would make his own name in the athletics world.

Although Allan enjoyed the technical and practical classes at school, he was not a keen scholar and left at 15 to take up an engineering apprenticeship. However, he did not decide to devote his sporting efforts to athletics for another few years. When he did, it was the long jump and triple jump that he pursued, winning a Scottish junior triple jump title in 1971, and dabbling a little in the sprints, which were dominated at the time by the young David Jenkins. He earned a couple of international vests for Scotland as a long jumper, but his personal best in the event meant that he could never excel in the way he wanted. Even though his relay times showed much promise as a sprinter, the best he could manage by the time of his twenty fourth birthday was a 10.9 for the 100 metres, but despite that he decided to switch events and devote his attention to improving his sprinting times.

It was in 1976 that Allan joined a group of athletes trained by the wily old professional coach Wilson Young, a man who even today is totally ignored by the Scottish athletics powers, but who steered Allan on to the road towards the Olympic Games. Wells considers the switch to be the watershed in his athletics career, a time when he began to pursue the sport seriously. 'I think I

was looking for a new method in training and also a motivation factor,' he says, 'and they both came together in one. I was still a long jumper and he was happy for me to join the group and gain more speed for my long jump, but I think it took me about a fortnight to realise that I was going to be a sprinter. I think Wilson Young realised I was going to be a sprinter whether I was thinking of being one or not.'

The atmosphere of competition and motivation created by Young catapulted Allan into the national arena, and his performances began to reflect the new lease of life he was getting from working with the group. One of the first to see the change was coach Tom McNab, who was still the British sprint coach at the time. 'Allan came from the tradition of professional sprinting in Scotland, trained by a professional coach and that's a very closed world. Allan carried a lot of professional attitudes with him into the amateur world, qualities like the ability to concentrate and work hard in training. He was very single minded and I give credit to him for being the catalyst in the revival of modern British sprinting.'

It might have been a closed world but Allan's training included many of the old pro techniques, such as the emphasis on strength and power, built up with special exercises, including the speedball, a device more familiar in a boxing gym than in the athletics world. But the new training and the highly charged atmosphere created by Young served to spark him into life and he recognises the debt he owes his old mentor, though sadly they fell out just as Allan was getting into high gear and they have rarely spoken since. Says Allan: 'I feel it was something that was always going to happen. He was motivating everybody in the group, not just me, there was no way that I was getting any more attention than anyone else, though maybe there are some people who would say otherwise. But I think that was the thing that spurred us on, he had one against the other, fighting each other physically and mentally. But the coach and I had our differences and me leaving the group was the best thing. I don't think the two of us came off any better, but at the time it was the only thing we could do. It was a sad day when we parted and I regret it now, and I'm sure he does too.'

Thanks to Young's influence, Allan began to attract attention as a sprinter, running the best legal time in Britain in 1976 of 10.55 and earning a Great Britain call-up for the sprint relay team in an international against Canada. In the following year, he continued to improve, although his 100 metres time stayed the same, and managed to get

*Above: the famous speedball,
part of Allan's training
Right: a perfect illustration
of Allan's powerful start*

a second place in the British championships, but it was the winter training between 1977 and 1978 that pushed him into the major league. Allan adopted some of his own training ideas and allied them to the tried and trusted ones he had been using, a regime of punishing exercises that would make a hardened SAS man wince. He was working under the auspices of coach Charlie Affleck, but also taking a more prominent role was his wife Margot, a guiding light in Allan's career and a formidable force to anyone who got in his way.

Wells put himself through hell during the winter, using a training system he maintained right up to and beyond the Olympics, leaving work at Brown Brothers Engineering and meeting Margot and a training partner at a local park at about 5pm for a session of bounding, hops, skips and other exercises which lasted for about 45 minutes. Having finished in the park, they would travel to the gym, a freezing converted single garage in Leith, so cold that on some nights they had to shovel the snow away from the door to get inside. The one-bar fire made little difference to the temperature inside, especially with so many holes in the walls, but despite the conditions Allan pushed himself through an hour of constant exercising, including speedball sessions, press-ups, squat thrusts, chin-ups and all kinds of variations, using so much effort that by the end of the evening the sweat would rise like steam from his body and he could squeeze about a half pint from his vest. The training went on six days a week throughout the winter, and when the 1978 season began the new super-powerful Allan

Wells bounded onto the scene ready to take the sprint world by storm.

'It was complete concentration during the training,' says Allan, 'and I was a Jekyll and Hyde. I would go to training and be somebody else and when I stopped I became Allan Wells. But when I was training I was Allan Wells, the athlete, though a lot of people could probably find other words! I was accused of being a right sod, but I didn't do it to make friends, it was an attitude of wanting to be the best.'

The early season of 1978 did not witness the explosion, owing to a shin problem he suffered, but in July he burst on to the scene by equalling Peter Radford's 20-year-old British 100 metres record of 10.29, and doing so with his hands in the air five metres from the line. A week later he broke the record with a 10.15 on his home track in Meadowbank, and suddenly people were beginning to talk about the new 'find' from Scotland and how ironic it had been that he should arrive in the same year that the last British gold medallist, Harold Abrahams, had died. Allan's performances earned him selection for Scotland's team at the Commonwealth Games, in Edmonton, where he won two golds and a silver, firmly establishing himself on the international scene, running a sensational, though wind-aided 10.07 to finish second behind Quarrie in the 100 metres, but beating Crawford; winning the 200 metres in a windy 20.12 and taking another first in the relay.

Running against some of the world's top fast men was tough enough, but meeting Hasely Crawford meant he had to undergo another test of

Allan Wells flings up his arms in celebration as he wins to equal the UK 100 metres record at Gateshead on 9 July 1979

Allan and his wife Margot, the centre of the photographers' interest, take a break from training at the 1980 Moscow Olympics

character. 'Wells was running very well and I knew he was the one I had to beat,' recalls Hasely, 'so I went to the dressing-room before the final and his wife Margot was giving him a massage. I walked up and shouted at him, "I'm gonna beat your white ass" and said a lot of other things besides. I was really trying to upset him, to throw him off, but he just looked at me without a change on his face and I realised I couldn't move him. He was like a rock.'

Crawford has always had enormous respect for Allan and admits that throughout his own long career there were only two men he could not intimidate with his own bizarre brand of racing tactics – Wells and Borzov. Allan returned home triumphantly from Edmonton, but he did not have the experience to cope with the European Championships four weeks later and finished sixth.

A member of the British teams at both Edmonton and Prague, Margot Wells was a good sprinter and an even better hurdler, but she decided to forgo her own athletic career and work full-time on Allan's. 'She decided to take a back seat in her athletic world and help me a bit more,' says Allan, 'but I felt I'd lost something, because

when she ran it spurred me on. There was one occasion when we did train together, running 50s, and it brought the best out of both of us, but I couldn't have taken many sessions like that.' Margot's role in helping Allan drew a lot of publicity – there were not too many top-class athletes coached by their wives – but she still winces when she hears the description of her role as Allan's coach. She was much more than just a coach, because by this time Allan did not really need much coaching, but he needed other help: motivation, organising and someone with sprinting knowledge to be his eyes during a race and point out anything that was going wrong. 'I always said to her after a race, "How did it look?"' says Allan, 'and it got to the stage when she was criticising me all the time. To some extent it motivated me, sometimes it could break me, because she could be over-critical and that would kill me, because it's your wife, not the guy who comes and coaches you for an hour and a half each day. So you go home and fight for 24 hours!'

From 1978 onwards, Allan and Margot were seen on tracks around the world, and it was Mrs Wells who earned the reputation as a tough lady who would not take any nonsense from anyone. 'I just tried to let Allan run and think about his running, I did everything else,' explains Margot, 'I made sure his vests were there, he had two spikes, he got the right bus and all he had to worry about was preparing for the race. I wouldn't let anything get in the way and I wouldn't stand for officials hassling him or causing him problems. If

The new and the old pictured together. Hasely Crawford welcomes his successor Allan Wells to the exclusive 'Fastest Men on Earth' club

boycott had, because it had absolutely no impact on the Afghan situation, was that the Eastern Bloc stayed away from the next Olympics in Los Angeles; eight years of pointless political gesturing which served only to frustrate hundreds of athletes and satisfy the politicians who wanted to be seen to be doing something, without affecting trade or the stock and currency markets.

Allan was among the many British athletes who received piles of letters aimed at persuading him to pull out of the team. But he had other things to worry about, apart from the problems caused by the pro-boycott lobby, and they included the IAAF's insistence that starting blocks would be compulsory at the Games. That was a problem for Wells because until three months before Moscow he had not used them in competition, preferring to start with his feet firmly on the track. In the winter prior to Moscow, he was told that he would be forced to use them, so he practised a little, but did not start using them competitively until just 12 weeks beforehand. Until then he had been happy to run without blocks, even at major championships like the European or the Commonwealth Games, because it felt more natural to him and he could start a fraction further forward than the other athletes. The only time it had worked against him was in Turin, for the Europa Cup, when his foot slipped on the track and he could only finish third. Margot suggests that there may have been another reason for Allan's reluctance to use them, and that was his laziness. Training at Meadowbank meant sharing the track with many other athletes, so each time Allan used blocks he would have to come back, pick them up and move them because other people wanted to use the track. So he began starting without blocks and soon realised that he could start just as fast that way. Allan himself thinks that other people worried more about him making the transition than he did, because he had used blocks before in training, and they were not totally foreign to him, so it was just a case of getting used to them in competition. However, it was an added complication in the run-up to the Games and it would have been interesting to see whether he could have been the first man to win the 100 metres title without blocks since Jesse Owens.

To ensure that Allan arrived in Moscow in first-class condition, his company kindly gave him six months' leave from work to prepare. He used the time wisely, running in the warm climate of Australia during the inhospitable British winter, then training with some of the Olympic team in the South of France before returning

anybody did get in the way it was always me that went to them and told them to stop. If I annoyed someone, but Allan won a race, then that was the price I had to pay. I always tried to be polite, but leading up to an Olympic final the last thing you're thinking about is being polite.'

During the 1979 season there were no major Games, but Allan managed to win the 200 metres in the Europa Cup in Turin, finished third in the 100 metres, although he slipped at the start, and placed second in the Golden Sprints in Zurich, behind the American James Sanford. The next major championships were the Olympic Games, in Moscow in 1980, but these Games were already being dogged by political rows over the Russian invasion of Afghanistan and there were calls from all over the world to boycott them, led by the United States. Finally, the British team did go to the Games, whereas many Western countries did not, including the United States, but the athletes took a battering from some conservative quarters about taking part and although the British team fared well, they also served to illustrate the petty attitude of the Government which tried to stop the athletes participating. The only influence the home to complete his preparations in the familiar surroundings of Edinburgh. The break from his job was crucial because it would have been almost impossible to have reached the level of fitness and race freshness attained while still working in a regular job five days a week. But all this preparation could have counted for nothing when he injured his back just a fortnight before leaving for the Games and until a few days before the team got on the plane for Moscow he was unable to do any sort of training. There were genuine fears that he would not be ready for the competition, but thankfully the injury healed and he was able to begin working on his starts on arrival in the Soviet Union. Interestingly, Allan believes the injury may have been an advantage, because it helped him recover from the heavy pre-Olympic training sessions he had been putting himself through and acted as a buffer for the two weeks left before the Games. When he started serious training in Moscow he began to look like a real champion, starting like a train on the practice track.

Allan's dedication to the challenge of becoming Olympic champion prompted his team manager Lynn Davies to say: 'For want of a better word he really is a fanatic. Training, athletics and the build-up to Moscow are everything. I'm not saying other athletes are not dedicated or committed in their approach, but Allan is totally committed. In many ways I see some of my qualities in Allan that I used to have 10 or 15 years ago in approaching the Olympic Games. It's a life or death situation, whether you are going to do well or not. Unless you are totally committed these days you are not going to win an Olympic gold medal. He really does live for athletics and to Allan a feeling of slightly less well-being than yesterday can affect his mood. For that day the quality of training is the most important thing.'

The intensity of Allan's preparations did, on occasions, alienate some officials and media people, particularly the press, who often saw him simply as a moaner, but they never bothered him. He was not the marketable kind of star, in press terms, that Sebastian Coe or Steve Ovett were, and as far as the British were concerned, it was the middle-distance races they were keen to see rather than the sprints, where Allan was given a chance of a medal, but not the gold.

Even though the three Americans Stanley Floyd, Mel Lattany and Harvey Glance were missing because of the boycott, and Floyd had the year's best time at 10.07, there were still a fine collection of sprinters in Moscow, including the talented Cuban Silvio Leonard, hoping to make

up for his 1976 disappointment, and the Polish star Marian Woronin, who predicted that he would win the title. East Germany's Eugen Ray and the home fans' favourite, Aleksandr Aksinin, were also tough competitors, so it was not going to be easy for Allan. But he breezed easily through round one, beating his old rival Don Quarrie into the bargain, looking relaxed and comfortable. It was the next stage, the quarter-finals, when he made everyone sit up and take notice, running a new British record of 10.11 to win a heavily loaded heat, which included defending champion Crawford, Italy's Pietro Mennea, Cuban Osvaldo Lara and the Bulgarian Peter Petrov. He continued to improve through the semi-final. 'That was his best run,' says Margot. 'The semi was phenomenal. He felt really good, he looked really good and he was supremely confident, but some people were saying he was too confident. Allan had gone back to the village after the race and I went down to the warm-up area to get the results, the wind-reading and get all the details about who was trying and who was easing up. When I got there everybody was in a panic, they were saying he was too high and that I would have to get him down. Everyone was running around like their heads had been cut off.'

The hysteria was mostly on the part of the British team officials who, for the first time, saw the real possibility of a British victory in the 100 metres in a few hours' time, but when Margot returned to the village she found Allan lying quietly on his bed reading his book, *40 Years of Murder*. Perhaps he was also thinking about the dream he had had before the Games in which he saw himself winning the 100 metres, but intriguingly it was transformed into the 200 metres when the dream ended before the finish of the race.

Allan and Margot then went back to the stadium, where she said simply, 'I'll see you when it's finished', and they went their separate ways – she into the stands, he into the dressing-rooms. Strange things happen before Olympic finals and this one was no exception: the first was the bizarre appearance of the Russian Aksinin, who Allan remembers walking into the dressing-room wearing just his underpants and making a point of moving around so that everyone present could see there was blood on them, possibly the result of an injection. Of course, it was unlikely that an injection could cause that amount of blood, or whatever he had smeared on them, but it was a psychological ploy that might have worked with someone else – not with Allan. 'I just thought, "You sod, you're going to have to run ten times harder for that".

Above: Allan wins the gold, just beating Silvio Leonard
Right: Allan delights in his 100 metres Olympic success

Once in the collecting area the Russian officials would not let anyone out, and Wells had to get special permission to pay a visit to the toilets, a disgusting, wooden shack at the back of the stands, where the stench was so bad that the officials advised the athletes to wear masks. 'It reminded me of the old rugby clubs and their old changing rooms,' says Allan, 'and it brought back to me that here I was at an Olympic final. It really brought me back to earth. I was standing in there and thinking what the hell am I doing here, with this stench, and I was actually praying for help.'

When he lined up at the start, in front of a crowd of nearly 100,000 inside Moscow's magnificent Lenin Stadium, he was drawn in the dreaded outside lane nearest to the stands, whereas his main rival, Leonard, was six athletes away, on the inside. From the gun it was Leonard who appeared to have the lead, and as the halfway mark passed he began to push out in front and away from the rest of the field, but he could not have seen that way out in lane eight Allan Wells was powering down the track, passing the rest of

the athletes inside him, and with five metres to go began to dip. He seemed to hit the finishing line at almost the same instant as did Leonard. There was confusion in the stadium and no-one seemed to know who had won. It was a photo finish for the first and second, with Wells and Leonard well clear of the third placed man, Petrov.

Allan recalls: 'It felt like I was in a tube, with that one lane stretching out in front of me and you are sort of outside yourself. You've done it all before, you've run it a hundred times before, you've slept it a hundred times before, but now it's real and you can feel the ground, but it's like you're looking through your own eyes at yourself.

'Lara was in the lane beside me and I passed him in a flash and I could see the line coming up in the distance. With about 40 yards left I allowed my eyes to glance across and I saw the Cuban Leonard. He was right up there and I thought to myself, "Well I'm going to get a medal anyway, I'll bloody well make a dive for the line and give it everything, that's why I'm here." But I wasn't sure and neither was Leonard.'

Margot, screaming memorably from the stands, remembers: 'I was just past the finishing line and from the angle I was in, I thought Leonard had won. The blood just seemed to drain from my body, I think it was all in my feet, I was disappointed for Allan.'

Everyone in the stadium, including the athletes, stood on the track and waited for the action replay to come up on the stadium's giant electronic scoreboard. It was transmitted in slow motion and frozen on the line, showing clearly that Allan had dipped in front of the Cuban at the finish. Allan leapt into the air and began a victorious lap of honour, something he had promised himself if he won a gold medal, but when he returned to the finish a Russian official approached and told him that he had not won after all. Horrified that he had just embarrassed himself and his country by taking a lap of honour he had not earned, Allan watched in anguish for the scoreboard to put up the names of the winners. Finally it came up – in Russian – but he correctly assumed that even in Cyrillic his name was shorter than Leonard's and the shorter name had won, so it must be true. As he walked off the track and into the drugs testing room, Margot was receiving a bunch of flowers which he had organised before the race, but they did not see each other for several hours. The medal ceremony was an anti-climax to Allan's success – another petty act on the part of the British Government meant that the team would not see their flag rise nor hear the national anthem. Instead the Olympic flag and anthem were used, a sight that also greeted Britain's other major winners, Coe, Ovett and Thompson.

'It hadn't really dawned on me that if I won I wasn't going to see the flag or hear the anthem,' says Allan, 'and it was really sad, a real anti-climax, to see the Olympic flag and hear their anthem. I suppose it wasn't a really significant thing, but these are the moments you cherish and they weren't there.'

But standing on the rostrum with the gold medal around his neck was a proud moment. He was the oldest man in Olympic history, at 28, to win the 100 metres. As Margot described it: 'Winning an Olympic gold medal has a kudos about it, a respect, because it's the one thing that you step on the track for, to race, to run, to train, whether you're five or fifty five, it's the one thing you never dream about because you never think it can happen. When it does it takes a while to sink in.'

Allan was piped into the post-race press conference in Highland style, but the first question fired at him was about the late Harold Abrahams, the last Briton to win the title. One writer asked him if he had won it for Harold and Allan quick-fired back, 'No, that one was for Eric Liddell.' It brought the house down for the Scottish pressmen. Although there were many celebrations, Allan had to be careful because he had plenty of running still left to do, and a double sprint victory was on the cards with his best event, the 200 metres, coming up. Again he made the final in some style, but standing in his way was the Italian 'Blue Arrow' Pietro Mennea, who was still smarting from his Europa Cup defeat over 200 metres on his home soil at the hands of Wells. After that defeat Allan became known as 'The Beast' in the Mennea household and the 1972 bronze medallist in the 200 metres was fired up to win this time.

The race progressed as in Allan's dream, with him tearing into the lead, making up the stagger on Mennea, who was running just outside him in lane eight, and taking a perfect curve leaving Mennea some three yards in his wake. But the Italian did not give up and, as Allan began to tire, Mennea fought back and just as Allan's dream had ended, Mennea nipped by him in the last few metres to win, with Allan second and Don Quarrie third. However, in coming second, Allan had set a new British record of 20.21, so he was not too disappointed, but significantly neither the first nor the third placed man in the 200 metres final had run in the 100 metres final, and Allan had to work hard to get the silver.

After taking fourth place in the sprint relay the British team set off for home, but the typical reaction to Allan's victory was simply that he would not have won had the Americans been there. Even in Britain people were sceptical, while in the United States the little coverage that the Olympics received added to the general feeling of apathy about Wells. *New York Times* track writer Frank Litsky explains: 'The American reaction was who? Scotland don't have sprinters. We knew an American sprinter hadn't won because we weren't there, but the record books don't have an asterisk by Allan Wells' name saying the Americans were not there. He was the right man at the right time and after those Olympics he raced against the Americans who were missing from the Olympics and he beat them. He won the Olympic title legitimately and won his number one ranking legitimately.'

Naturally the American sprinters felt that they could have given him a tougher challenge and their opportunity came in the first major post-Olympic meeting in Cologne, when Allan proved his point by beating the previously undefeated Stanley Floyd over 100 metres.

'I could never say that the Americans wouldn't have won the gold medal,' says Allan, 'and I have never said I would have won if the Americans were there, because it's total speculation. Politics came between us, but what I would say is a couple of weeks after Moscow I was given the opportunity to run against the Americans and if you look back they were second and I won.'

Although Floyd did manage to beat him in a couple of subsequent races, by then it was academic as far as Allan was concerned, although he made the point far more forcibly at the Golden Sprint the following year. At his triumphant homecoming where thousands of fans turned out to see the fastest man on earth, the police had to control the Edinburgh crowds as Allan's open-topped bus moved slowly along the streets to a big reception at Meadowbank stadium. As reigning Olympic champion he was invited to scores of meetings around the world, but if 1980 had been a good year then 1981 was probably his greatest, with victory in the European Cup 100 metres in Zagreb, and second place in the 200 metres; followed by his most decisive victory over the Americans, by winning the Golden Sprints in Berlin, taking second behind the flying Frenchman Herman Panzo in the 100 metres, and winning the title on aggregate by storming to victory in the 200 metres by five metres from Mel Lattany – a win that he feels was probably his finest run. He followed that with victory in the World Cup 100 metres in Rome and despite a nagging stomach bug, still managed to finish second behind Lattany in the 200 metres.

When the following season got underway, Allan was 30 years old and many people were writing him off, but he pushed himself hard through the winter and the run-up to the Commonwealth Games – so much so that Margot even admitted to reporters that their marriage had been under enormous strain, but the effort certainly paid off. Allan took three medals at the Commonwealth Games in Brisbane, Australia, winning the 100 metres from the emerging Canadian Ben Johnson, running a memorable tie for first in the 200 metres with England's Mike MacFarlane, and adding a bronze from the relay. His subsequent performances in major championships have not lived up to his own expectations, but he has consistently surprised the experts by making finals and winning international meetings around Europe.

At the 1983 World Championships he qualified for both finals and was placed fourth in the 100 and 200 metres, and the following year, despite a toe injury, he elected to defend his title in the Los Angeles Olympics. It ended disastrously with him finishing an embarrassing last in his semi and as he trotted forlornly back down the tunnel, he could see the future champion in front of him – Carl Lewis. It was a symbolic moment and one that convinced Allan that he was not finished, so he battled back. An operation on his toe caused him to miss the entire 1985 season, but he came

Allan Wells wins the 1981 Golden Sprint title in Berlin. In both the 100 and 200 metres he beat the Americans who had not competed in Moscow

back in style in 1986 to finish fifth in both sprints at the European Championships, at the grand old age of 34. Although he did not warrant selection for Scotland's team for the Commonwealth Games in Edinburgh, he answered the selectors in ideal fashion by beating both the 100 and 200 metres Commonwealth champions at a famous meeting at Gateshead, where he turned out in long, 'Chariots of Fire-style' shorts and beat Ben Johnson and Atlee Mahorn into second and third place in different races. It was the last race that the current world 100 metres record holder Johnson lost. Allan went on to run some impressive times during the early part of the 1987 season, which earned him selection for Britain's World Championship sprint team, but injury forced him to pull out. However, he set a different kind of world record, becoming the first man over 35 to run under 10.30 for 100 metres.

In November 1987 Allan underwent a hernia operation, but is still preparing to be selected for the 100 metres in Seoul. He wants to take a trip back to his athletic roots and take up long jumping again, too, before he finishes his athletic career. When the Seoul Games begin Allan will be over 36 years old. 'It's not the money that's made me carry on for so long,' he says. 'It's the sheer enjoyment the sport has given me and the pleasure I still get from training and competing. Maybe my concentration is not as good as it was, but the competitiveness and aggression are still there. But I won't be too sad to give up because I've had my share of injuries and I won't forget the good moments. The feeling of running fast is unforgettable; the exhilaration you experience running around a bend, it's like you're in charge, you're like a Ferrari.'

In 1982, he moved down south from his native Scotland to Surrey where he teamed up with locally based physiotherapist John Allen, who had helped him through some of his best performances, but the move did little to improve his athletics. His best years were 1979, 1980 and 1981. If he were the Olympic sprint champion now, Allan would probably be a millionaire, but at the height of his track powers the 'big break' had not yet arrived and payments were a closely guarded and haphazard affair. 'I do regret there's not been the financial rewards,' says Allan, 'but my event at the time wasn't as financially rewarding as the middle distance events. Even though I was the first British gold medallist in the sprints for more than 50 years it still didn't seem to have much power behind it. But the way things have changed now I would certainly be getting top notch money.'

Conversely, Margot values the gold medal more than wealth, and believes that athletics has suffered from loaded races and ridiculously high payments to mediocre athletes.

Allan Wells has always been a racer rather than a record breaker, although he has had his fair share of national records. He never really received the credit he deserved as a sprinter, even in his own country, where he always ran in the shadow of Coe and Ovett and played second fiddle to them on the European circuit, with the middle distance men getting the money, the publicity and the kudos. Allan never courted popularity and maybe that is why he never attained real superstar status in Britain. In fact, even during his most successful years he was never voted athlete of the year. However, he was awarded an MBE in 1982.

Today he still lives in Surrey and enjoys his work as a technician in the mechanical engineering department of Surrey University, which gives him enough time to do some promotional work for a sportswear firm and train and compete in occasional odd races. At home he and Margot have two 'tiny terrors', Zoe (3½) and Simon (1).

To many people Allan has always been an enigmatic, almost mysterious character – typecast as a dour, difficult Scot by the press, something that track fans around the country actually believed. Allan admits that as an athlete he is interested only in winning races, but off the track he's a different person: a quiet, unassuming man who enjoys family life, his children and his job and talks engagingly about his sport.

'He's totally the opposite to the commentators' portrayal on TV,' says Margot. 'They say he's dull and he never smiles, but actually he smiles quite a lot and he's got a very dry sense of hunour. The problem is that he's a perfectionist in everything.

'It doesn't matter what he does, everything has to be just so. In his job he's working to thousands of an inch and if he does anything in the house it has to be exactly right. He does everything at a snail's pace and he's always late, in fact the only thing he does fast is run.'

Margot's influence on Allan's career has been fundamental, and without her it is difficult to imagine how he could have achieved half of the things he did. He is driven by an almost insatiable pursuit of excellence, and during his long career his intense dedication and hard work have brought to the sport a sense of professionalism which has encouraged a new generation of sprinters in Britain and perhaps elsewhere in the world. There may have been greater sprinters, but in fighting his way to the top with guts, determination and sweat, Allan was simply outstanding.

THE SUPERMEN

1984 Carl Lewis

'*It was more like a religious experience . . . I remember feeling very tall, very strong like I had just conquered the world*'

Ben Johnson 1987 World Champion

'*I got out so quickly over the first 10 metres I thought I'd come out of my lane . . . by 60 metres I knew that people would have to do something quite remarkable to pass me . . . I want to be remembered as the best sprinter of all time*'

1988 Seoul XXIV Olympic Games

'*The twenty first Olympic Games and the 100 metres comes of age . . . Will there be another new star or will the current Olympic champion make history and re-claim the title "The Fastest Man on Earth"?*'

1984 Carl Lewis

It is difficult to believe that the age of Carl Lewis as the world's fastest man may be at an end. For four years, a considerable span for a sprinter and one that embraced the 1984 Los Angeles Olympics, Carl reigned supreme in both sprints and the long jump. But since 1986 he has been forced to take a back seat in the premier 100 metres event by the emergence of a new star, the muscular figure of Canadian Ben Johnson.

Carl, who has just turned 27, is still the world's number one in the long jump, where he has eight of the 10 best jumps in history, and at 200 metres, a distance Johnson chooses to avoid, Carl is still the master. The astonishing performance of 'Bullet' Ben in shattering the world 100 metres record in 9.83 during last year's World Championships in Rome, has served to dull Carl's achievements in the eyes of the public, yet he is still undoubtedly the best natural athlete in the world, the greatest of his era and possibly the greatest of

Carl Lewis accelerates past a top-class field of international athletes to easily win the 100 metres 1984 Los Angeles Olympic title

all time. The mere mention of his name at a track meeting is enough to send the box office tills jangling, and he is one of the most sought after and highly paid athletes in the world, presenting an unprecedented 'larger than life', almost Hollywood image of the sport.

Johnson might have knocked him off his 100 metres pedestal, but Carl is still the reigning Olympic champion, a track millionaire and only the second man in history to win four gold medals at a single Olympic Games. His achievements, like those of his guiding light Jesse Owens, will be remembered forever. However, his astonishing success as a competitor has proved that even exceptional athletic ability is no guarantee of popularity, and he has become a curiously unappreciated champion, especially in the United States, where his behaviour has earned him disdain in some quarters and closed doors from the commercial world. The latter seems scarcely credible, given that a presentable, articulate, multi-gold medal winning athletic superstar like Lewis should present the perfect image to the marketing world, yet his much vaunted career as a corporate megastar hardly took off.

It is here that the story of Carlton Frederick Lewis takes a different turn to those of his predecessors. He could not have had a better grounding in track and field, born into the sports crazy Lewis family in Birmingham, Alabama, in 1961, where father Bill was a 49 second quarter-miler and mother Evelyn one of the world's top hurdlers during the early 1950s. His older brothers, Mack and Cleve, were also quality sportsmen, with Mack an impressive 9.7 100 yards man and Cleve a professional soccer player, whereas younger sister Carol would become one of the world's top long jumpers and the first American woman to clear 7 metres. Carl has no memories of the deep south because he was only

two years old when his parents moved to the pleasant Philadelphia suburb of Willingboro in New Jersey, where his parents worked as high school teachers and coached at the local track club.

With his sporting background, it seemed natural that young Carl should follow in the family tradition, but he was a slow developer and at one stage it seemed that he might be the only member of the Lewis family not to excel in sports. He was shy, quiet and, for a time, smaller than his sister Carol, who was two years his junior, thus earning the nickname of 'Shorty'.

'I was kind of a slow learner, and a non developer, or whatever you want to call it,' says Carl, 'and it was interesting to see my brothers and even Carol far exceeding the things I could do. They were all very successful at a young age and I was just the opposite. I was reserved and shy, but as time went on I started to evolve, to mature and grow a little bit, then the talent just came to me.'

He was always quiet at school, and it was not until he attended high school that he began to develop physically and then as an athlete, finally fulfilling the hopes of his parents. He loves to tell the story about a maths teacher at school who lambasted him for turning up in class on crutches to support a damaged knee. 'I had a knee problem which was associated with me growing so fast at that particular time,' remembers Carl, 'and when I explained the problem he just said, "Yeah, you little jerk you're not going to be an athlete or anything like one!" He just blew me off and it was frustrating, but at the same time it helped because it made me want to go on and prove him wrong.'

Similarly while Carl was playing soccer he fell foul of the school coach who complained he was uncoachable and would never amount to anything in sport. Both incidents served to drive him on to better things. Thankfully, Carl had the sporting knowledge and encouragement of his family, so when things became difficult he always turned to them for help. But life with the Lewis family was not all sports and Carl's parents were acutely aware that they had to create other diversions for their children. Young Carl became an avid visitor to the cinema, sang with his sister in the local church choir and even learned to play the cello – all leisure activities that gave him an appreciation for the unusual, cultural pursuits he enjoys today.

At the age of 12 he was introduced by his father to a man who would become a constant source of inspiration and whose achievements he would one day emulate – the great Jesse Owens. Carl met him at an Owens track and field meet, which was part of a nationwide programme for youngsters, and was immediately impressed. The ageing Owens joined sprinter Steve Williams and long jumper Arnie Robinson as Carl's childhood heroes. A year after meeting Owens he began to take a more serious interest in long jumping, which he had first tried as a nine-year-old jumping into some sand his father had put down as the foundations for a patio. His imagination was fired by Bob Beamon's miraculous world record jump of 29ft 2½in (8.90m) during the 1968 Olympics – a distance Carl then marked off in his front garden.

He began dreaming of making a 28-foot jump long before the idea of competing in an Olympic Games entered his head. It was not until 1979, the year before Moscow, that he realised he had a chance of making the US team. The metamorphosis began in 1976 and in one month he grew an amazing two-and-a-half inches in height and was attracting the attention of discerning people within the sport. During that year his 100 yards time dropped from an ordinary 10.6 to a world-class 9.3 and he began to jump regularly over 20 feet. He was placed fourth in the AAU junior championships in the long jump and ran the 100 metres in a personal best 10.5, but it was in 1979 that his athletic career really took off. Still under the careful coaching guidance of his parents, he leaped an impressive 8.07 in an Illinois high school meeting, taking the US high school record and a world best for a 17-year-old. Soon after that triumph he came second in the US senior championships with an 8.09, a jump that prompted the *Track & Field News*, the most respected track and field journal in America, to describe Lewis as 'a tall, lean high schooler with mind boggling potential'.

His performances earned him a place on the US team for the 1979 Pan American Games in Puerto Rico, where he took a bronze medal with a jump of 8.13 just six days after his eighteenth birthday, a leap that helped rank him fifth in the world in the long jump at the end of that year. Carl Lewis had arrived.

In 1979 he had joined the University of Houston, where he came under the keen eye of coach Tom Tellez, who had been a key man in the athletic careers of triple jumper Willie Banks and high jumper Dwight Stones. Tellez, who is still his coach, began working with Carl to completely change his long jumping style and also helped improve his sprint skills, so much so that he was able to make a clean sweep of the sprints in the 1980 US junior championships. For Tellez, Carl is something of a perennial experiment, where he is feeding in information and seeing the results on

the track or in the long jump pit – like programming a computer. Although the Americans had decided to boycott the Moscow Olympics, the so-called Olympic Trials were held as planned, with Carl making the 'shadow' team in the long jump and as fourth placed man in the sprints, he was also selected for the relay team, alongside Floyd, Glance and Lattany. Missing the Olympics did not bother him unduly. 'It really wasn't that bad for me, because I was 18 when I made the team and 19 when we made the alternative tour in Europe. I was young and I felt the world was in front of me. I don't think I would have won anything anyway, but I think I would have got a medal in the long jump and I might have run in the relay, but I just looked to the future and I knew I'd be back and I'd have another opportunity.'

Despite a nagging foot injury, Carl ran well in the post-Olympic tour in Europe, but he could only manage fifth in the 100 metres race in Cologne in which Allan Wells beat Floyd. His year ended with him being ranked sixth in the world in the long jump and seventh for the 100 metres. During the winter of 1980-81, Carl toiled through a gruelling weight-training programme devised by Tellez to develop his build and strength. The benefits were apparent when the indoor season opened in February 1981 and he ran a 6.06 60 yards, which was just outside the world record, and then jumped 8.49 to smash Larry Myricks' indoor long jump world mark. A week later in the US Indoor

Carl Lewis is airborne in his attempt to beat Beamon's long jump record of 29ft 2½in and to become the greatest long jumper of all time

Championships in New York, he could manage only second place behind Myricks with a jump of 8.06 – but it was the last time he lost a long jump!

'We've had a lot of rocky times,' admits Carl, 'and there were times when I almost didn't win, but right now the long jump is the best it's ever been. There are a lot of good jumpers out there, but the key factor for me is that I just know a lot more about the event. I understand the approach, the adjustments, what I need to do at the board and how to leave it.'

Naturally his ultimate target is to break Beamon's record, something that once seemed impossible. The distance is probably more important to him than any other record or title. 'It may not make sense, but 29 feet is more important than 29ft 2½in, he explains. 'I believe in barriers and 29 feet is my next barrier, my goal, and if I achieve that then we're talking such a small extra distance that I don't think that will be such a big deal. Because once I jump 29 feet I'll know why I did and how I did it and I'll know how to duplicate it. I'm not saying I'll go out and jump it five times a meet but I definitely believe that when I do it I'll understand it so well I'll be able to do it again.'

Despite his defeat at the hands of Myricks, 1981

turned into a special year for Carl, and in Dallas in May he performed the greatest double in history, leaping 8.25 and running a 10 seconds flat 100 metres beating his previous legal best by 0.21 of a second. Carl followed this success with another major double, taking the NCAA titles in the long jump and the 100 metres – the first man to do so since Jesse Owens in 1936 – and then followed suit at the TAC championships in Sacramento. That summer he toured Europe, where his appearance at the World Cup in Rome was eagerly awaited, but a hamstring problem dogged him throughout, and although he won the long jump he was unable to give his best in the 100 metres and finished a miserable last in a career-worst 10.96, in a race won by Allan Wells.

Despite this one poor performance, Carl was ranked number one in the 100 metres, ahead of Wells and his countrymen Floyd and Lattany. *Track & Field News* voted him the US Athlete of the Year, and second to Seb Coe in the world. To cap it all, he was presented with the prestigious Sullivan Award by the AAU, the first black athlete to win the title of the top sportsman or woman, since Wilma Rudolph back in the 1960s. 'It was a very gratifying end to a great season,' said Lewis, 'especially the number one ranking, because after Rome I didn't know if I would get it. I felt very good about that and I really felt I deserved it, because I had run better than anyone, except for one race. But being number one really motivated me and helped me to move on, because a year before everyone had said I couldn't be a world class jumper and sprinter.'

It was a ranking that Carl would retain for the next four years in the 100 metres and one he still holds in the long jump. The following year began with problems when the University of Houston declared him academically ineligible by virtue of failing a history course. Carl maintains that the reasoning behind the university's action was fear of a much-heralded NCAA investigation into college track programmes in the USA. He had taken a history test but claimed that the school subsequently lost his paper and refused a re-test. Therefore he lost his athletics scholarship and had to pay his own fees to complete his degree in TV and radio communication – not really a hardship as one of the school's worries about the NCAA probe was how to explain away Carl's new Porsche.

He continued studying and was able to carry on training at the university, but he also joined the Santa Monica Track Club, under the auspices of his manager Joe Douglas, who began to negotiate on Carl's behalf for his appearances on and off the track. He stayed in school until the spring of 1984 and then worked at a local ABC-TV station to get some 'hands-on' experience of television outside the classroom, a medium he hopes to work in when he retires from the track. Having left the university track team, he had a greater freedom to compete anywhere he chose. The announcement by America's great hurdler Renaldo Nehemiah to quit the sport and play American football enabled Carl to fill the gap he left and to become a major sporting figure in the United States.

Carl now projected himself onto the national sports scene, so much so that the Dallas Cowboys, trawling for another Bob Hayes, wasted a twelfth round draft pick on him, but manager Douglas came up with the immortal line: 'He couldn't afford the pay cut.' Such was the attraction of Carl's prodigious athletic talents that the National Basketball League's Chicago Bulls even tried to draft him, despite the fact that he had not played the sport at high school level. But it was in the following year, 1983, when the fluent, graceful running and easy smile of Carl Lewis were really launched on an international audience, at the inaugural World Championships in Helsinki. Until then, apart from the occasional foray into Europe, his best performances had been reserved for the few home fans who turned up at the various track meets around the United States. During 1982, the best of these included the TAC Championships in Knoxville, Tennessee, where Carl ran a breathtaking 10.11 into a headwind while turning to wave at the crowd at the finish. The real highlight of the year proved to be the controversial officiating during the long jump at the US Olympic Committee Sports Festival at Indianapolis.

Carl leaped a magnificent 8.76, a world best at sea level and generally regarded as a superior jump to Beamon's world record set at altitude, but some people believe he was cheated out of a genuine world record during the same competition. In the fourth round, he literally took off into the pit, a jump that had everybody on their feet, but it was greeted by a red flag and universal groans from the crowd. Carl examined the take-off board to see where he had fouled, but there was no mark on the plasticine line at the front of the board. The officials claimed the toe of his shoe had been slightly over the edge and that had prompted the foul call, but the IAAF rules state that a foul occurs only if the athlete actually touches the ground beyond the board. This would be impossible without making an indentation of some kind on the plasticine indicator line, but the officials refused to change their decision and the foul stood. There have been various suggestions as to how far he jumped: one competitor estimated it to be over 30 feet, whereas Carl himself reckoned that he had cleared 30ft 2in (9.19).

All his performances that year convinced the track world that he was going to be a mighty force during the World Championships, but he decided not to compete in the 200 metres, where he was most inexperienced, and to concentrate instead on the 100 metres, long jump and the relay. He qualified to run in all three at the TAC Championships (the trials for Helsinki), easily winning the 100 metres, leaping an incredible 8.79 – the second longest jump in history at the time – and clinching his spot on the relay team. He ran in the 200 metres at the trials, clocking the second fastest time ever in 19.75, just two-hundredths of a second outside Pietro Mennea's world record, set at altitude. But his own inimitable style cost him the record, as he looked both left and right with 10 metres to go and, seeing that no-one was near him, he broke into a huge smile, threw his arms into the air and coasted through to the finish.

In Helsinki, he was simply in a different class to the rest of the athletes present and he comfortably won his two main events, the 100 metres and the long jump. In the former, he accelerated smoothly

past everyone at about 75 metres, leaving fellow countryman Calvin Smith, the new world record holder, in his wake. Smith had come to the Games confident of beating Lewis, especially after shaving two-hundredths of a second off Jim Hines' long-standing world record of 9.95 in the thin air of Colorado Springs a month before arriving in Finland. Considering that Carl was behind both Smith and Emmitt King at 70 metres, his margin of victory (about a metre and a half) and his time of 10.07, was nothing short of remarkable and demonstrated perfectly what later became known as the Lewis 'gas jets', an almost turbo-charged extra gear into which he clicked with about three-quarters of the race gone – a spectacle that made the rest of the field look as if they were moving in slow motion.

His form continued in the long jump: his first jump of the competition, an 8.55, proved to be the winner and he only bothered to jump once more before withdrawing from the event convinced that he would win. Finally, he anchored the USA's formidable relay quartet of King, Willie Gault and Smith to victory in a new world record of 37.86. By the end of 1983, Carl had recorded the fastest ever sea-level time in the 100 metres (9.97), the second longest jump in history (8.79m), the fastest sea-level 200 metres (19.75) and a share in the world 4 × 100 relay record. He had all the credentials with which to establish himself as the greatest athlete in the world, so when he emerged from Helsinki to tell the eager media that he would shoot for four golds and try to emulate Jesse Owens in Los Angeles, it seemed as though he was on the threshold of mega-stardom.

He started the crucial 1984 season where he left off the previous year, with a series of stunning sprinting and jumping performances leading up to the US Olympic Trials in Los Angeles, where he reeled off an incredible 10.06 into a 2.2 metre per second headwind, regarded by some track experts as the greatest 100 ever. He then leaped 8.71m to win the long jump and clocked an impressive 19.86 in the final of the 200 metres to ensure that he qualified for all four events as the undisputed number one.

The Los Angeles Olympics, boycotted by all the Eastern Bloc states with the exception of Rumania because of their so-called fears over the safety of the athletes and concern about commercialization, opened at the famous Coliseum on 3 August. Naturally, everyone expected Carl to take his

Carl Lewis pleases the Los Angeles Coliseum crowds by taking a victory circuit around the track and waving the American flag

place among the track immortals and walk away with four gold medals. But that was the heart of his problem. The American public not only expected him to win – in their eyes, he already had won. Scores of newspaper and magazine stories about him appeared around the world, with the first wave eagerly detailing his imminent assault on Jesse Owens' haul of four gold medals. The media began to look around for new angles on the Carl Lewis story – they did not have to look far. In the build-up to Los Angeles, Carl and his associates had made some wild claims about the financial potential of winning four gold medals, and the commercial bunfight for Carl's signature began.

He had been doing commercials for the sports firm Nike and the Japanese company Fuji, but in a report in the respected *Newsweek* magazine, his manager Joe Douglas, described his search for a high-class corporate giant for which Carl could be a marketing front man. Even the Association of National Advertisers suggested that if Lewis won four gold medals he would be 'very hot property.' It was nothing new for athletes to cash in on their Olympic fame – the new rules regarding payment to competing athletes enabled them to earn money both on and off the track. Swimmer Mark Spitz and decathlete Bruce Jenner had both made handsome fortunes in the commercial world after their Olympic feats. What was different in Carl's case was the advance planning for his marketing after the Games. He was already earning about 500,000 dollars a year from Nike when the Games began, but Douglas was keen to broaden his commercial appeal. In the *New York Times* he said: 'We hope he'll be a multi-millionaire, but we'll wait and see. I don't think anyone knows how much he'll be worth.'

Thus while Carl was busily preparing for the track, his backers were already doing battle in the boardrooms of potential employers, a tactic that actually dampened his appeal because at the start of an Olympics it appeared somehow unseemly and served to devalue his sporting contribution. Douglas even admitted to the *New York Times* that a marketing plan had been drawn up to cash in on Carl's ability as far back as 1981, designed to turn him into a national hero whose commercial value would rocket after the Games. However, other stories were appearing, too, but not the usual flattering tributes like the two cover stories in *Time* during the three weeks running up to the Games. First, there was a particularly vitriolic piece about him in *Sports Illustrated*, then a Scandanavian scandal sheet printed some unpleasant allegations about his sexual preferences, and yet another publication suggested that he was taking drugs. Suddenly, instead of being hailed as the all-conquering American hero, he was being hounded by the popular press. Turning up late for the few press conferences he gave did not help his cause, dressed outrageously and often attended by an entourage that would befit a heavyweight boxer. He had already won the medals, taken his place on the champion's pedestal and been knocked off it, all before he had set foot on the track in Los Angeles. If he did not win all four golds he would be branded a failure. If he succeeded, no-one would be surprised because he was expected to do so.

Stories about his opulent lifestyle began to appear in the press, detailing the splendours of his Victorian mansion in Houston and his penchant for collecting fine crystal. A *Newsweek* article described how their reporter was greeted by a uniformed servant and led into a luxurious living room for an interview with Carl, who appeared in a blue silk Japanese bathrobe and complained that the athletic authorities were 'very strict' about billing furniture to his trust fund. Even the other athletes on the US team joined in, including the respected hurdler Ed Moses who accused Lewis of 'showboating'. Larry Myricks, for so long the bridesmaid to Carl in the long jump, bleated: 'There's going to be some serious celebrating when Carl gets beat.' Carl dealt with the adverse publicity the only way he knew: by denying the more unpleasant stories, especially about drugs and his private life; and by refusing to live in the Olympic village and shunning the accepted daily press conferences. This did not improve his profile in the eyes of the public at the very time when he was about to make his greatest sporting strides forward. In the middle of the pre-Olympic storm was the respected track writer of the *New York Times*, Frank Litsky. 'Carl Lewis is a superb athlete, make no mistake about it. But he has a problem with a bad public image. He went into the Olympics with an opportunity to win four gold medals and become one of the great merchandising stars of our generation, of our century. He won four gold medals and actually went downhill as a merchandising attraction. I think it was just bad handling by his people, many things went wrong and any opportunity they had to present him in a good light they either forgot or did the opposite.

'At a press conference before the Games he arrived 45 minutes late, dressed outlandishly with his huge entourage. During the Games he didn't hold a daily press conference like most of the other athletes, saying he would only speak to the media after the gold medal events, that's four times in something like 11 days. Instead of spending 15 minutes a day answering questions and getting the media off his back, he stayed away and the media got angry, especially those members who were not track writers and had no knowledge or interest in track and just wanted to ask the guy a few questions. He just seemed to lose ground everywhere.'

With all this going on it was a miracle that Carl managed to perform as he did on the track, but he is philosophical about the experience. 'The problem I had was that everybody had their idea of what they wanted me to be or how I had to act. In most cases I didn't fit the mould and people created things. Reporters sought out athletes to say negative things about me and I never went out and said a lot of things about the money, it was just taken out of context. Joe made a statement once that if I won four gold medals it would put me at the same level in sport that Michael Jackson is in music. That was turned around to read Carl should be as rich as Michael Jackson.'

Carl brushes off some of the scurrilous things that were written about his private life and suggestions that he was involved in drug taking. 'It didn't hurt me as much as people think it did,' he says, 'because I knew where it was coming from. It was other athletes in my sport and a lot of the press people wanted something like that to write about, but they couldn't say it until someone else did. Once they got a little bit they snatched it like a baton on an anchor leg. It didn't bother me that much because only a couple of these athletes made the team and they didn't do well.'

He managed to reduce the pressures by avoiding newspapers and living away from the village, thus earning strong criticism in the United States, even though other top athletes like Mary Decker, Ed Moses and sprinter Ron Brown also stayed clear of the mayhem. Carl decided to treat his mammoth task simply, taking each race as it came and not putting pressure on himself by expecting to win every one. His philosophy was that winning the four gold medals was important, but going out and doing his best was even more so.

The first event was the 100 metres, in which his toughest rivals came from the USA, with reigning champion Allan Wells injured and no Eastern Bloc surprises. It was a copybook run and Carl totally outclassed a good sprint field, turning on the 'gas jets' at about 60 metres and hurtling past everyone to win by the biggest margin ever in an Olympic final, an amazing two-and-a-half metres

Carl Lewis on the gold medallist's rostrum having received his medal; Sam Graddy was awarded the silver and Ben Johnson (right) the bronze

from second-placed American Sam Graddy, in 9.99 seconds. The improving Canadian Ben Johnson took third, but he was nowhere near Carl. 'I didn't react well at the gun,' recalls Carl, 'and when I stood up at about 15 metres I saw Sam was ahead of me, in fact quite a few people were ahead of me, but I just stayed relaxed and the whole time I new I was going to win. When I hit the finish line I really didn't know what to feel at the time because you're always so removed, it didn't really sink in until I saw my parents.'

Carl's mother Evelyn could not bear to watch the race and father Bill would not let her go down to the track to congratulate her son, waving Carl away to do his own lap of honour, something he did in some style, grabbing a huge American flag and trotting around the track waving it enthusiastically as the 92,600 sell-out crowd cheered wildly. Carl eventually got to Coach Tellez, who proved to be just as outwardly emotional as his father. 'He just stuck out his hand, shook mine and said, "You should have had a world record". So this is what I have to deal with. The man wants perfection.'

The medal ceremony was a highlight for Carl even though he would go through the routine another three times before the Games ended, but he remembers it particularly because Graddy was on the podium with him. 'It was nice to have another American there and the crowd was very vocal and very pro-American and every move you made they just cheered. It was really a great experience to think that the whole world was sharing the moment with you, it was more like a religious experience because it was really spiritual and really special. I remember feeling very tall, very strong, like I'd just conquered the world.'

It seemed as though all the bad publicity had been blown away in less than 10 seconds of explosive running, but a few days later events took another wrong turn, this time during the long jump competition. The long jump final was held on the Monday afternoon, just a few hours after Carl had run a couple of heats in the 200 metres, and he was feeling a little soreness in his leg. He opened up with a leap of 8.54, just a fraction over 28 feet, fouled the second and then decided to sit out the rest of the competition, just like the 1983 World Championships, confident that no-one would exceed his jump. Again he was right, but when it became clear to the enormous crowd, who had paid top prices to see the competition, that Carl was not going to jump again they began to get frustrated and then angry. They even booed him during the medal ceremony that followed.

'People were very upset,' remembers Frank Litsky, 'because they'd spent 60 dollars a ticket. Carl was supposed to jump six times, that's 10 dollars a jump. If he and his people had thought about this they could have got him to clutch his hamstring in agony after the second jump and he would have had all the sympathy in the world, but he didn't do it and he lost more ground with the American public.'

Carl was philosophical about the incident at the time, commenting that it was flattering that they were booing because they wanted to see more of him, which was partly true. Today he explains: 'I remember having a problem with my leg and as the afternoon went on the temperature began to drop and I didn't want to take a risk on getting injured, because I had two more events still to go.

'I don't fault the crowd at all for booing, because I don't think most of them were very knowledgeable about track and field. I do fault the media for making a big deal out of nothing.'

In the 200 metres a couple of days later he produced another awesome piece of running, perhaps the best demonstration of curve running ever, to win his third gold medal, hitting the finish line well clear of his two American rivals, Kirk Baptiste and Thomas Jefferson, in a new Olympic record of 19.80, despite a fairly strong headwind that was blowing down the home straight.

A few days later he trotted back onto the track to complete the formalities of his quadruple gold by anchoring the USA relay team to victory in another world record time of 37.83, alongside Sam Graddy, Ron Brown and Calvin Smith. His personal clocking from a flying start was an incredible 8.94 and he stormed away from the rest of the field to double the American winning margin to an astonishing eight metres. It was his thirteenth competition in just eight days. 'To duplicate one of track and field's greatest feats is an honour,' he told newsmen. 'Everybody said it couldn't be done, even I said over a year ago that I didn't think I could do it. Jesse Owens is still the same man to me he was before – he is a legend.'

So Carl's job was complete: he had taken the four gold medals he was expected to win, emulated the achievement of the great Owens and was now ready to accept the predicted avalanche of commercial offers and the cascades of dollars that would obviously be coming his way. However it did not happen that way at all. The pre-Games publicity and some of the poisonous stories that had been appearing about him during the Olympics had hurt him more than he knew. Worse was still to come when Britain's decathlon gold medalist Daley Thompson took his lap of honour around the stadium wearing a T-shirt bearing the slogan: 'Is the world's 2nd greatest athlete gay?' It was a slur that had dogged Carl for some time before the Games and an unworthy snipe on Thompson's part. Daley tried to laugh it off at a press conference by pretending that the word gay in England meant happy, but understandably Carl was far from happy about the whole affair, although to his credit he managed to keep cool and never let it show.

'I never developed the macho side as a lot of boys do,' he told one newspaper. 'Even my sister Carol shows more masculinity, but that doesn't make me a homosexual. They say I am, but I'm not. They say it because nobody knows what I'm doing. I don't even stay in the same hotels as the other athletes, I could be sleeping with a horse for all they know.

'Basically I'm a loner and that's why they say it. They say it about Michael Jackson for the same reason. If I was weak minded I could become paranoid about the accusations, instead I feel that as long as I know what I am it doesn't matter what people say.'

So much mud had been thrown at Carl during

the Games that some of it was obviously going to stick, true or not, and as a result the offers from major companies did not materialize. Even the giant Coca Cola corporation, which had been keen to link up with Carl and use him as a marketing weapon, backed off after the Olympics. 'Some of the offers before the Games were very, very good, but then came the negative publicity,' said manager Douglas, at the time. 'We are very disappointed. We lost Coca Cola and we've not had the kind of deals we'd expected since then.'

Looking back at the Games and the way in which Carl was treated, it is clear that he was the victim of a major smear campaign by the press. He had created some friction by failing to attend conferences or extend the normal pleasantries to reporters, and they reacted in the time-honoured way. He could have been faulted had he not performed on the track in the way he did, but he came away with four gold medals. 'I don't think a lot of the media know how much it takes to compete in four events at an Olympics,' says sister Carol, who saw the campaign at first hand. 'He competed almost every day and they didn't realise that to run qualifiers at nine in the morning, you can't get up at 8.30, take a shower and leave, like you're going to work. You have to get up at five in the morning, then nap in the afternoon, between heats, then go home and eat dinner and be in bed about 8.30 so you can be back up the next day functioning correctly.'

The general public, however, did not care about the hard work and dedication that went on behind the scenes – all they wanted to see was the finished result. As it turned out the real hero of the Games, as far as the USA was concerned, turned out to be the gymnast Mary Lou Retton, who thrived in the absence of the sport's 'heavyweights' from the Eastern Bloc and won the hearts of the nation in much the same way as Olga Korbut had done back in Munich in 1972. Carl admits that after the Games he felt very different, but for perhaps the wrong reasons because his profile was higher than ever before. As for the commercial disappointments, he can now afford to laugh at some of the things that were being said about him. 'After the Games some of the companies were saying, "Oh, he's so strange, his haircut is strange," and this and that. But a few months earlier I wanted to change my hair and one corporation said, "Don't change it, because it's unique". I don't think they really knew what they wanted.'

After the Olympics there were no further major titles for him to aim at until the next World Championships in 1987. Thus in 1985 Carl tried to

Another Michael Jackson? 'I can't sing as well as he can, but he can't run as fast as I do', says the Carl Lewis of the future

beat Beamon's long jump record, but despite remaining unbeaten and coming very close once or twice, it proved to be a frustrating time. Towards the end of the season he suffered an injury during a long jump competition and decided to use the time it would take to get back to peak fitness to have a break from the track. He concentrated on his acting and singing careers, a decision that led to a couple of movies, some TV appearances and some records and live shows, including a TV special in Japan, where he is regarded as the new Michael Jackson. It is a comparison that is often repeated and Carl once answered a reporter who enquired whether he felt he might be as big as Jackson, 'Physically definitely. I can't sing as well as he does, but he can't run as fast as I do.' However, he is serious about wanting to make acting and music his future career after athletics. He has studied at New York's Warren Robertson Theatre Workshop and enjoys writing and producing his own songs. 'To me it almost feels like athletics,' says Carl, 'because there's the preparation, the hard work, study, practice, dedication and the satisfaction of doing it, finishing and sitting back to enjoy it. I'd like to be recognised as a singer. If I sell 50 or 50,000,000 records a year it doesn't matter, I just enjoy it. But right now we're not even into the athlete who sings yet, but I'd like people to respect me as a singer. As far as the acting goes I'd like to play in some action adventures. Of course the good thing about it is that after the financial success I've had in track and field I don't have the pressure of trying to be a millionaire out of entertainment.'

Carl can identify certain similarities between himself and Michael Jackson, especially in their appreciation of the bizarre and the pleasure they both take in being eccentric. 'He's his own person and he keeps people dancing as to what he's like. In my track world I do the same thing. People don't see me very often, but when I'm out I'm very flashy and outgoing.'

Actually, the real Carl Lewis is a much more reserved and quiet person than perhaps even he cares to admit, and it's rare to see pictures of him appearing in the newspapers or magazines taken at clubs or big events. A few months after the Olympics he was no longer in the headlines, and after his injury in 1985 he even disappeared from the sports pages, choosing his competitions sparingly during 1986. He moved from his much publicized house in Houston, which had suffered two robberies and a constant stream of tourists, some of whom would camp on his front drive waiting to catch a glimpse of him. Today he keeps his address a closely guarded secret and few people outside his own close circle of family and friends are allowed there.

On the track he still managed to merit a number one ranking in 1985 in the 100 metres, despite his injury, and that upset the fast improving Ben Johnson, who felt that he warranted more than second place. However, it spurred Ben on to greater things and gave him the desire and the hunger to return in 1986 and ensure that he became the undisputed number one and stayed there – something he achieved.

Ben Johnson is a remarkable athlete in so far as he had been on the athletics scene for some time before making the jump into world class in 1985 – the year after he finished third in the Olympics. Today both he and Carl have changed the perception of the 100 metres, and the event is now one of the most eagerly awaited of the 1988 Games in Seoul. It surprises people when they realise that Ben Johnson is almost as old as Carl whose dominance overshadowed practically every other sprinter in the world until 1985, when Ben started to make some impressive runs around Europe. Until then, Ben had had a reputation as a fast starter who would burn up after 80 metres and could be caught by fast finishers. However, from his determination and his colossal efforts in training, a new-look Ben Johnson has evolved. The difference between the athlete of the 1984 Olympics and today's version is striking – the former a

A picture of power: Ben Johnson pictured after his incredibly fast start, shows just why he is feared around the tracks of the world

mere shadow of the muscular man who dominates the event today.

Ben was just 12 years old when he and his family emigrated to Canada from Jamaica, but it was another three years before his brother took him to the local track club in Toronto for his first taste of running on a proper track. 'I wanted to quit after two weeks,' says Ben, 'because I couldn't even make it around the track. But his brother and the club's coach, Charley Francis, persuaded the skinny teenager to stick at it, and six months later they were rewarded when Ben ran a 100 yards race in 10.3 in a pair of donated spikes. It was a performance, Francis felt, that warranted spending more time on the young Johnson. By 1979, he had gained over 40lbs and was competing internationally for Canada. The following year he came second in the national championships and would have gone to Moscow had the Canadian Government not joined the boycott. Within 12 months, Ben had run a 10.25, in Venezuela – the turning point of Ben's career according to Francis. 'From that point on I was sure his potential was virtually unlimited. Everything from then on was up to him.'

Ben began weight-training seriously to lay the foundations for the impressive physique he has today. It also gave him the extra strength to keep going for another 20 metres and not to burn out before the finish of a race. However, that came later, because in 1982 he was still fading after 80 metres, although he was widely regarded as the fastest man to that mark, and indoors he was simply amazing. One man who helped him in his early days was the ageing ex-Olympic champion Percy Williams, who taught Ben several of the old exercises he once used, some of which Ben still uses today. He took a silver in the 100 metres, behind Allan Wells, in the 1982 Commonwealth Games, and two bronzes at the LA Olympics, in the 100 metres and the relay. By this time Ben had dropped the mechanic's course he was taking at college and decided to take up athletics full time with a dedication and concentration probably never before seen in an athlete; he even made the training routine of Allan Wells seem lightweight!

In the autumn of 1984, he lowered the Canadian record to 10.12 at the giant Weltklasse meeting in Zurich, returning the following year to win the same race *and* beat Carl Lewis. In 1985, he lowered his personal best to 10.00 in the World Cup in Australia, and took the world record to 6.50 over 60 metres in Japan. Despite this success and the huge demand for Ben on the European circuit he was still only rated number two behind Carl Lewis when the rankings were published in January 1986. This upset him for a number of reasons, not just because he felt he deserved to be number one but also because the ratings were not merely a paper excerise but genuinely affected appearance money, sponsorship and endorsement possibilities, all of which had been thin on the ground in his native Canada, where ice hockey star Wayne Gretzky and swimmer Alex Baumann were dominating the field. The situation may be partly responsible for the apparent rivalry between Ben and Carl, but talking to the athletes themselves there is clearly little animosity between them. 'I don't think there's a real rivalry because Ben is really low key,' says Carl. 'I think

it comes from his coaches and management, they like the idea of the rivalry. To them I'm like the old war horse against the new rising star – who's actually the same age as me – and I'm not into all that and I'm not sure he is either.'

Smiles Ben: 'He doesn't want to say I'm better than he is because he's not running any slower than he was in '84, but I've got better over the years. I think he tries to make something big out of it.' Certainly Ben has not enjoyed Carl's degree of success off the track. He has two things running against him, the first being his nationality – in Canada track and field is even less popular as a spectator sport than it is in the United States, and although interest in the sport is growing fast since he broke the world record he has not received the financial incentives available in America. The second is a problem that he has been fighting to overcome for years – a stammer. A penalty, he says, for teasing his brother as a child, but it is something that before the 1987 World Championships deterred commercial offers.

Early in 1988 he signed the world's biggest individual sports sponsorship deal, worth an estimated £2,000,000 with the Italian sportswear company Diadora. It will be interesting to see if he becomes the world's richest athlete ever.

For Ben, winning a gold medal in the 100 metres in Seoul is the solution to many of the problems that have dogged him over the years. His whole race is geared to his start and it is a lethal weapon. It has even inspired scientists to study it at length, because his speed off the blocks deceives the eye and sometimes even the start computer, which leads to accusations that he jumps before the gun. Coach Francis insists that the start computer is set at either 0.1000 or 0.1200 of a second and the average reaction time for a sprinter is 0.16; for Ben it is only 0.0997 and sometimes that can cause problems. A scientific study conducted at the University of Ottawa suggests that his speed is unique among sprinters. The researchers' evidence has been gleaned from poring over slow-motion film of his technique during last year's indoor Winternational Games in Canada, when Ben set a new world record best for the 50 metres in 5.55. They found a number of stunning facts: first, that Ben uses 3,000 watts of energy in one stride, which is more than enough to light up an average mansion; and second, that he brakes more efficiently than a car. Ben also intrigued the scientists by running in what they described as a completely different style to that of other sprinters. Leading the inquiry was Professor Gord Robertson, who explained: 'We

Athletics history in the making: Ben Johnson smashes the world 100 metres record in 9.83 seconds at the 1987 World Championships

have always felt that sprinters landed high on their toes and the heel would barely touch the ground. But this is not what happened in Ottawa. Everybody was landing on their heels, but Ben wasn't.' The professor explained that Ben ran high on his toes with the ankle fully extended upwards, just like an animal. 'Dogs run like that,' says Robertson. 'They run on their fingers with their heels inches off the ground.' The scientists concluded that this strange style was responsible for Ben's incredible spring.

Other studies have revealed that Ben accelerates through the first 60 metres and then holds his speed, about 43 kilometres an hour, to the line. He used this style to great effect during 1986, when he won a series of top races in exceptional times, including a sea-level best of 9.95 in the Goodwill Games in Moscow. For the first time in four years, Carl Lewis was relegated to the number two position in the 1986 world 100 metre rankings, with Ben Johnson taking over at the top. So the 1987 season began with Carl announcing that he was casting aside his 'other interests' for the time being to concentrate fully on training for the Rome World Championships at the end of August.

The scene was set for an exciting build-up to their classic confrontation on the track in Italy, billed by the media as the greatest head-to-head sprinting clash of all time and reminiscent of the great sporting rivalries of Ali-Frazier or Borg-McEnroe. There have, of course, been other great sprint rivalries, such as Hines-Greene, Morrow-Sime or Owens-Metcalfe, but the new popularity of track and field, brought into millions of homes through television ensured that this confrontation was going to be enjoyed and debated all over the world by a massive audience.

Throughout the year, both athletes provided evidence on the track that they were running up to peak form in Rome, especially Ben, who did not have to worry about competing in the long jump, where it was suspected that the true loyalties of Carl Lewis actually lay. In their first and only meeting on the track prior to the World Championships, Carl was convinced that he had pipped Ben on the line in a meeting in Seville, Spain, but the race was awarded to the Canadian by just one-hundredth of a second, in 10.06. That made the official scores in the ongoing sprint match: Lewis eight, Johnson five. As Carl had not beaten Ben since 1985, the favourite was still the Canadian, who had put together the six fastest 60 metres times ever and had not been beaten over the 100 metres since his surprising defeat at the hands of Allan Wells in Gateshead in 1986 after emerging as the sprint champion from the Edinburgh Commonwealth Games. After defeating his rival, Ben embarked on a series of sprint races unrivalled in track history, starting with a new season's best in Canada of 10.02, followed by an impressive tour of Europe, then back to Canada for the national championships, where he registered a 9.98, returning to Europe where he ran in 9.95 in Cologne and a 9.97 in Zurich. He had been threatening to blast Calvin Smith's world record all summer and Coach Francis thought it might happen in the World Championships, while Ben would say only that he was confident that he would run a 9.8 by the end of the year.

Meanwhile, all Carl could offer was to place second in the US trials behind his Santa Monica training partner Mark Witherspoon, so the scales were continuing to tilt Ben's way. Now everyone wanted to know about 'Bullet' Ben, and even the Americans, who had been predicting that Carl would retain his 100 metres title, were beginning to make worried noises. Ben was now in the best shape of his life, fired up to prove to everyone that he was the undisputed number one in the world, and he wanted to do it in the ideal setting – the 100 metres final at the World Championships. For 10 years, he had been training towards one goal, to be number one, and for the last five years he had submitted himself to a daily tortuous four-hour training regime in which he was lifting increasingly heavy weights to get stronger and more powerful. He is now believed to be bench-pressing more than twice his own body weight – more than 350 lbs – but he can squat-lift more than 500 lbs – more than the giant linebackers in the NFL.

It was difficult for the press to build a picture of the new star because Ben is a shy, quiet and introverted man, preferring to live almost anonymously in a Toronto suburb in a house he built for his mother. He shuns the limelight and lets his running do the talking. He certainly is not the most loquacious athlete on the circuit, despite his quiet sense of humour; so when the clans began to gather in Rome in August, it was to Carl Lewis that the pressmen flocked for news of the coming confrontation and they listened attentively while Carl held court at his palatial rented villa high up in the hills overlooking the city.

Intriguingly it was Carl who looked the part in the heats, running an almost embarrassingly casual first round in 10.05, a championship record, and cutting that to 10.03 in the semi-final. Meanwhile, Ben was doing only what he had to in order to qualify for the next round, but in the semi-final he gave warning of his intent by springing into a three-metre lead right from the start and shutting down all engines just after halfway, lost two metres on the rest of the field in the last 10 metres and still won in 10.15. Now it was time for the final, the most eagerly awaited clash of the championships, where eight of the world's best sprinters were ready to do battle, but in their heart of hearts six of them knew that they were racing only for third place. This was essentially a match race between the two greatest sprinters of the era, Ben Johnson with his incredible start and Carl Lewis with his incredible finish, but which would prevail?

At the gun, Ben seemed to explode out of the blocks as if fired by a cannon and his start was so powerful that he almost lost control and veered into Carl's lane beside him. But by 10 metres he was so far ahead of the rest of the field, particularly Carl that the race was effectively over. By 50 metres the Canadian was bombing, and though Carl began to gain fractionally towards the end the gap was simply too big to close, and Ben powered through to the finish.

Astonishment filled the stadium as the crowd looked at the clock which read unofficially 9.84, a mark that was quickly rounded down to 9.83. Ben Johnson had dismantled a record that had only been nipped at down the years in hundredths of a second, but he had lopped one-tenth of a second off Smith's altitude record and had achieved it at sea-level with a negligible wind behind him.

Lewis was so astonished that his face was almost frozen in dismay as he too looked up at the clock in disbelief. So far behind Johnson was he that he was convinced he had run about 10 seconds flat, while Ben had run another 9.95 or 9.97, but Carl had just run the fastest 100 metres of his life, a 9.93, which equalled the old world record but gave him only the silver medal. The race was the highlight of the World Championships and overshadowed the remainder of the proceedings. It was a record of Herculean proportions and one that may not be beaten for another 50 years.

'I got out so quickly over the first 10 metres I thought I'd come out of my lane,' admitted Ben. 'By 60 metres I knew that people would have to do something quite remarkable to pass me.' Carl just could not catch him and it was his sixth straight defeat at the hands of the Canadian, bringing the match score to Carl eight, Johnson six. Said Carl: 'I feel I've been KO'd.'

In financial terms the victory has done wonders for Ben Johnson as a marketable force both on and off the track, and his form continued early in 1988 where he twice broke the world 50 yards record indoors, but his ultimate goal, and it is one that will finally set him apart as possibly the greatest sprinter in history, is to win the 100 metres gold in Seoul. Carl Lewis feels that he can run better and the Olympic 100 metres may well be a closer result than the World Championships.

Carl was never out of the headlines throughout the championships and he made the front pages all over the world when he decided to stand up and voice some of his fears about the level of drug-taking in the sport, a subject that has caused furore in practically every country and still threatens to endanger the future of track and field. It is widely known that drugs are used at the highest levels of athletics and not only by the weight men or the heavy throwers. Drug abuse has become more sophisticated, with the manufacturers light years ahead of the drug detectors. There are now calls for a major investigation worldwide and a better system of detection followed by irrevocable life bans for offenders.

It is impossible to say which athletes are taking drugs in the sport, although one top sprinter suggested that it was easier to identify those who were not involved because the level of dependence is so high. During the championships, Carl told a British TV crew: 'There are gold medallists here already who are definitely taking drugs.' That remark upset Ben's coach, Charley Francis who felt that Lewis was pointing the finger at Ben, although Carl insisted that he was not singling out anyone. 'Some people always have an excuse to make if they lose,' said Francis. 'I can tell you that Ben is very much against drugs. He has never taken them and he never will.'

Carl is unrepentant, however, about his stand on the drugs issue and believes firmly that someone has to speak out before the sport is irreparably damaged. 'There have been two or three people in the history of this sport who have been very outspoken – and I'm one of them. I'm not ashamed because I've never taken drugs and I believe that if I didn't take a stand and left the sport, who else is going to stand up?

'Are we going to be in a situation where for my kids to run in the future they have to take drugs? It's getting noticeably out of hand and we have a duty to let people know that and then to start a

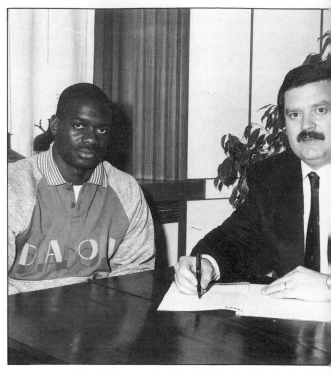

Ben Johnson sets another record as he signs a $3.5 million contract with Italian sportswear company Diadora's President, Roberto Danieli

programme to counteract the spread of drugs, because it is the number one problem in our sport.'

'I find it very difficult to look on modern sprinters with the same sort of admiration as those from the earlier age of innocence,' says former British sprint star Peter Radford, a bronze medallist in the 1960 Olympic 100 metres and now an acknowledged worldwide expert on physical education and sport. ' I don't know why some of the contemporary great sprinters are great, you can never be sure if they have done it legitimately and to my mind that's destroyed the whole ethics of the sport.'

Another man who has been prepared to speak on an otherwise taboo subject for athletes is the great Jamaican sprinter Don Quarrie, who stays close to the sport as a coach. 'When I was competing you only heard about drugs as far as the weight men were concerned, now it's all over. I think that eventually the IAAF will corner the market as far as drug users are concerned because they're putting in a lot of money to make sure parents don't say to their child in the future: "I don't want my child in athletics because of the drugs."

'So I think the IAAF has a lot at stake and

they're determined that people are not ing to get away with it. I know for sure that when I was running a few guys I competed against were taking drugs, but I can't prove it. But I can tell you I beat them and my advice to young athletes out there is that regardless of what an athlete is taking, if you are determined to win, you are well coached and perform at your best, you can beat these people.'

The subject of drugs will be uppermost in the minds of the athletic administrators at the Seoul Olympics and if any athletes are detected taking illegal substances they may well be made examples to the rest of the sport and treated with the utmost severity, which means an almost certain life ban.

As far as the 100 metres in Seoul is concerned it is the big race of the Games and the one that everyone is looking forward to seeing. Can Ben break his own world record? Can Carl run faster? For the first time in recent years, the middle-distance races have been forgotten and the sprint is the talking-point of the Olympics. It should be a classic encounter and probably a much closer race than Rome, but opinion is divided as to who will win the gold medal. Ben Johnson is certainly hungry for the medal and for that reason alone he may prevail, but since Rome, Carl's pride has been wounded and he is not only going to Seoul to defend his own title but also to erase the memory of that stinging defeat.

Carl believes that he can win and knows that no-one has ever come back and retained an Olympic gold medal in the 100 metres. 'It means more to me than a world record,' he says. 'To be the first person to duplicate a gold in the 100 metres at the Olympics would be a great feat, but I also have the opportunity to do that in the long jump and the 200. I think it is possible for me to duplicate all four gold medals in Seoul, though the toughest event will certainly be the 100, but I'm training better, I'm smarter and stronger and I know I have the race to win if I can run it.'

It will be the last time that Carl will be seen on the Olympic stage, because he has maintained his vow to retire after his twenty-eighth birthday, in 1989, and return to his music and acting careers. There could even be a Mrs Lewis in the not-too-distant future, an event that would silence a few scandal-mongers, particularly in the United States. 'Actually I hope so,' says Carl, with a wry smile, 'because I love kids and I'm sure I could take the 'mom because I know I'd love the kids!'

Whatever happens in Seoul, Carl would like to be remembered as an athlete who changed the perceptions of his event, particularly in the long jump, where his ultimate goal is to break that elusive world record and be regarded as the greatest long jumper of all time. He will not be satisfied until that barrier of Bob Beamon's is broken.

The 100 metres final in Seoul, as long as both athletes avoid injury and arrive in South Korea in good health, should be another match race. However, there are several other sprinters who would clearly disagree, including the fast improving Jamaican Ray Stewart, who is developing in terms of physique as well as speed. Third behind Johnson and Lewis in Rome and the dark horse for the Olympic final, Stewart has convinced the 1976 champion Hasely Crawford that he will surprise everyone and win. As for the others, there are Britain's Linford Christie, who finished fourth in Rome and can get better, the USA's Mark Witherspoon, who actually beat Lewis in the trials and then picked up an injury that ruined his chances in the world championships, and Nigeria's Chidi Imo.

The 100 metres has changed very little over the years in terms of the way it is run, with historians suggesting that throughout the last century Man's basic speed has increased by about 10 per cent. Therefore the sprint in essence is still a lifetime's training for just 10 seconds of hard running. 'It's reaction, driving and hoping,' says Don Quarrie, 'because there's not much time to think about what you have to do. There's just enough time to do what you're supposed to do.'

After talking to the scores of people involved in this project, my favourite description still has to be that immortal line uttered by Harold Abrahams' eccentric old coach Sam Mussabini, just before the 1924 Olympic final and made famous in the film *Chariots of Fire*. 'Just think of two things,' he told Harold. 'The pistol and the tape. When you hear one run like hell till you break the other.' Even today this remark still sums up the 100 metres and remains the very essence of sprinting.

Winning an Olympic title has had a marked effect on the lives of all the sprint champions, but a gold medal is not a ticket for life; it does not endow everlasting success, fame and fortune. Of course, for some athletes it did prove to be something of a golden key which opened doors that perhaps might otherwise have remained closed, but for others it was a golden millstone which left the rest of their lives empty and exaggerated their faults in hard times. For the fastest men on earth winning their Olympic gold medals was a ticket to somewhere, but while they alone chose their destinies on the track, they were not always able to choose where the journey later took them.

Acknowledgements

Special thanks to Richard Hymans and Dave Terry

AAAs
Athletics Weekly
Austin American-Statesman
Baldwin-Wallace College
Boston Athletic Club
British Columbia Sports Hall of Fame
British Museum Library
British Newspaper Library
British Olympic Association
British Veterans Athletics Federation
Cleveland Board of Education
Cleveland Plain Dealer
Daily Mirror
Dallas Cowboys
Dallas Morning News
Detroit News
Detroit Public Libraries
Duke University
Florida Times-Union
Fogarty, Professor John
Gateshead Public Libraries
German Press Association
Hammersmith & Fulham Libraries
Harlingen Public Libraries
Hartford Courant
Hauffer, Armin
IAAF
International Olympic Committee
Jamaican AAAs
Kearney, Jim
Kelly, Kevin
Mallon, Dr. Bill
Michigan, University of
Milwaukee Journal
Mirwis, Sam
National Centre for Athletics Literature
(Birmingham University)
New York Times
Northwestern University
Ohio State University
Patent Office
Powderhall Stadium
Princeton University
Rodda, John
South African Press Agency
Soviet Sports Committee
Sports Information – USA
TAC – The Athletics Congress
Temple University
Texas Monthly
Times Newspapers
Track & Field News
Trinidad Guardian
US Olympic Committee
Vancouver Sun
Wright, Harold

Picture credits

We would like to thank all the people and organizations who allowed us to use their pictures in this book. We apologise if we have omitted to mention any picture sources used in the following list.

Abrahams Collection
All-Sport
Associated Press
Associated Sports Photography
British Columbia Sports Hall of Fame
Cambridge Syndics Inc
Chicago Defender
Cleveland Board of Education
Colorsport
Daily Mirror
Diadora
Duncanson, Neil
German Press Agency
Harriet Mae Bottorf Collection
Hartford Courant
Herringshaw, George
IOC
Mary Evans Picture Library
Michigan, University of
Morrow Collection
Northwestern University
Novosti
Ohio State University
Paddock Collection
Photosource
Princeton University
Rex Features
Shearman, Mark
Temple University
Terry, Dave
Thomas, Bob
Topham Picture Library
Wells, Allan